PUBLIC
POLICY
AND
PROGRAM
EVALUATION

Evert Vedung

TRANSACTION PUBLISHERS
New Brunswick (U.S.A.) and London (U.K.)

First paperback printing 2000
Copyright © 1997 by Transaction Publishers,
New Brunswick, New Jersey 08903

This book is printed on acid-free paper that meets the American National Standard for Permanence of Paper for Printed Library Materials.

Library of Congress Catalog Number: 96-52816
ISBN: 1-56000-299-9 (cloth); 0-7658-0687-8 (paper)
Printed in the United States of America

Library of Congress Cataloging-in-Publication Data
Vedung, Evert, 1938–
    [Utvärdering i politik och förvaltning. English]
    Public policy and program evaluation / Evert Vedung.
        p.   cm.
    Includes bibliographical references and index.
    ISBN 0-7658-0687-8 (paper : alk. paper)
1. Political planning. 2. Political planning—Evaluation.
3. Policy sciences. I. Title.
H97.V4313   1997
320'.6—dc21   96–52816
                                                                CIP

PUBLIC POLICY

POLICY

AND

PROGRAM

EVALUATION

For Young–seek Choue and Peter Gerlich
without whose invitations
this book would never have come about

Contents

List of Figures

Preface to the English Edition

In August, 1991, I stayed for a couple of nights at the Bildungshaus Sankt Virgil in Salzburg. In the lobby I found a postcard that read in German: "Our life is the history of our encounters." This adage captures important events in the developments that have led to the publication of this book in English.

It all began in 1985 in a workshop on evaluation in Barcelona, arranged by the European Consortium of Political Research, where I presented some ideas from a Swedish manuscript of mine on public policy assessment. In the sessions, I had the exceptional luck of encountering Professor Peter Gerlich, who one year later unexpectedly invited me to lecture at the Vienna University International Summer School, located in the picturesque Alpine village of Strobl am Wolfgangsee, not far from the illustrious Gasthaus Im Weissen Rössl, made famous by Benatzky in the operetta. I decided to teach administrative control and public policy evaluation and have the rest of my unfinished Swedish manuscript translated into English. The 1987 course was repeated in 1989 and 1991.

Before my first visit to Vienna University, however, I had another unexpected opportunity to improve my English manuscript. This happened after the Barcelona meeting in the late fall of 1985, when I taught at the Kyung Hee University's recently inaugurated Graduate Institute of Peace Studies in the Kyonggi Province outside Seoul, Korea. Behind this invitation were Professor Sookon Kim, Professor Kwan–Bong Kim, and Chancellor Young–Seek Choue. The first trip to Korea was followed by two more, in 1988 and 1990, arranged by, among others, Professor Sung–chul Yang. Also, I further expanded and rewrote my English manuscript in a room in the Bursa im. st. Pigonia on Ulica Garbarska, Cracow, during short sojourns between 1987 and 1991, partly supported by the exchange program between the Uppsala and Jagiellonian universities in the Office of International Affairs, Uppsala, and organized by my good friend and colleague Professor Marian Grzybowski of the Jagiellonian University's Political Science Department.

When I received my fourth invitation from Kyung Hee University to teach in the spring semester of 1994, I decided to finish the manuscript and try to find an English publisher. Since the Swedish book was issued already in 1991, the English version that took form on the flowering Kwangnung campus turned out to be a very different work. The last point should be emphasized: the present work is *not* a mere translation of my 1991 Swedish book, but an entirely revised product.

Through the years, excellent computer literati in Uppsala and Seoul have helped me to install and taught me to use several versions of WordPerfect and PC Tools. In particular I wish to acknowledge the invaluable assistance of Woon–ho Kim, Soon Park Park, Joon–ju Yoon, and Young–chul Kim, all of Kyung Hee University. Dean Yoon–hee Suh, Rector Sung–kuk Lew, and Rector Jae Shik Sohn provided material and moral support. In addition, I take this opportunity to recognize the invaluable help of Pour Mitrahi–Bijän in matters of copying, telefaxing, and mailing, and of my Uppsala colleague Anders Westholm and my competent and spirited brother Tage Vedung in computer matters. The latter has altruistically worked for nights and days to provide the manuscript in camera-ready form.

I have also received inspiration from members of the NOGA Group on research evaluation, headed by Associate Professor Ola Nyquist and financed by the Council for Building Research (BFR) in Stockholm, and from colleagues in the Working Group on Public Policy and Program Evaluation, sponsored by the International Institute of Administrative Studies in Brussels, to which I have belonged since 1992; its chairman and spiritus rector Professor Ray C. Rist of George Washington University recommended me to send the manuscript to Transaction Publishers, advice that I was fortunate enough to heed.

My colleague Alexander Davidson, then in the Uppsala Department of Government, now back in New Zealand, carefully read an earlier version of the whole English manuscript and painstakingly corrected my linguistic inadequacies. Anders Weström did some last-minute reference checking. A substantial part of the work was done when I was the lucky holder of a special research position on evaluation research in the National Research Council for the Humanities and the Social Sciences (HSFR) in Stockholm. The research has also been supported by the Scientific Advisory Board of the Council for Building Research (BVN) in Stockholm.

To all the people and institutions mentioned, and among the latter particularly the HSFR, I wish to express my profound gratitude. As a special token of appreciation, I dedicate this English–language book to my good friends and respected colleagues Young–seek Choue and Peter Gerlich.

Of course the usual caveat applies: none of the institutions and persons mentioned are in any way responsible for the content of what I have written. The manuscript was finished in January, 1996.

Teatrum Œconomicum,
Uppsala, 10 January 1996

Preface to the First Swedish Edition

Unintended effects of intentional action fascinate. Few can fail to be gripped by King Pyrrhus' victory or Columbus' voyage to discover the western sea route to India. This phenomenon has been formulated in various ways and observed in diverse fields. Adam Smith thought he saw the Invisible Hand at work, Hegel discovered the Cunning of Reason, and Elster regards friendship and love as essential side effects.

This insight into the reverse consequences and unintended side effects of human planning has been a major force behind the shaping of mechanisms for results–oriented analysis and information feedback in the public sector. Since the 1960s, evaluation has been promoted in democratic states as an important example of such a mechanism. Evaluation has been institutionalized in ministries, public agencies, public investigatory commissions, and particular watchdog agencies.

However, the advance of evaluation has been accompanied by criticisms and crises. Not only have the contents and methodological quality of the evaluations been questioned, but their relevance, inadequate utilization, and even their tendency to "cost more than they taste," if I may use a Swedish proverb. Evaluation researchers have responded by developing new methods and approaches to the application of evaluation in political and administrative decision–making processes. The star of evaluation is currently in the ascendant, not least in Sweden, where so–called results analysis is to constitute the life force in the new triennial budget cycle.

The present work has been written to be used as a qualified introductory volume in evaluation at academic institutions as well as within public administration. It can be used in courses on administration, administrative technique, and organizational management.

My own interest in evaluation, and thereby the production of this book, is also originally an unintended by–product of the nuclear energy issue.

It was nuclear power that turned me into an energy researcher, which impelled the director of the then Energy Research and Development Commission (*Delegationen för energiforskning*), Sigfrid Wennerberg, to entice me into a project about energy policy instruments. The project, which also put me in contact with Yngve Boye, gradually became directed toward the evaluation of tools of government, and was presented in 1982 in the work *Energipolitiska utvärderingar 1973–1981*.

The continuation was a humble paper on evaluation methods, written in 1982 for the Energy Conservation Commission (*Energisparkommittén*). The inspiration came from the Commission's secretary Ulf Karlsson. The Commission's evaluator, Jan-Eric Furubo, who later transferred to the National Board of Energy (*Statens energiverk*) and who now works at the National Audit Bureau's (*Riksrevisionsverkets*) methods department, has been an indispensable sparring partner in matters of evaluation for more than a decade.

A period at the University of Texas at Austin (1982–1983) helped me to find what has become the American Evaluation Association. Its annual assemblies have not only put me in contact with the ferment of the American evaluation community, but also with a natural catastrophe which could have brought that community to an end, namely the San Francisco earthquake of 1989.

The work has been continued within the research program for public policy "Forskningsprogrammet Offentlig Politik," funded by the Swedish Council for Building Research (BFR) and the Council for Planning and Coordination of Research (FRN), Stockholm. The program director Leif Lewin has not only expressed his views on part of the manuscript, but has also—with unobtrusive efficiency—ensured that his colleagues at the Department of Government in Uppsala have enjoyed a peaceful working environment.

The manuscript has been completed under the exceptional working conditions that a special research position on evaluation research in the National Research Council for the Humanities and the Social Sciences (HSFR) in Stockholm provides.

The Council for Building Research (BFR) and its Scientific Advisory Board of the Swedish Council for Building Research (BVN), through the tandem team Sture Blomgren and Ola Nyquist, have been a decisive support. No other persons I have come into contact with have worked in such a powerful and goal–conscious way to build up evaluation environments in Sweden. For me, the cooperation with Sture and Ola has been vital. Their evaluation network has provided contacts, infused courage and created material and intellectual conditions for the development of theory and methods. Amongst other members, I would like especially to mention my political science colleague Michael Nydén, who is now working on evaluation questions at the Swedish Agricultural University at Ultuna, Mette Qvortrup, Østfold Distriktshøgskole in Halden, Norway, and guest researcher in Uppsala, and Örjan Eriksson.

In the National Audit Bureau's (RRV's) results analysis community have I found people with similar interests. These people include particularly Rolf Sandahl, with whom I have conducted an ongoing dialogue for several years, and who has read and given comments on the entire final version; Bo Andersson; Ulrika Barklund, who for a few short months was my research assistant; Shirin Ahlbäck, who read the section on the stakeholder model; Anne-Marie Fallenius; and Hans Grohmann.

For a brief period of time the National Council for Cultural Affairs and its work with reviews of national cultural policies in Sweden and other European countries was also a source of contacts and impulses. Valuable insights have been conveyed by Carl Johan Kleberg, Göran Nylöf, and Kjell Eide from Oslo.

The Nordic Summer School of Evaluation Research in Båstad (1985) propelled me into the company of Tore Nilstun and Göran Hermerén. That we engaged Joseph Wholey and Michael Quinn Patton as lecturers opened enduring connections to the American evaluation research elite.

During the passage of years, a great number of friends and colleagues in my own discipline, political science, have supported me with criticism, encouragement, advice, and opinions. Amongst these I would like to mention: Anders Berg; Stefan Björklund; Axel Hadenius; Nils Karlsson; Bo Månson; Olof Petersson; Bo Rothstein and Sven-Erik Svärd, Department of Government, Uppsala; Rune Premfors and Björn Wittrock, Department of Political Science, Stockholm; Ulf Bengtsson, Department of Political Science in Gothenburg; Peter Gerlich, Institut für Politikwissenschaft at the Universität Wien; Hans Ring, Växjö University College; Bo Jonsson and Stig Montin, Örebro

University College; Sven-Olov Larsson and Alf Gunnmo, Östersund University College; and Joachim Schäfer, Kriterium AB in Knivsta. In addition to giving substantive opinions, Anders Westholm at the Department of Government in Uppsala has always been prepared unselfishly to solve troublesome computer problems. In connection to computers, I would also like to name my colleagues Göran Blomberg, Sverker Härd, and Jörgen Hermansson, and last but not least Lars Bruzelius at the Uppsala Data Centre.

Laila Grandin has promptly and reliably sent out conference papers, taken care of travel accounts, ordered reports, and photocopied. Barbro Lewin has maintained order over funding and employees. I suspect that my wife Siv, head librarian at the Psychology Library in Uppsala, has in silence bitterly regretted that she once taught me to borrow and not to buy books, as she has had to locate them in databases and catalogues, and transport them to and from the Carolina Rediviva. That she has furthermore, between rounds of the libraries, bought us a new apartment and given other meaning to my life; I hope that she does not have any regrets.

To all the above institutions and persons I convey my deeply felt thanks. None of those named can be accused of the inadequacies of the presentation, as the responsibility is completely and fully my own.

Uppsala, 12 April 1991

1

Evaluation: A Semantic Magnet

Evaluation:
1. *The action of appraising or valuing (goods, etc.); a calculation or statement of value; = valuation.*
2. *The action of evaluating or determining the value of (a mathematical expression, a physical quantity, etc.) or of estimating the force of (probabilities, evidence, etc.).*
—Oxford English Dictionary, *1933 (1978)*

As early as classical antiquity, scholars were summoned to Court to become counsellors to the Prince. Aristotle was hired by King Philip of Macedon as the youthful Alexander's teacher in statecraft. During the siege of Syracuse, the Roman legionnaires were forced to protect themselves from Archimedes' burning mirror and catapults. The tendency has continued in Europe's nation states. Heeding a request from King Christian IV, the prominent astronomer Tycho Brahe took residence at the Court in Copenhagen to read the monarch's horoscope in order to aid the King in the crafting his foreign policy. Members of the Nobel family, in their efforts to invent and supply the Czar with modern weapons, made several tests of explosive substance on the ice of the Neva river in St. Petersburg.

Public sector evaluation is a recent addition to a great chain of attempts by princes to use the brainpower of scholars and scientists to further the interests of the state. The services requested from evaluation experts are, of course, completely different from the ones hinted at in the examples cited above. Evaluation scholars are asked to provide retrospective assessments of the administration, output and outcome of government measures in order to effect self–reflection, deeper understanding, and well–grounded decisions on the part of those who are in charge of government operations. Discarding the hackneyed political notion that honorable intentions are enough, evaluation is predicated upon the opposite idea that good practices and solid results are what really count. Evaluation implies looking backward in order to better steer forward. It is a mechanism for monitoring, systematizing, and grading government activities and their results so that public officials in their future–oriented work will be able to act as responsibly, creatively, and efficiently as possible. The interventions of the modern state are so extensive, their execution so complicated, and their potential consequences so far–reaching that science and social research are needed to monitor operations and establish impacts.

However, systematic evaluation is not for contemporary princes alone, but can also be called upon by the political opposition, the professions, the citizenry, or the clientele of government programs. For political scientists, the political opponents' and the citizens' perspectives on evaluation are of particular concern.

Careful retrospective assessment requires systematic data collection, data analysis, and source documentation. In addition, pertinent criteria of merit and standards of performance about how well the intervention must do on these criteria are needed, because evaluation is a normative enterprise.

Evaluation Defined

"Evaluation is the process of determining the merit, worth, and value of things." These words by Scriven (1991:1) capture the basic, natural meaning of the term *evaluation*. Evaluation is the process of distinguishing the worthwhile from the worthless, the precious from the useless.

Evaluation is a key analytical procedure in all disciplined intellectual and practical endeavors. While acknowledging that the process of determining the merit, worth, and value of things permeates every domain of thought and practice, in the present work evaluation will be delimited to suit the demands of public service and governmental affairs. For the purpose of this book, I propose the following definition:

> Evaluation = df. careful retrospective assessment of the merit, worth, and value of administration, output, and outcome of government interventions, which is intended to play a role in future, practical action situations.

This definition of evaluation is controversial. Evaluation is circumscribed in numerous ways. Actually, the term evaluation has attracted so many different meanings that we may call it a *semantic magnet* (Lundquist 1976:124). It has come to signify almost any effort at systematic thinking in the public sector. It is easy to agree with the very first sentence in Carol Weiss' early textbook *Evaluation Research* (1972): "Evaluation is an elastic word that stretches to cover judgments of many kinds."

Since evaluation comes in many guises, I shall try to compare in more detail other scholarly definitions of evaluation with the one proposed here. The purpose of the exercise is to put my own definition into a larger perspective. I shall start with the subject matter of evaluation.

Evaluation Concerns Government Interventions

Since evaluation is a truly general analytical process, it can be applied to any area of social endeavor. A special thing in the present context, however, is that evaluation is limited to government interventions only, that is, politically or administratively planned social change, like public policies, public programs, and public services.

Contemporary public interventions cover substantive as well as process–oriented programs (Lundquist 1990). Substantive measures concern diverse functional domains such as energy, environment, natural resources, land use, housing, social welfare, health, transportation, economic development, and many other fields of endeavor. It also includes foreign policy, an area left entirely untouched by systematic evaluation (Vasquez 1986).

Process–oriented interventions—administrative reform—refer to ideas and measures directed at the organization and function of public administration itself (Petersson and Söderlind 1992:7ff). Administrative reform is concerned with management by objectives versus detailed process–oriented management, decentralization, new budgeting systems, changes in local administration, and other institution–building processes. A central problem in modern administrative reorganization is which institutional arrangements are used and ought to be used in implementation of public policies and programs: regulatory agencies stacked with neutral and competent executive officials, personnel appointed on political merits, execution through municipalities, corporatist arrangements, professionals, client involvement, or contracting out to private business (overview in Lundquist 1985).

It goes without saying that evaluation embraces the assessment of substantive as well as process–oriented government interventions. Evaluation is targeted at all kinds of public sector activities.

Evaluation is Focused on Administration, Outputs, and Outcomes

As defined here, evaluation is not concerned with the entire policy cycle, but only with the back end of it. To clarify this idea, I shall introduce systems thinking, which is so prevalent in political science study of public administration.

Political scientists tend to view public administration as a system (see figure 1.1). A system is a whole the component parts of which are dependent upon each other. In its most rudimentary form, a system consists of input, conversion, and output in the following fashion:

FIGURE 1.1
The Simple System Model

In the field of public administration, the general–systems notion is applied to the civil service, which is viewed as a system. It could be one separate government agency, but also a conglomerate of different organizations. The agencies or conglomerates could be at any level, for instance at the global, the interregional, the national, the intraregional, or the municipal level. The input to an agency from the environment, particularly from its principal (e.g., the government), may be funds with some strings attached to their use, written instructions, oral support or criticism, and appointed people. Within the agency, funds, people, and instructions are coordinated and converted into something else. The conversion is what is going on in the agency. Output is what comes out of the agency.

In public policy studies, the conversion stage of the general systems model is roughly equivalent to administration, and an outcome phase is often tacked to the output stage of the general system model. By output is meant phenomena that come out of government bodies in the form of, for example, prohibitions, enabling procedures, grants, subsidies, taxes, exhortation, jawboning, moral suasion, services, and goods. Outcomes are what happen when the outputs reach the addressees, the actions of the addressees included, but also what occur beyond the addressees in the chain of influence. We may distinguish between immediate, intermediate, and ultimate outcomes. Another term for outcomes is *impacts*. *Results* will be used as a summarizing term for outputs and outcomes. Results may also indicate either outputs or outcomes. The term *implementation* usually covers conversion and output. The reasoning is summarized in figure 1.2.

FIGURE 1.2
The System Model Adapted to Government Intervention Evaluation

Let me illustrate this with an example. Some years ago the Swedish government instituted a program to help refugees from the civil war in Afghanistan, who lived in camps in Pakistan. To this end, the government allocated funds to the Swedish International Development Agency, abbreviated SIDA. SIDA struck an agreement with the International Red Cross in Geneva, which promised to funnel the money to the National Red Crescent in Pakistan. For the funds, the Red Crescent was instructed to buy tents and blankets from local dealers, and provide the equipment to the refugee camps. In the camps, the local Red Crescent branch was expected to put up the tents, and distribute the blankets to the refugees. Then, refugees were supposed to use the tents and blankets in order to alleviate their plight.

To qualify as an evaluation, a study of the Help–to–Afghani–Refugees Program must concentrate on either the outcome (if the refugees were actually using the tents and the blankets and if that alleviated their plight), the output (the distribution of tents and blankets through the local Red Crescent), or the administration (what happened to the funds once they had reached the SIDA through the purchase of blankets and tents by Pakistani authorities). Admittedly, outcome evaluation may be considered more important than output or conversion evaluation. However, I do not want to equate evaluation with outcome evaluation. The concept, as defined here, includes concern with administrative processes and output as well. In the refugee case, for instance, everybody can see that administration is a long process with several levels of authority involved.

The limitation to outcomes, outputs, and administration excludes studies assessing *ex post* the merits and drawbacks of features in the policy formation phase. For instance, actual or past policy formation can be assessed against such evaluative criteria of merit as comprehensive and reliable information base or participation by various affected interests. One may evaluate measures on the books, using such dimensions of merit as comprehensibility or consistency with other programs. In this context, however, such studies will not be reflected upon.

One additional clarification is probably justified. The limitation to administrative processes, outputs, and outcomes is not concerned with explanatory factors in evaluation. If the evaluation sets out to explain what influenced variations in administrative procedures, outputs, and outcomes, my definition allows for explanatory factors to be drawn from anywhere. It would be abjectly inappropriate to delimit the concept of evaluation with respect to the determinants that may be discerned.

Now, I have ventured to justify the delimitation of the subject matter of evaluation to "administration, outputs, and outcomes of government interventions." In the next section, I shall address what it means for evaluation to be "retrospective".

Evaluation is Retrospective

Evaluation is retrospective assessment of public interventions. Prospective appraisals (i.e., scrutinies of courses of action considered but not yet adopted even as prototypes), are not included in my definition. Also this limitation is controversial, particular in the North American context. Leading theoretists argue that prospective assessment—*ex ante* assessment, forethought evaluation, needs assessment, analysis for goal–setting—does belong to evaluation. To them, evaluation becomes an umbrella, covering all kinds of analyses of, in, and for public intervention. Is it reasonable to let "evaluation" refer to almost any intellectual effort in the public sector? Cases of this large perspective on evaluation can be taken particularly from economists, who perform cost–benefit and cost–effectiveness analyses of potential, future options, maintaining they practice evaluation. Also Rossi and Freeman (1989:18) adopt this large perspective when they maintain: "Evaluation research is the systematic application of social research procedures for assessing *the conceptualization, design,* implementation, and utility of social intervention programs" (italics mine; also Anderson and Ball 1978:3, 11, 15ff).

"If planning is everything, maybe it's nothing?" Aaron Wildavsky (1973) ironically wondered two decades ago on the then strongly fashionable fad, planning. Can the same question be raised today, when *ex ante* assessment is included in evaluation? Of course, it is both futile and foolish to legislate about the use of a word. But if evaluation is allowed to embrace all kinds of analysis in political and administrative life, will not the concept become too diluted? Here, perhaps, we face another instance of the semantic magnetism of the word *evaluation*.

The major argument against including *ex–ante* assessments in evaluation is drawn from the origin and history of evaluation research. The demands of the early evaluation movement for empirical data on policy and program results emerged in opposition to the prevailing emphasis on analysis of planned interventions. If evaluation is allowed to embrace even planning, this significant historical line of conflict will be obscured.

Hence, in this context I have confined evaluation to after-the-fact assessments. Such assessment concerns adopted interventions in the sense of ongoing or terminated policies, programs, program ingredients, and the like, no matter whether they are veterans or recently introduced small–scale prototypes. Before–the–fact analysis of potential, not-yet-adopted interventions, however, is not included in evaluation in my usage in the present book.

Evaluation is Assessment of Ongoing and Finished Activities

Sometimes evaluation is restricted to *ongoing* activities, leaving out assessment of finished policies and programs. This quite narrow perspective is clearly discernible in David Nachmias's textbook *Public Policy Evaluation* (1979:3f):

> One method that can reduce the number of erroneous decisions is the formal scientific approach to knowledge. . . . Viewed from the scientific perspective, policy evaluation research is the objective, systematic, empirical examination of the effects ongoing policies and public programs have on their targets in terms of the goals they are meant to achieve.

Actually, the narrow perspective on the subject matter of evaluation is a commonplace in American and Canadian literature. According to Rutman, "program evaluation refers to the use of research methods to measure the effectiveness of operating programs" (1980:17). Wholey et al. write: "Evaluation assesses the effectiveness of an ongoing program in achieving its objectives" (1970).

Indubitably, ongoing interventions clearly belong to the subject matter of evaluation. They may even constitute the core subject of public sector evaluation. But should evaluation be confined to ongoing activities *only*? The answer must be no. Lessons can be learned also from assessments of terminated operations. Why exclude these from evaluation research? I would argue that careful assessment of terminated public activities—summative evaluation to use Michael Scriven's famous expression—may very well assist in improving ongoing operations. Terminated policies and programs may also be scrutinized for accountability. Delimiting evaluation to the study of ongoing activities would unduly fence off important parts of policy evaluation research. Evaluation should include all retrospective or *ex–post* study of policies and programs, ongoing as well as terminated. According to my definition, evaluation comprises all kinds of *ex–post* analyses of administrative processes, outputs, and outcomes of public sector activities.

Evaluation is More than Impact Assessment

On some rare occasions, eminent methodologists have also defined evaluation as impact assessment. In his *Planning Useful Evaluations,* Leonard Rutman (1980:17) states:

> In this book program evaluation refers to the use of research methods to measure the effectiveness of operating programs.

And effectiveness, he adds, is the extent to which a program achieves its goals or spawns certain effects.

Thus, evaluation is restricted to studies raising the impact issue. I do not accept this unduly narrow definition here. In my view, apart from impact assessment, evaluation should also include efficiency assessment, administration and output monitoring, as well as simple goal–achievement measurement where the impact issue is not raised. Furthermore, in the evaluation of research, libraries, museums, public health, public parks, and other government services, the quality of the output is assessed, for instance, by expert panels, peer arrangements, or client groups, but in these studies the causality issue is frequently not raised at all. Still, the studies are referred to as evaluation, and justifiably so. Eventual criticism of these practices ought to be advanced by means of substantive argument, not by definitional fiat.

Intervention Goals are not the Only Permissible Value Criteria

In the discourse on evaluation, there isn't even general agreement on a seemingly fundamental point: that evaluation is concerned with the determination of merit, worth, and value. Charles Atkin, for instance, includes no reference to valuing in his definition, which goes like this: "evaluation is the collection and presentation of data summaries for decision–makers" (quoted from Scriven 1991:156).

My position is that evaluation by definitional fiat involves the assessment of merit, worth, and value. The value component of evaluation presupposes at least one criterion of merit against which public interventions are judged. Some authors, particularly in the past, took a rigid view of what value criteria were permissible for something to be called an evaluation. Evaluation was equated with assessments against premeditated, avowed *intervention goals*. Argues Carol Weiss (1972a:4):

> The purpose of evaluation research is to measure the effects of a program against the goals it set out to accomplish as a means of contributing to subsequent decision making about the program and improve future programming. (See also quotation from Nachmias above.)

Admittedly, the traditional formulation of the program evaluation question is: To what extent does the program succeed in reaching its goals? But why should intervention goals be the *only* permissible criteria in judging the merit of public policies? Why shouldn't assessments using other criteria of merit than intervention goals be referred to as evaluation? Why shouldn't judgments using concerns and expectations of the clients or of other stakeholding audiences be called evaluations? Why shouldn't appraisals using yardsticks drawn from political philosophy—that is, equality, freedom, and justice—be regarded as evaluations? The selection of criteria of merit is a crucial, albeit little debated, issue in evaluation. Excluding all yardsticks except the avowed intervention goals is in my opinion to circumscribe the concept too narrowly. It will by fiat preclude discussions concerning what criteria are to be applied to our evaluands. Therefore, the definition propounded here contends that evaluation engenders appraisal but leaves open what kinds of value criteria may be used.

I wish to make another point with regard to criteria of merit. Evaluation may apply either descriptive or prescriptive theories of valuing, to use the illuminating distinction by Shadish, Cook, and Leviton in their masterful treatise *Foundations of Program Evaluation* (1991:46ff). A descriptive theory of valuing implies that evaluators use the merit criteria of others—such as intervention goals—as evaluative yardsticks, as opposed to a prescriptive theory that advocates the primacy of particular values. My definition is neutral with respect to these two approaches. It is also neutral in relation to subdivisions within the two approaches. Within descriptive valuing, some authors prefer to use premeditated goals, whereas others suggest a kind of division of labor on this account between formal evaluators and recipients of the formal evaluations. In complicated cases, formal evaluators may resist from applying premeditated value criteria in the expectation that the assignment of weights to the information provided is best performed by the recipients afterwards once the study is finished. Also this would pass as evaluations according to my definition. In order for something to be an evaluation, it is not necessary that the researcher–cum–evaluator actually performs the valuing. Some valuing must be executed, but it might be executed afterwards by some recipient. If this is what Atkin had in mind, the difference between my position and his is probably negligible.

Evaluation is Careful Assessment

Evaluation is *careful* assessment of public interventions. This means that an evaluation must meet some minimum standards of quality such as systematic data collection and the conscientious application of criteria of merit and standards of performance.

Many celebrated authors have proceeded further and made the explicit point that evaluation by definition is social research. The following statement by Elinor Chelimsky (1985:7) is typical for these scholars:

> Program evaluation is the application of systematic research methods to the assessment of program design, implementation, and effectiveness.

It is obvious that Chelimsky is preoccupied with cases where the canons of social science methodology are used to make the judging process more accurate. She attempts to draw a sharp line between evaluation research and offhand evaluations that rely on intuition, opinion, and trained sensitivity. The same attitude is displayed by other authors as well. In his pioneering *Evaluative Research* (1967:12; cf. Mann 1972, Caro 1971), Edward Suchman stated: "We do not view the field of evaluation as having any methodology different from the scientific method; evaluative research is, first and foremost, *research* and as such must adhere as closely as possible to currently accepted standards of research methodology" (also Meyers 1981:50ff; Nachmias 1979:1ff).

I disagree with Chelimsky, Suchman, and others that evaluation should be minimally *defined* as research, although I use research in a relatively wide sense. Research is not equated to science and the application of quantitative methods. It also includes humanistic research and qualitative methods. Furthermore, research encompasses commissioned research as well as research under the scholars' own program responsibility. Nonetheless, I shall not equate evaluation with research, because there are alternative ways of regarding evaluation which it would be outrageous to discard by linguistic stipulation only. For example, evaluation is often an integral part of the political and administrative decision–making processes in which careful research plays a role, albeit not a dominant one. I shall also refer this to evaluation, provided there is some careful *ex post* assessment involved.

Evaluation Should be Useful

On a general level, evaluation should be delimited according to purpose as well. Evaluation is not any careful appraisal; it is appraisal intended to play a role in future practical action situations. By this I do not necessarily mean that a study must have immediate relevance to a pending decision to be called an evaluation. The purpose may be to contribute to public policy debate, that may or may not lead to some authoritative decisions. A straightforward aim, on the other hand, is to perform evaluation to provide reasoned judgments based on solid empirical ground to be employed in decision making. Another, more dubious intention, would be to conduct evaluation to give outsiders the impression that the organization is handling things well. The general practical orientation is so central that it must be included in the definition.

On the other hand, further specification of the practical orientation would make evaluation too circumscribed. Some veterans of evaluation research argue, for instance, that evaluation always aims at intervention refinement. Lee Cronbach et al. (1985:14), among others, have defined evaluation with respect to the intervention improvement idea:

> By the term *evaluation,* we mean systematic examination of events occurring in and consequent on a contemporary program—an examination conducted to assist in improving this program and other programs having the same general purpose.

True, future intervention betterment is an important purpose of evaluation. The problem with Cronbach's definition is that numerous evaluation studies are undertaken for practical purposes other than improvement; still, it seems reasonable to call them evaluation. Exercising evaluation for accountability reasons, that is, principals undertaking evaluation with the aim of holding their executives responsible for what they have done, is a perfectly valid purpose for evaluation (see chapter 6). True, accountability studies can lead to intervention improvement. However, they can also end up with intervention termination. Furthermore, evaluations are undertaken for political purposes, for instance, to save time or divert public interest from the issue. In order not to preclude far–ranging and deep–probing discussions on why evaluation should be exercised, it seems preferable not to limit evaluation only to the intervention improvement purpose. By definition, evaluation is an enterprise intended to play a role in future practical action situations, such as, for instance, kindle public policy debate or more directly provide useful materials for some pending decision. However, the concept ought not to be further delimited with regard to purpose.

This ends my justification for defining evaluation as careful, retrospective assessment of merit, worth, and value of the administration, output and outcome of government interventions, which is intended to play a role in future practical action situations.

2

Evaluation Between Intervention
and Feedback

Evaluating engenders looking backwards to improve forward direction. The specific role of evaluation is to systematically amass and assess information on intervention outcomes, outputs, and administration to produce adjustments, or more rational future decisions.

Spinning Top Models

To illustrate this ex post facto orientation, the public intervention process is usually regarded as a cyclical operation divided into a number of stages, where evaluation constitutes or is included in a later such stage, which points to the next decision cycle. The stage models are often drawn as spinning tops, cycles or spirals. (see Figure 2.1) Presumably, the stage models do not purport to picture public sector realities, but are heuristic devices to facilitate thinking or tools by which realities can be investigated.

A drawback with the spinning top models is that public policies and other public sector activities seem to swirl around on the same spot. There is no development or direction involved. Another demerit is that evaluation is on apar with all other processes.

Intervention Process, Evaluation Process, and Feedback Process

A superior way of illustrating the afterthought idea is to detach the evaluation process from the intervention process and view them as two different subprocesses of the larger political– administrative gov-

FIGURE 2.1
Evaluation According to the Spinning Top Model

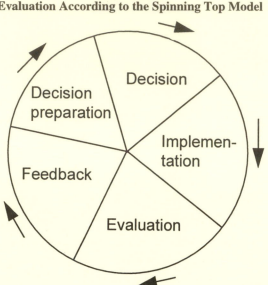

ernance system. The evaluation process in turn can be regarded as one component of a more general administrative retrospective control system. Administrative control is the means used by an organization to elicit the performance it needs and to check whether the quantities and qualities of such performance are in accord with organizational specifications. Evaluation, as part of such a control system, is a systematic reflection on the final stages in the primary public intervention process. One of the crucial problems in governance processes is to link this secondary process—metaprocess—to the primary intervention process. This is achieved through a feedback mechanism in which the evaluation is utilized. Also the feedback can be perceived as a separate process. In the governance model presented in figure 2.2, the primary public intervention process stages are limited to six, with evaluation and feedback drawn as two distinct metaprocesses.

It must be stressed that the governance model does not provide an empirical description of any reality. It is a heuristic, an instrument to support thinking. It should guide reflection and research on public intervention processes, evaluation and utilization of evaluation. It is a tool of analysis designed to provide hypothetical insights, and create ideas on appropriate research problems. The model neither contributes a realistic picture of public policy or evaluation reality, nor is this its purpose.

FIGURE 2.2
Evaluation in the General Governance Model

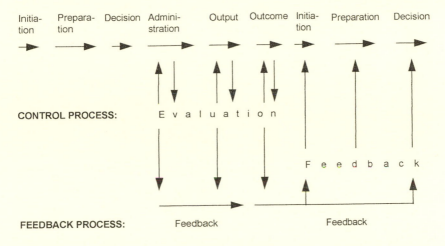

In general systems terminology, accounted for in the previous chapter, initiation, preparation, and decision in the intervention process would belong to the input stage; administration would be conversion and output would be output. Outcome is usually not covered in the general systems model, but must be included in any heuristic which purports to be fruitful for evaluation purposes.

According to the general governance model, the public intervention process starts with *initiation*. Initiation concerns the identification of a problem, the solution of which supposedly demands public action. Demands for government consideration may arise from within the political system, by for instance an administrative body, or from some external source such as interest organizations or the media. When political officials address the problem it has entered the political agenda. When national politicians start to become concerned and attempt to bring it up in some national political channel, then it has been brought up on the national political agenda.

Aside from the substantive issue, *decision preparation* is concerned with implementability of proposed measures and evaluability of results to be achieved. First, efforts are made to pinpoint the nature of the problem for the purpose of creating a base for an upcoming decision. Information concerning alternative courses of action is gathered and organized, the presumed consequences of the alternatives are calculated, the costs of the consequences are assessed, goals are set, and the alternatives are assessed in the light of what is to be achieved. Second, decision preparation is attentive to before–the–fact implementability in the sense that investigations are performed to determine the legality of the options, and the available organizational, managerial, and manpower capabilities in order to establish the degree to which the proposed intervention alternative can be specified and implemented. Third, decision preparation may also involve considerations concerning how a future intervention should be evaluated. Ideal–type decision preparation, then, not only includes substantive concerns with goals, means, costs, and benefits, but also amenability to successful implementation and evaluation.

Decision preparation may involve numerous actors and procedures for example appointment of a formal investigatory body, presentation of preliminary options for action, review by interest groups and other stakeholders, reworking of the original proposals, presentation of one or several final suggestions for action. Decision preparation ends with the presentation of proposals for decision.

Decision preparation, consequently, is concerned with goals, means, costs, benefits, implementability, and evaluability. But it also involves actors, conflicts, clashes between different stands of the issue, negotiations, and compromises. Preparatory work for political and administrative decisions can never be turned into pure intellectual problem solving. Invariably, it also contains features of conflict and conflict resolution.

Decision implies that a formal, authoritative, legitimating resolution is made. Who will make this resolution varies of course from intervention to intervention. If the decision concerns legislation is must be made by the parliament. Furthermore, intervention decisions can be made by the government, the national agency and the regional agency. At the municipal level, decisions are taken by the municipal councils, the municipal commissions, or the municipal agencies. The decision function is much less comprehensive than for instance the decision preparation stage.[1]

Decision in my heuristic model concerns the formal intervention decision. Where the real decisions about the adoption are made is held open for empirical investigation. Often the real decision is made already in the preparation stage.

Administration is a wide and diversified category. The basic idea is that intervention decisions should be brought forward to their realization. Even though decisions to intervene and administrative decisions to achieve the purposes of intervention decisions are sometimes hard to differentiate, it is important to make the distinction. Through administrative decisions, efforts are made to plan, design and make interventions ready for delivery to the targets. This can be thought of as the core process of administration. The core process needs support processes, however, like for instance hiring and training of personnel, purchase of technical equipment, payments of salaries, and gatekeeping functions like communication with the outside world.

Administration involves intervention specification and preparation for field execution. Specification includes such things as diffusion by upper–level decision makers of information on the contents of general decisions, specification by governments of general regulatory regimes adopted by parliament, and specification by regulatory agencies of regulatory mandates through the issuance of detailed norms and rules. Preparation for field execution refers to political attempts to affect government agencies, upper management attempts to influence lower management, and lower managements attempts to influence street–level operators. The addressees may also contribute to administration, for example, through active participation in the formation of the grass–roots agency's intervention delivery. In public administration language, this is called client or user participation.

Outputs are the means through which street–level operators and other agents in the administrative system attempts to influence intervention targets. Outputs are the things actually pouring out of the administrative system. Outputs include social services and goods delivered, laws and ordinances applied to individual cases, taxes and levies collected, grants and loans disbursed, campaign messages distributed to targets, and the like. In more concrete terms, what happens is that teachers teach in the schools, senior citizens are taken care of in the nursery homes, highways are built, trash is hauled, and books are borrowed from the public libraries.

Sometimes, outputs are included in the administration stage. The reason why they are treated separately here is a wish to facilitate for the readers to see the parallel between the public intervention model and the general, simple system model. Since the simple system model clearly differentiates between conversion and output (see figures 1.1 and 1.2 above), I have also made the separation in my heuristic intervention model.

Outcomes are what happens on the addressee (client, recipient) side in the intervention model. Outcomes can be measured in several stages. In some circumstances, they are gauged as addressee attitudes, addressee actions, and addressee urges to act. In other situations outcomes are essentially constituted by primary, secondary, or even tertiary societal repercussions beyond the addressees. Outcomes are then thought to be effects of addressee actions.

It may be difficult to pinpoint exactly the factors in the governance process that in a special case actually produce an outcome. An outcome may ensue because some addressees anticipate a future intervention decision and adjust before they are formally obligated to do it. The adopted intervention may directly impact upon the addressees, as when they without compliance measures comply with a regulation. Finally, the outputs may also produce the outcomes in the general population. What is important to realize is that outcomes are not always produced only through formal administration of higher level policies and outputs, but also through anticipation before the formal intervention decision is made.

In all organizations, a fundamental management task is *after–the–fact control*. Some device for monitoring and redirecting the diverse and specialized activities of large complex organizations such as a public bureaucracy is necessary, if the system is to be effective. In the present context, after–the–fact control is viewed as a metaprocess, as a separate, ongoing cycle of monitoring the primary public intervention process, including the collection of information about the performance of subordinates, and the screening of addressee compliance. After–the–fact administrative control comprises traditional auditing, simple monitoring, and evaluation. Administrative control also includes self–control in the sense that intervention operators themselves may control their work and work results in order to be able to adjust and accommodate.[2]

Evaluation is one type of after–the–fact administrative control. Decision makers, upper management, lower management, and street–level operators authorize their subordinates or external researchers and consultants to find out how the various stages in the administration process are unfolding, what the outputs and outcomes look like, whether the outcomes are produced by the intervention, and whether there are more cost–efficient means to reach the same goal. Evaluation may also be conducted as self–assessment for the purpose of learning and self–adjustment.

Findings dug out through after–the–fact control and particularly evaluation are supposed to be used as information for learning in the primary intervention process. Evaluation findings might be communicated to different audiences, such as agency managers, program operators, or outside decision makers. By itself a metaprocess, the delivery of control information is called *feedback* in figure 2.2. On the basis of the information supplied, the various evaluation users can take action in or directed at the intervention process. Feedback is supposed to produce redirection and reconsideration. In this stage of redirection and reconsideration, three things can happen as a consequence of learning: continuation as before, change, or termination. On the basis of these new circumstances, the intervention process is supposed to run another round and be subjected to after–the–fact control, which gives rise to new feedback.

Metaevaluation

As a final note, I would like to add that metaprocesses like evaluation and feedback can be evaluated as well. At a first glance, auditing evaluation may seem a peculiar activity. But evaluation, as a part of management in an organization, is as auditable as other management processes, such as policy implementation. To continue with the terminology previously used in this chapter, metaevaluation is a metameta–process in the general governance process. The relationships between the various levels are illustrated in figure 2.3.

Also, insights produced by evaluation of evaluation and feedback evaluation should be fed back to appropriate decision makers in order to be utilized. This metafeedback mechanism is not illustrated in figure 2.3.

Metaevaluation may be applied to one particular evaluation, for

FIGURE 2.3
Metaevaluation: Evaluation of Evaluation

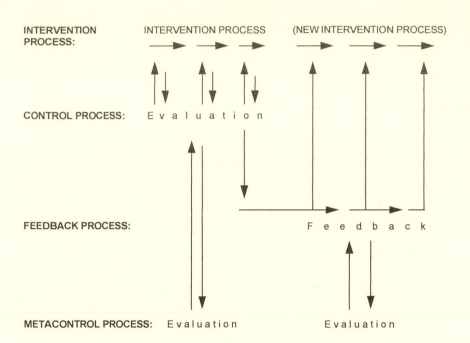

INTERVENTION
PROCESS:

INTERVENTION PROCESS

(NEW INTERVENTION PROCESS)

CONTROL PROCESS: E v a l u a t i o n

FEEDBACK PROCESS: F e e d b a c k

METACONTROL PROCESS: E v a l u a t i o n   E v a l u a t i o n

example, before it is sent to the commissioner or prior to its publication. It may be carried out by the evaluator herself, by some external scrutinizers, or preferably by the evaluatees. The purpose is to check for methodological quality, readability, faithfulness to facts, and other properties. Metaevaluation may also be carried out as a summary of findings from several evaluation studies.

Still another possibility is to audit the evaluation function of some government agency. A frequent subject in the evaluation literature (Hoogerwerf 1992:215ff), metaevaluation in this sense is especially appropriate when superiors want to evaluate the performance of some subordinate body with strong professions. University research is a perfect case of such a government supported activity where professionals reign almost supreme. The idea is then to let the professionals themselves manage the evaluation function—professors are asked to evaluate other professors and their performance, because outsiders do not have the necessary competence—but that the superior decision maker may ascertain whether the evaluation mechanisms actually function and function well.

Let me once more emphasize that the governance model is a heuristic model, which is supposed to facilitate thinking on evaluation. It is supposed to help evaluators and commissioners of evaluation to place themselves into a larger context. It neither provides not does it purport to provide a realistic picture of what is going on in governments. The realistic picture can be painted only on the basis of careful empirical studies.

Notes

1. Decision stands for program decision. Evidently numerous decisions are made also in the other stages in the primary governance process. Decisions are made to appoint investigatory commissions, how implementation should be carried out, how ex post facto control should be organized, and so on. This obvious complication will be overlooked here.
2. The idea of regarding evaluation as a meta–process is clearly expounded in Fernández–Ballesteros (1992a:207), who distinguishes the public policy intervention cycle from the evaluation (assessment) functions. Also in the same author's 1992b.

3

Evaluation, Rationality, and Theories
of Public Management

All evaluation rests upon the minimal rational supposition that goals, intentions, perceptions, judgments, opinions, schemes, plans, even ideologies—in short everything concerned with the world of human consciousness—play such interesting roles in public sector action, that their functions are worth investigating. Humans are seen as calculating actors, capable of choosing among options and judging, albeit crudely, their consequences. Through experience they may learn from past actions.

In recent times, attempts have been made to marry evaluation to various top–down management doctrines, particularly management by objectives and management by results. This is by no means necessary. Evaluation can be part and parcel of more bottom–up or pluralist management doctrines as well, such as professional evaluation, client–oriented evaluation, and stakeholder evaluation (see chapter 4). In addition, evaluation may be a one–shot event. In this chapter, I shall scrutinize briefly the top–down management doctrines, and discuss other possibilities in the next chapter.

Evaluation and Radical Rationalism

Elementary evaluation is ancient. According to Daniel's account of the Babylonian Imprisonment, King Nebuchadnezzar's courtier, Aspenas, systematically tested if a special diet given to the Jews Daniel, Hananya, Misael, and Asarya had any effect. As controls, Aspenas used Babylonian adolescents, who were given the King's food to taste (Dan.1:1–21; and Chelimsky 1985:2)

Yet, however ancient after–the–fact assessment is, contemporary evaluation research undoubtedly was part of a mighty rationalistic tide, the main philosophical thrust of which was to convert politics into a more rational, even scientific enterprise. This rationalistic, technocratic tendency grew particularly strong in the 1960s and the first part of the 1970s. According to dominant wisdom between 1960 and 1975, makers and administrators of public policy ought to apply the whole spectrum of methods for program–budgeting, zero–based budgeting, strategic planning, futures studies, systems analysis, cost–benefit and cost– effectiveness analysis, methods commonly referred to as policy analysis. Then ever–changing, fickle, and ill–considered public policies might be avoided and government interventions would become well–grounded, sound, and efficient. Through use of science or sciencelike analysis, well–co
nceived, long–range, and reasonable public policies would influence, if not replace, the shortsighted games between parties and special interest groups, which through simple rules of thumb attempt to muddle through arising societal problems (Wittrock and Lindström 1984).

The most far–reaching element of this rationalistic current in politics and administration was "radical rationalism" (Wittrock and Lindström 1984). Radical rationalists argued that decisions should be made only once researchlike policy analysis had answered a series of questions, somewhat simplistically summarized in figure 3.1.

FIGURE 3.1
Radical Rationalism

1. What ends are the decision makers trying to reach and what is the problem in need of a solution?

2. What alternative options may contribute toward achieving the end?

3. What are the consequences of the different options and the probabilities of each of these consequences?

4. What are the costs and resource requirements of the various options?

5. How can the options be arranged with respect to costs and consequences, and which criterion of merit should be used in the choice of option?

In the United States, Wittrock and Lindström (1984:11ff) continue, radical rationalism originated at the Rand Corporation and spread via Robert McNamara's Department of Defense to units of planning and analysis throughout the Federal administration in Washington. In Sweden, the diffusion was accomplished by systems analysts in the National Defence Research Establishment (FOA), the Agency for Administrative Development, and the National Audit Bureau. In both cases, the defense research communities seem to have played a role. Streamlined planning systems were created for physical, regional, and economic planning, for traffic and environment, higher education, and energy. Thinking in terms of clear goals, systematic data collection on problems and exhaustive before–the–fact analysis of measures dominated.

The combination of researchlike analysis and extensive programs marks the breakthrough of what Wittrock and Lindström call "the era of the great programs." While in the United States the new methods were part of president Lyndon Johnson's Great Society, in Sweden, they were intended to strengthen the Social Democracy's "Strong Society."

Radical rationalism, in my interpretation, emphasized the future–oriented, decision–preparing, planning stages in public decision–making operations. The essential requisite was that interventions were wisely and synoptically designed in a central planning machinery before they were established; execution and actual goal achievement were seen as relatively unproblematic. Actually, radical rationalism's trusting belief that results come up as effects of human design bears strong resemblance to what Popper and Hayek has called "naive rationalism" as opposed to "critical rationalism," which accommodates to the occurrence of unexpected side effects, reverse effects, and other limits to omniscient rationality.

With time, trust in radical rationalism's central–planning euphoria eroded. Observers realized that beautifully crafted plans are one thing, their transformation into practical reality another. More and more, administrative pundits started to argue the necessity of before–the–fact implementation analysis as a necessary missing link of rationalist policy analysis. And experts on administration came to the conclusion that a retrospective evaluation function had to be established in public policy, since reforms could lead to unexpected null effects, perverse effects, and side effects, while costs were skyrocketing.[1]

Evaluation and Management by Objectives

It was partly in this context that the focus of interest shifted toward *management by objectives,* and away from older notions like input–oriented and process–oriented management. Management by objectives incorporates three features that are thought to constitute good management practice in government: setting of clear goals, participation in decision making, and objective feedback of achieved results.

Management by objectives not only asserts that parliament, government, top managers, and other principals should set clear, measurable, intervention objectives. The objectives should be substantive and refer to results. Second, top management should involve senior administrators and their subordinates all the way down to the lowest hierarchical levels in objectives–setting discussions, which will result in the development of successively more specific objectives at all levels. Preferably the objectives–setting discussions should have a give–and–take character. Finally, efforts should be made to monitor progress toward the objectives and evaluate the results in terms of effectiveness. These results should be fed back to top management and senior administrators, but also to low–level subordinates because in the management–by–objectives doctrine, the latter are supposed to react to evaluation results and adjust their behavior accordingly. In the Swedish version of management by objectives, currently under implementation, a fourth step is added: those levels that are most successful in fulfilling the objectives should be awarded; the unsuccessful ones punished.

The stages of a management by objectives process are outlined in figure 3.2 (adapted from Rosenbloom 1989:159f).

The opposite to management by objectives is process–oriented management. In *process–oriented management,* politicians formulate rules for the decision–making processes in the public agencies and other executive bodies in the hope of influencing output, outcome, or costs. Immediate objectives are targeted at internal administrative processes, not at results.

While placing strong emphasis on participatory goal determination, management by objectives on the other hand attaches less weight to the setting of goals for the input into or the decision–making processes within the public agencies; instead it emphasizes what should come out in the form of impacts on society and to some extent outputs. Another crucial feature is learning from feedback and knowledge of

FIGURE 3.2
Management by Objectives

1. The top managerial level determines overall, organization–wide goals and sets priorities and posteriorities among the goals; the goals are formulated in terms of results to be accomplished, preferably as outcomes but also as outputs;

2. Top management principals involve lower–level agents—such as senior administrators, middle managers, and their subordinates—in the work of breaking down the overall organization–wide goals into subgoals for each organizational unit, even for each individual, operationalizing the subgoals into fully measurable results, making priorities and posteriorities between the subgoals, and indicating the time frame within which the subgoals are to be achieved; top managers are actively supporting and participating in the objectives–discussion;

3. Units and individual staff members develop plans for accomplishment of the intended results;

4. The superior liberates his subordinates from directives concerning how the goals ought to be achieved so that the subordinates themselves can decide by which means and methods the subgoals and objectives should be accomplished;

5. The principal allocates resources to his agents, preferably as block grants—unspecified lump sums—to provide some degree of freedom in developing means for the achievement of objectives;

6. People in the agencies are involved in implementation of plans, with emphasis on communications for responsiveness and on broad sharing in establishing authoritative objectives, priorities and posteriorities;

7. A system of performance review is instituted to track progress toward goals and objectives, with specific intermediate milestones indicated;

8. The results are frequently reviewed and evaluated in terms of effectiveness;

9. Evaluation findings are disseminated not only to top–level management, senior administrators, and middle managers but all the way down to the staff members at the lowest hierarchical levels of the organization to enable everyone to compare his performance with others in order to generate and implement improvements in objectives and results;

10. Successful work toward goal accomplishment is awarded by the principal (salaries, merit pay, promotion), shortcomings and failures are punished.

results. It is thought that both goal setting and performance evaluation will contribute to increased productivity. Some researchers have actually found that "it is the goal originally established that produces most of the 'motivational force' in the situation rather than the provision of feedback alone" (Carroll and Tosi 1973:4).

Evaluation and Results–Oriented Management

Evaluation can also be seen as a vital feature of *results–oriented management* (Wholey 1983; Shadish, Cook, and Leviton 1991:233). Like management by objectives, the term results– oriented management is ambiguous. I have to admit that I am not sure what the differences, if any, between the two doctrines actually are. I shall address two interpretations of the management–by–results doctrine.

Characteristic of results–oriented management is that the principal early on signals to his agents that the results will be controlled after the fact. Also he indicates what results he expects them to achieve. Furthermore, the superior makes clear that the results will be disclosed to the public and compared to the results produced by other units. To this end, the principal institutes mechanisms for after–the–fact monitoring and evaluation of outcomes and outputs. In management by results, the evaluation mechanism is intended to have a double function. It is intended to give signals to the agents which results the principal is expecting. This is largely to be effectuated by means of the evaluation process, that is, the agents are thought to be influenced by what the questions posed in the evaluation reveals about the value criteria and value standards of their superiors. In addition, the evaluation results are also intended to furnish the principal and the agents with continuous and systematic feedback of reliable information concerning real results. The idea is that the agents themselves voluntarily will correct their activities when they get to know their own position in relation to others. For the evaluation will cover not only one unit but many, which makes comparisons possible. But the reporting of the results shall also be an instrument for the principal to give signals to the agents in which directions they ought to change their efforts. Not only may these signals come as advice and recommendations but also in the form of increased or decreased appropriations and funds.

Obviously, evaluation is a fundamental feature of results–oriented management. Naturally, the results accounted for in the evaluations are important. Management by results is based on the notion of continuous and systematic feedback to principals and agents of reliable information on policy and program results. Public policy and planning should, above all, be grounded in a firm foundation of real results. By results is meant either outcomes or outputs, or both. Management by results is an outgrowth of a just–give–them–the–facts philosophy. Just present the facts, but leave it to the principal and his agents to apply criteria of merit to the facts and perform the overall evaluation. On the basis of this, principals and staff at all levels in the organization can start to calibrate the goals and objectives for the continued program activities. But it is also important to note that in management by results not only the evaluation findings, but also the evaluation process, is supposed to give critical clues to agents for their future activities.

One similarity between management by results and management by objectives is that the agents are given full freedom to choose means to reach the signalled goals. The principal provides unequivocal result–oriented comprehensive goals, but does not interfere with how the agency or the unit act to accomplish these goals. Management by results is thought to function largely through the force of example. Subordinates should be stimulated by comparing themselves to others, not by being mandated to perform specific tasks through detailed compulsory regulations and directives.

What is meant by results in results–oriented management is not always clear. According to one interpretation, results means substantive results minus resources consumed, that is, costs are taken into consideration. But results also seems to refer to outcomes, outputs, or both without any specification of the costs involved.

According to a second, somewhat different rendering, results–oriented management is regarded as the incipient stage in the development of a management–by–objectives system. Before clear and determinate objectives can be worked out on higher levels, lower–level agencies must account for their actual results. When this is accomplished, higher levels can start to set realistic and feasible goals for future action. Results–oriented management will then become a process that starts bottom up, while management by objectives starts top down, at least in the incipient stage.

The reformation of the Swedish government budgeting process currently under way is dominated by management–by–results rhetoric.

Dissatisfaction with traditional budgeting has been growing for a long time. Critics have argued that budgeting to a preciously small extent is concerned with achieved results; the result–oriented evaluations that are carried out lead lives of their own, isolated from the budgeting process, which mostly concerns appropriations to different purposes. The present reform is an attempt to remedy this unhappy situation by tying output and outcome evaluation stronger to budgeting.

Agencies are placed in a triennial cyclical pattern, so that each of them is subjected to extensive assessment every three years. On these occasions, the assessment should be strongly results–oriented, which presupposes that the agencies themselves continuously evaluate their own programs and disseminate this information to their superiors. In the years when no extensive assessment is performed, the agencies will be subjected to a so–called simplified assessment. Even simplified assessments will contain an evaluative component, since their purpose is to monitor whether the results objectives set in the extensive assessment are met. Furthermore, the government should define comprehensive output and outcome objectives and provide some general guidelines concerning agency activities, but leave the agencies considerable leeway to choose the appropriate ways and means to attain the results objectives. The focus will also be switched from budgeting and other constraints toward results analysis, evaluation, and achieved results (Sandahl 1992; P 1987/88:150, app. 1, FiU30, rskr394, SOU 1990:83).

The attention that management by objectives has received in scholarly journals has seen a dramatic demise. Extensive discussion of the subject could be found in any public administration outlet during the 1970s; articles are rare in the 1980s and 1990s. After the initial euphoria, it has also attracted massive criticisms from the academic community. In government it is impossible to manage by goals or results, it is argued. Politicians cannot determine clear goals because they lack necessary knowledge or hesitate to reveal their operative motivations because they are regarded as inopportune. Furthermore, the official goals are often too hazy to be employed as meaningful criteria of evaluation. A more principal criticism asserts that some activities, such as academic research, simply should not be managed by goals or results. Academic research is an innovative enterprise that cannot be managed by goals for the obvious reason that it should produce something new, which is not known at the moment when goals should be set. It is also alleged that decisions on means cannot be left to the bureaucrats, because means are sometimes more politically contested than goals. Often, political parties hold widely differing views about means because they are immediate and concrete, while they agree on the goals, which are regarded as cosmetics to garner acceptance and legitimacy for the programs. For instance, it is difficult to see the choice between private or public day care for children as an empirical question of best available means to reach a commonly approved goal: best possible care for the young generation. On the contrary, in cases like this, political parties agree on the goals but widely disagree on the means to reach the goal.

Note

1. The historical development of retrospective evaluation in various countries is charted in works by Derlien 1990a and others in Ray C. Rist 1990, by several authors like Nioche, Gray and Jenkins, Leeuw, Kordes, and Sandahl in Mayne and Bemelmans–Videc et al. 1992, and by contributors to the volume edited by Gray, Jenkins, and Segsworth 1992.

4

Models of Evaluation

There is acrimonious disagreement on the methodological foundation and practical orientation of evaluation research. Scores of advocated approaches have been sufficiently formalized to appear in the literature. To create an overview, this multitude of approaches ought to be collapsed into a few basic schools. For this an Occam's razor is needed, but unfortunately no such sharp, universally recognized instrument is available. The most pertinent basis of division is the evaluation's "organizer", that is, its logical point of departure. The organizer is the basic question posed in the evaluation. Often, the chosen criterion of merit is the organizer of an evaluation. But since this is not always the case, I prefer the more abstract concept of organizer.

My approach is based on what Guba and Lincoln (1981:8, 11ff.) have suggested about organizers in their treatise on education evaluation. Since I shall attempt to apply both a political science and a broader social science perspective on evaluation, my scheme will in practice be considerably different from theirs.[1]

A taxonomy of evaluation models, ordered according to organizers, is provided in figure 4.1.

An important line of demarcation distinguishes models focusing on the substantive results of government interventions on the one hand, and models checking for legality, equity, representativeness, and other qualities of the procedures according to which the interventions are supposed to be handled by ministries and agencies on the other. The former are called substantive, the latter procedural models. While of long-standing importance, procedural models will not be dealt with

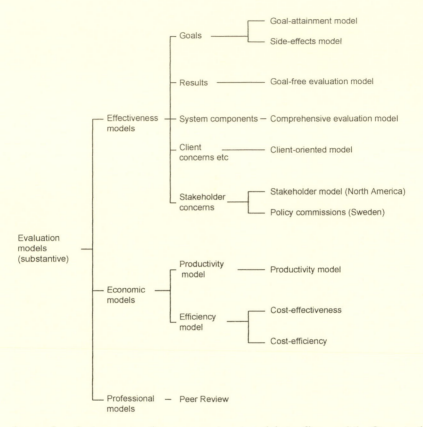

here; for that reason, they are not entered into figure 4.1. Our study will focus entirely on some important substantive models: effectiveness models, economic models, and professional models. Effectiveness models constitute a fairly large and varied group. In addition to the classic goal–attainment evaluation, effectiveness models include side–effects evaluation, goal–free evaluation, comprehensive evaluation, client–oriented evaluation, and the stakeholder model.

While effectiveness models address only the results of alternative interventions, economic models pay heed to costs as well. The latter property differentiate them from effectiveness models, which are cost blind. The two basic variants among the economic models are the productivity and the efficiency models.

Economic models integrate cost and effectiveness aspects of public interventions. Yet just as evaluators often consider only the results aspect (effectiveness), administrators sometimes deliberate only the costs. In the 1980s, in fact, there has been an increasing emphasis on the management of resources rather than the management of policy. However, pure cost models are not included here.

Before proceeding, a caveat must be inserted concerning "effectiveness" and "efficiency." In efficiency measurement costs are included, while effectiveness assessment concentrates on results only without taking costs into consideration. This was clear to Herbert A. Simon already in 1945 when he wrote his chapter "The Criterion of Efficiency" in his renowned book *Administrative Behavior* (1976:180f.). "Until practically the end of the nineteenth century, the terms 'efficiency' and 'effectiveness' were considered almost as synonymous," Simon asserted. But then, efficiency acquired a second meaning: the ratio between input and output. To sustain his assertion, Simon quoted *The Encyclopedia of the Social Sciences*:

> Efficiency in the sense of ratio between input and output, effort and control, expenditure and income, cost and the resulting pleasure, is a relatively recent term. In this specific sense it became current in engineering only during the latter half of the nineteenth century and in business and in economics only since the beginning of the twentieth.

Consequently, intervention effectiveness in English has nothing to do with costs.

Professional models, the third basic category in figure 4.1, focus on the subject matter only indirectly, in that immediate stress is put on who should perform the evaluation. The most celebrated professional model is the peer review approach, in which for instance professors evaluate professors, engineers, and surgeons.

My exposition will start with effectiveness models, proceed through economic, and end with professional models. As already mentioned, the procedural models will not be treated in the present context.

Goal-Attainment Evaluation

The classical way of approaching the evaluation problem is goal-attainment evaluation. The two basic ingredients of goal-attainment evaluation are called goal–achievement measurement and impact assessment. The key question in *goal-achievement measurement* is: Are the results in accord with program goals? And the *impact assessment* issue can be formulated: Are the results produced by the program? Another name for goal–achievement measurement would be *results monitoring*.

Goal–attainment evaluation is a paragon of simplicity and lucidity. After identifying the goals of the program, teasing out their actual meaning and rank order, and turning them into measurable objectives, the second step involves determining to what extent these premeditated goals have been realized in practice. The third step in goal–attainment evaluation implies ascertaining the degree to which the program has promoted or dampened goal realization.

Goal–attainment evaluation is an effectiveness model because it asks questions about the substantive content, output, and outcomes of the program, not about program procedures like equity of treatment, due process, and the like. It differs from economic and institutional models in that it raises substantive issues only, but pays heed to neither program costs, nor the organization of the evaluation.

In adopting the yardsticks of others as criteria of merit, the goal–attainment model applies a descriptive theory of valuing. Actually, it supports a particular descriptive theory of valuing, since it takes premeditated program goals as criteria of merit and organizer for the evaluation. Ernest House writes that

> [it] takes the goals of the program as stated and then collects evidence as to whether it has achieved those goals. The goals serve as the exclusive source of standards and criteria. The evaluator assesses what the program developers say they intend achieving. The discrepancy between the stated goals and outcomes is the measure of program success. (1980:26)

This does not imply, in practical terms, that evaluators should first of all search out the goals. The crucial point is that goals are the *logical* point of departure. After all, the major task of evaluation, advocates of the goal-attainment model claim, is to determine if the premeditated program goals have in fact been achieved and then try find out to what extent the program has contributed to goal achievement.

The simple anatomy of goal-attainment evaluation is outlined in figure 4.2.

The first part of the goal-attainment model, goal–achievement measurement, engenders two distinct activities to be kept apart: (1) the clarification of program goals (the goal function); and (2) the mea-

FIGURE 4.2
Goal-Attainment Evaluation

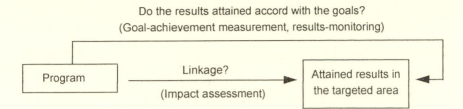

Do the results attained accord with the goals?
(Goal-achievement measurement, results-monitoring)

surement of actual completion of premeditated program goals (the goal accomplishment function). The second part of the model implies finding out to what extent the program has contributed to goal achievement (the causal function) (Lane 1987).

Let me provide a straightforward example. The goal of the 1978 Swedish Energy Savings Plan for Existing Buildings was that "annual net energy consumption" in the 1978 building stock would in 1988 be approximately 35 TWh lower than in the benchmark year of 1978. This meant a reduction of approximately 30 percent. To achieve this goal, state funds were channelled into home insulation, retrofitting of industrial and commercial buildings, and energy auditing and counselling. A goal–attainment evaluation of the Energy Savings Plan would entail investigating whether annual net energy consumption—however measured—in the 1978 building stock actually was 35 TWh lower at the end of 1988 and whether this actual outcome might be attributed to the adopted reform.

The example makes it clear that the goal–attainment model also presupposes some idea about the time span that may pass before the goals are supposed to be achieved. In other words, goal–attainment evaluators must know when it is appropriate to pass a judgment on goal completion. In my example, a full summative evaluation can only be carried out in 1989 or later. However, goal–achievement evaluations can also be performed as intermediate reviews during this period to check whether things are moving in the right direction.

The goal–attainment model may be applied to government interventions at all political and administrative levels; for example, programs adopted by:

1. municipal commissions;
2. municipal assemblies;
3. county assemblies;
4. national agencies;
5. national parliaments;
6. the Nordic Council;
7. the European Community; or
8. the United Nations.

A program might be a broad regulatory mandate espoused by a United Nations body or by a national parliament, or tiny planks in small substantive programs introduced by a municipal decision–making body. Embraced by most OECD countries and truly global in magnitude, the 1987 Montreal Protocol regulating emissions of substances thought to destroy the global ozone layer is a program, as is the peat heating scheme enacted by the city of Uppsala in Sweden.

All types of government programs can be evaluated for goal attainment. Programs may concern organizational change in the public sector or substantive issue areas. A program can be many different things: a planned public social service, an actual social service, a stream of commodities, a law, a norm derived from a law, a planned information effort, and the like. The intervention concept also covers conglomerates of individual programs, for instance Swedish environmental policies, which include numerous important laws, subsidy schemes and grants for research. Neither the kind of program nor the political or administrative level at which it is instituted is of importance to the subsequent reasoning on goal–attainment evaluation.

While "goal-attainment evaluation" is a common expression in the literature, the term "goal–achievement evaluation" is frequently used as well. Other denominators include "the rational model," "the objectives-oriented approach," and "the behavioral objectives approach."[2]

The Strength of the Goal–Attainment Model

In earlier literature, the goal–attainment model reigned supreme. Program evaluation was even identified with goal–attainment appraisal, a curious fact that was discussed in chapter 1 on the evaluation concept. Since the 1970s, however, goal–attainment evaluation has been under constant attack. Presently, almost no one is able to, or has the stamina to stand up in its defense.

There are, however, three important reasons in favor of goal–attainment assessment. I shall label them the democratic argument, the research argument, and the simplicity argument.

The *democratic argument* is a compelling one, grounded in the notion of the *primacy of the parliamentary chain of control* and, consequently, in a democratic perspective.

Government program goals differ from goals in other walks of social life due to their institutionalization through a formal decision–making machinery. They are publicly and officially adopted in political assemblies by the representatives of the people. Decision–making procedures of political bodies are circumscribed by formal rule systems to an extent that has no counterpart in, for example, corporations, voluntary associations, or families. Political leaders are supposed to honor the rules of the constitution, and the rules of procedure in parliament and government. Once a decision comes out of this system, it has a status that cannot be compared to decisions in other social bodies. The fact that program goals are the product of the formal decision–making machinery of the state makes them all the more significant. It is a merit of the goal–attainment model that it recognizes this fact, which is often overlooked by students of general organizations.

The goals of the democratic state also occupy a special position because they have emerged under responsibility. In principle, political officials must contemplate not only their own wishes, but also available resources. Partial interests, like the various pressure groups, can pursue demands and set goals without considering the general public interest or the financial situation.

In the extension of this conviction of the special status of the parliamentary chain of command there is a deeply rooted ideal of public administrators as the obedient tools of the elected representatives. Civil servants must attend to their political principals regardless of personal idiosyncracies, feelings about the worth of the programs, and partisan allegiances. In serving their masters, they should subscribe to Tacitus' famous *maxim sine ira et studio*, "with neither anger nor partiality."

In sum, I am sympathetic to the descriptive theory of valuing underlying the goal–attainment model.

Two of the criticisms periodically raised against the goal–attainment model are insensitive to the democratic aspect. One of them brands the model as dangerously *elitist*. It is geared to the needs of reform makers and other peak groups in the decision–making system, since it is these power wielders who want to know whether program goals have been accomplished.

The elitist criticism disregards that goal accomplishment is of the utmost importance from a citizen's perspective. It must be of interest to citizens to be informed about whether the adopted policies really deliver what they promise. Assume that the representatives of the citizens, the elected politicians, have promised in an election to introduce a pension reform that will give everyone an economically secure retirement. It eventually becomes obvious that these goals are not being fulfilled. It must be valuable for the electorate to get to know about this when they are to judge the performance of their representatives, and past policies in the next election.

The second objection that overlooks the accountability and citizen perspective intimates that initial program goals might become *obsolete* as evaluative yardsticks. In adopting initial goals as points of departure, the evaluator runs the risk of using an antiquated baseline when her paper is presented. The result cannot be applied in the next round of decision making.

The compelling force of this objection hinges upon which goals that change and to whom the evaluation is addressed. If goal displacement occurs among politicians, evaluation against official, allegedly obsolete goals will be of no interest to them. But it will be of great concern to the citizenry in its role as principal, because to them the official goals still hold true, and they may want to hold the politicians accountable for discarding them. If goal displacement subtly transpires in the national agency or even further down in the implementation process and the program is modified radically due to this, evaluation against antiquated official goals will be of no substantive concern to these groups, but will be of the utmost relevance to citizens and responsible politicians, since agencies and low–level implementors are their proxies and executives, whom they may want to hold accountable.

In sum, the goal–attainment model scores important points with respect to its inherent descriptive theory of valuing, which tilts toward the parliamentary chain of control, and representative democracy, particularly toward the frog's-eye perspective of the citizenry. The citizen perspective has been repeatedly stressed in this context, because it is rarely alluded to in international discourse on public program evaluation.

The second reason for goal–attainment assessment, *the research argument*, is based on the model's potential for bringing social research to bear on the evaluation enterprise. All evaluation requires dimensions of merit through which the program can be graded. Evaluation is a normative enterprise. The goal–attainment model seems to offer an objective solution to the value criterion problem in evaluation. Since program goals are explicitly stated in the original legislation or in the preparatory work, they can be established empirically, through an act of interpretation. By judging program results from program goals, the cautious evaluator can avoid taking a personal, subjective stand on the merits and demerits of the programs to be evaluated. Goal–attainment evaluation embraces a descriptive theory or valuing; it is what Scriven (1991:30) has called a secondary evaluation—evaluation from the point of view of others. Since the criterion issue can be settled in an objective fashion the whole evaluation can be conducted in an objective fashion as well. The goal–attainment model accords a large role to the objective evaluator. There exists a group in society who are trained to conduct objective research: the academic social scientists. Evaluation is best performed if the task is assigned to independent social scientists.

A third, admittedly less important reason for the goal–attainment model is its attractive *simplicity*. Involving only two major questions, it is very easy to understand and apply.

On the other hand, the goal–attainment model also suffers from persistent flaws and weaknesses, to which I shall now direct my attention.

The Shortcomings of the Goal–Attainment Model

The goal–attainment model disregards *costs*.[3] Goal accomplishment may have incurred substantial sacrifices in terms of money, time, and human efforts; these are completely ignored in goal–attainment assessment.[4] The lack of cost–consciousness alone reveals that the goal–attainment model cannot aspire to be the sole valid model of public policy evaluation.

Even more damaging is the case against goal–achievement evaluation in its own purported area of competence. One such momentous argument suggests that program goals are deficient as criteria of merit because of their *haziness*.

While a truism, the supposition of the pervasive haziness of policy and program goals is repeatedly stated in policy analysis literature. So accepted is the general idea that only rarely efforts are made to indicate in what ways public sector goals are muddy. There are good reasons, however, to distinguish between two major types of goal obscurity: goal indeterminateness and goal catalogues.

First, programs may be based on *indeterminate goals*. There is "terminological inexactitude," to use Winston Churchill's famous expression. Terminological inexactitude, in turn, is of two kinds. Particular goals may be *ambiguous* and carry two or more simultaneous meanings. Yet ambiguity is probably quite exceptional in political and bureaucratic language, and barely bothers evaluators. More confusion is caused by *vagueness*. A goal is vague if it does not delineate clearly cases where it is or is not applicable. The outer border delimiting the extension of a vague word is so fuzzy that within a certain range it is impossible to know what is included in the extension and what is not. Rampant in political rhetoric, vagueness is one favorite expedient to settle political conflicts without really resolving them.

The second major obscurity is produced by *goal catalogues*. In connection with most large social reforms, impressive directories of diverse goals are regularly presented. While a single goal may be hailed as the major one, it is often also said that this one must be balanced against all the others, maybe including potentially conflicting ones. Often, the particular items in the goal catalogues are vague. In addition, the necessary trade–offs between the several goals are not indicated, which makes it impossible to elicit from such lists of goals one distinct, transparent, expected outcome. Thus, program goals do not offer any safe guidance for the direction of continued empirical research work. They are not lucid enough to be usable as value criteria against which to measure successes, shortcomings, and failures.

The government regulatory regime concerning Swedish forestry management contains a catalogue of individually vague and collectively contradictory goals. The first paragraph of the 1979 Forest Management Act states that forests must be managed in such a way as to secure their sustained capacity to produce timber. However, the law also declares that nature protection and other societal interests must be paid heed to. The forestry business must operate with due concern for the functions of the forests as habitats for plants and animals, their role in water balance and local climate, for outdoor life and recreation. Attention must be paid to valuable cultural environments and landscapes.

Exactly how sustained high production of timber should be balanced against the other goals is not stipulated. This is probably wise, since it would be difficult to specify in central decisions how the weighing should be made in every local case. However, this wisdom creates difficulties for the goal–attainment model, since the program does not stipulate a clear expected outcome.

If the evaluator sticks to the notion of objectivity, which is a fundamental tenet in goal–attainment evaluation, she will not be able to tease out from the overall goal formulations one indisputably clear global outcome objective. To arrive at such an objective, she probably has to clarify the program goals and make priorities among them, which entails leaving the sphere of objective social inquiry and entering the area of subjective speculation.

The goal–haziness argument reveals an important misfit between the requirements of the goal–attainment model and the way public policies and programs are usually composed. If elected officials and program planners have not specified individual goals into measurable objectives, and if they have not balanced the various stated goals into one, global outcome or output measure, the goal–attainment evaluator cannot sum the results into a final evaluative judgment in any completely objective fashion. She can do so only after she has clarified the goals and prioritized among in a fashion that will cast doubts on the objectivity of the whole enterprise.

On the other hand, the goal–haziness argument, while pertinent, is not applicable across the board. Occasionally, political bodies find it appropriate to set clear, even quantified objectives; an obvious example is the above–mentioned 1978 Energy Savings Plan. In these cases, the goal–haziness argument has no bearing on the full applicability of the goal–attainment model.

A third objection, about *unintended effects*, is in my view the crucial one. Attempts at deliberate political control invariably lead to consequences that were not originally foreseen in the original decision situation. "It is difficult to forecast, particularly about the future," as Niels Bohr jokingly put it. Were the evaluators to confine themselves exclusively to researching the achievement of premeditated program goals, any serendipitous results or unanticipated side–effects would not be included in the main evaluation process. The evaluation would provide a tunnel vision of events, and produce a biased, if not fundamentally wrong, picture of what the program has attained. In all likelihood, a program generating some interesting spin–off effects must be better than a program producing several undesirable spillovers (Foss Hansen 1989:204).

In addition, the prevalence of intentional action resulting in unintended side–consequences is one of the strongest reasons—besides perverse effects—for performing evaluations in the first place (Meyers 1981:18ff.). Designing them in a way that does not allow for the possibility of discovering such side–effects must then be a serious mistake.

Suppose somebody made a goal–attainment evaluation of King Ferdinand and Queen Isabella's program of sending Christopher Columbus westward to find the sea route to India. Our evaluator concludes that the program is a failure because India was not reached and the program goal was not achieved. There is no reason to consider the side–effects, the discovery of America, the ensuing cruel and deceitful extermination of advanced ancient civilizations, and so on and so forth, since the goal–attainment model pays no heed to phenomena outside the target area.

A fourth seemingly compelling objection suggests that the goal–attainment model disregards the role of *hidden agendas* in public policymaking.

It has been suggested that policy analysts using premeditated, officially pronounced, substantive goals as measuring rods for evaluative purposes and organizers for data collection disregard something important in the political game situation. Manifest substantive goals resemble the tip of an iceberg. Far from revealing the real operative motives, they constitute only what decision-makers want to hold up to the public. Officially stated goals may have a symbolic character, not intended to be achieved, while real, hidden motives point to other directions. The hidden substantive political agenda behind a privatization drive of government–owned companies may not be to increase efficiency in the best interests of the consumers but to strengthen the power network supporting conservative and other nonsocialist parties. Hidden agendas include strategic motives as well. The point may be to strengthen party cohesion, to keep or attract voters in the next general election, or to prepare the ground for a coalition government. Once these hidden strategic goals are achieved, politicians lose interest in implementing the substantive provisions of the program.

To political scientists, this is a staple analysis of the motivating forces prompting public reforms. Of course, strategic considerations play an important role in public policymaking. But what is the real import of the hidden–agenda stricture against the goal–attainment model? Should the results also be evaluated against such strategic yardsticks as winning the upcoming election, strengthening internal party cohesion, or maintaining government coalitions? In that case, we have to admit, the goal–attainment model would be insufficient since it uses substantive and only substantive goals as yardsticks.

On the other hand, goal-attainment evaluators may rightfully argue that hidden agendas may very well be considered in their model. They might be used as factors *explaining* why substantive results did or did not occur. If, for instance, substantive program goals were not met, there is nothing in the logic of the goal-attainment model impeding evaluators from offering hidden strategic agendas as reasons why this occurred. Providing such explanations must be considered a major activity in evaluation research, and it seems to be reconcilable with a slightly widened goal–attainment model.

On the other hand, a strictly applied goal–attainment model does not emphasize nonprogrammatic explanations of the results. There is no separate box in the goal–attainment model for strategic considerations as explanations of outcomes. In fact, there are no boxes except for the one signifying the program. Naturally, the goal–attainment model must consider other explanatory factors besides the program but they are lumped together into one, large comprehensive factor, which is contrasted with the program factor. This comprehensive factor is treated like a "black box," never to be opened, but this is an obvious drawback, since if the program was partly a failure it would be very interesting to know exactly why.

In conclusion, the goal–attainment model has problems in considering hidden agendas underlying program decisions, but these problems are not insurmountable.

A fifth counter–argument maintains that the goal–attainment model *does not regard implementation as a problem.* Implementation processes are treated as black boxes. This is also a pertinent stricture, since if strictly applied according to figure 4.2, the model does precisely that. The model concentrates on the consequences of the program, not of the implementation processes. The organizations and networks of institutions and actors which are supposed to transform decisions into effects are uninteresting to goal–attainment evaluation.

A last objection maintains that the goal–attainment model proceeds from an all too *conventional view of the politics–administration relationship* according to which the administration not only in theory but also in practice promptly and faithfully executes the decisions of politicians. Implementation processes are actually mechanical, straight line, and controlled from the top. The goal–attainment model is accused of regarding public administration as a target–seeking robot fulfilling its mission with painstaking technical precision.

But this disparagement entirely misses the point. The goal–attainment model may well be associated with the normative conviction that the civil service ought to be the faithful tool of the elected representatives of the people. It does not, however, take for granted that civil servants always loyally execute the decisions of the politicians. There is nothing in the logic of the goal–attainment model compelling us to believe that the program has produced the intended results. On the contrary, eventual program impact in the target area is considered one of the two problems to be investigated in a goal–attainment evaluation, the second one being whether the achieved result accord with the original goals. The arrow from "program" to "attained result" in Figure 4.2 shows, not how the linkage actually is, but what the evaluator attempts to test in a goal–attainment impact assessment. She may very well come up with the conclusion that there is no causal relationship between program and result. The objection that the goal-attainment model treats programs as target–seeking robots has no bearing whatsoever on the logic of the model.

In sum, taking official subject–matter goals seriously is the major strength of the goal–attainment model. The reason why this is a strength is grounded in the theory of representative democracy. From a governance perspective, citizens as well as elected politicians need goal evaluation to check whether their executives actually carry out what they are obliged to do.

However, the goal–attainment model is also open to several valid objections. It overlooks procedural goals like equity of treatment and legality. It disregards costs. It has some problems with hazy goals, pervasive as we all know, in public policymaking. The most compelling rebuttal, however, emanates from the fact that the goal–achievement model is blind to side effects.

At this point, I would like to present a model that expressly considers the weighty side–effects argument, while retaining the fundamental goal–orientation of the goal–attainment model: side–effects evaluation.

Side–Effects Evaluation

An inherent difficulty with goal–attainment assessment using prespecified goals as the organizer is how to account for unintended and unrecognized effects. Political actions may culminate in unintended, unforeseen by–products. If an important set of side effects is unintended, how can they be considered and judged if the evaluator sticks to premeditated, substantive goals as the basic organizing principle? To solve this problem, the goal– attainment model must be extended to cover side effects. I shall call this approach side–effects evaluation.

Characteristic of the side–effects approach is that goals are retained as the fundamental organizer but supplemented by side effects. For the expression "side effect"—a side effect in relation to what?—presupposes knowledge of what the main intended effect is expected to be. Side effects must be defined in relation to the intended main effects. From the policy instigators' point of view, a side effect may be defined as an impact outside the program target area. "Main effects" can be defined as the central substantive impacts that the policy instigators *by intention* wanted to achieve. Consequently, main effects are associated with the substantive objectives of the policy–makers and with what they believe themselves capable of achieving. Furthermore, main effects are by definition anticipated as well as positively valued by the policy instigators.[5]

Thus, I contend that the model is *based* on goals in that program goals are retained as the focal organizer. But in addition, traits outside the target area preordained by program goals are also considered. The underlying idea is that public interventions may produce other things than intended results. They may lead to great discoveries embodied in names like Columbus and America. But they may also create more problems than they solve, turning solutions into problems. Solutions to puzzles become puzzles requiring solutions.

The side–effects issue is still grossly overlooked in evaluation research. I agree with the judgment of Sieber (1981:44f.): "Concern with unanticipated consequences of any sort seems to be a grudging exception [in evaluation research]. Textbooks on evaluation rarely mention the subject, and when they do it is almost entirely in the form of sheer admonition (along with a footnote reference to Merton, perhaps). Concrete guidelines for conceptualizing, detecting, measuring, or assessing a net balance of good and bad effects are not offered."

The basic skeleton of the side-effects model is sketched in figure 4.3.

It has been known since Machiavelli that political actions can be counterproductive. The liberator easily turns into an oppressor—the strength needed to break the bonds will be used to again put people into bonds, which in turn must be broken. This is what is known in public policy as *perverse effects*.

Perverse effects run exactly counter to the very intentions of the program instigators. To use a different but pertinent terminology, they are cases of counterfinality. Since these impacts occur in the target area of the public intervention they are not side effects. Neither are they main effects, since they are not coveted by the policy instigators. The side–effects/main-effects terminology cannot catch perverse effects. Perverse effects of purposive action ought to be treated as a separate category.

Perverse, or reverse, effects are also different from *null effects*. According to Sam D. Sieber, who to the best of my knowledge origi-

FIGURE 4.3
Side–Effects Evaluation

Do the results concur with ...

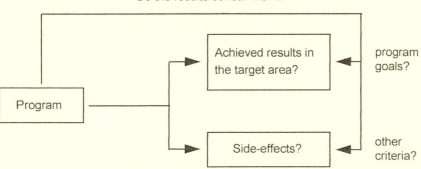

nated the distinction between perverse effects and null effects, which I am applying here (1981:10, 47, x), the expression null effects means that programs adopted because they are earnestly and fully expected to have certain effects wholly fail to spawn any such effects. The programs produce no impacts at all on their targeted areas. In the perverse effects case, consequences are produced but entirely contrary to the ones intended.[6]

A nearly universal fascination with the topic of perverse unintended effects of intentional action is manifested by an array of technical and historical terms—the Cunning of Reason, the irony of history, Pyrrhic victory, two–edged sword, counterproductive measures, backlash, and boomerang effect.

An alleged classic example (Sieber 1981:9, 166) of a self–defeating public policy is the Maginot Line, which lulled the French into a false sense of security and the consequent immobilization of military resources which contributed to their defeat by the German army in 1940.

Since by definitional fiat perverse effects occur and null effects do not occur in the targeted areas, the goal–attainment model with all its attention directed at what happens in these particular fields has no problem with handling them. But this also means that the model cannot discover and ascertain side effects because they fall outside of the targeted sectors.

Side effects can be *anticipated* and considered in calculations preceding decisions to adopt policies. Side effects are by far not always detrimental either. They may be detrimental to policy instigators, but, of course, beneficial as well. In spite of the fact that the term *side effect* has a slightly derogatory connotation in English, the evaluator must be open to the fact that public interventions may produce welcome as well as unwelcome side effects.[7]

In the aftermath of the 1973 oil crunch, governments all over the world instituted energy conservation programs. In Sweden, a government grant program was adopted for energy conservation in dwellings. Later it was converted into the above-mentioned Energy Savings Plan for Existing Buildings (from Vedung 1982a:85). State subsidies were offered to people willing to retrofit their properties. The intended outcome was to achieve more efficient energy use in existing buildings. Yet it was anticipated that the grant program might have an unfavorable impact on the distribution of wealth in the country, since home owners, owners of multifamily dwellings, and other prospective recipients of the program are generally wealthier than people at large. While not primarily coveted, policy-makers were prepared to create and accept this side effect in order to reach the overarching desired goal of energy efficiency.

On the other hand, policy sponsors also realized that the subsidy scheme might spawn a number of felicitous spillovers. It would boost economic activity in general and create numerous new jobs. Retrofitting and insulation of walls and attics would diminish draft, which would make indoor climate more comfortable. Insulation and the installation of three–pane windows would reduce noise.

A study geared toward investigating energy conservation as well as wealth distribution, employment, and comfort aspects would be a side–effects evaluation.

So far, I have considered anticipated side effects only. However, some side effects are no doubt *unanticipated* as well. Some policy analysts would probably even argue that most side–effects are unanticipated at the time the decision is taken. Like their foreseen counterparts, they might be felicitous or deleterious. Increased radon radiation in dwellings, and the increased incidence of allergies, both probable consequences of better insulation causing less draft, may be adduced as examples of deleterious, unanticipated side effects.

Beneficial inadvertent consequences are rare specimens, however, because reformers trying to sell a new policy are likely to list and exhaust all the positive impacts likely to follow. "The phenomenon of overselling a program at the time of policy formulation and legitimation is well-known and, in fact, characterizes much of policy–making in the United States," argue Ripley and Franklin in a recent book on implementation (1986:234f.). However, there are occasions when grim policies have unanticipated, happy spinoffs.

The demilitarized zone around the 38th parallel formed in 1953 across the Korean peninsula is an interesting story of how military conflict resolution unintendedly produced a last refuge for endangered species like, for instance, the rare Manchurian crane (*grus japonensis*), the ringneck pheasant, the native Korean bear, and the wildcat. The 4000 meter wide DMZ is one of the most militarized areas in the world as it is mined, has obstacles to foot or vehicle movement, and is constantly patrolled. It is also one of the least inhabited. It is the militarism of this area that inadvertently has created a safe haven for all wildlife as the habitats are saved from encroachments from intensive agriculture, industry, the building of roads, and the construction of cities, are protected from the industrial pollution that has threatened wildlife in more populated areas, and the animals very seldom find themselves as someone's supper.

The discovery that social phenomena may be "the results of human action but not of human design" is usually accredited to Bernard Mandeville and particularly to the moral philosophers of the Scottish Enlightenment such as Adam Smith and Adam Ferguson.[8] In particular, they predicated their case for the free, unfettered market on the idea of happy, inadvertent side effects. Mandeville's famous formulation "Private Vices, Public Benefits" refers to the market mechanism's capability of transferring individual evil egoism into collective welfare. The beneficial social results ensue unplanned, as side effects of the egoistic, self–serving behavior of individuals.

The central concept fashioned by Adam Smith in his *Wealth of Nations* (1776, 1937:423) was the "invisible hand." In an illustrious passage, Smith argued that each individual pursuing his own selfish interest would most effectively, but unintendedly, promote the common weal:

> Every individual necessarily labours to render the annual revenue of the society as great as he can. He generally, indeed, neither intends to promote the public interest, nor knows how much he is promoting it. . . . .By directing that industry in such a manner as its produce may be of the greatest value, he intends only his own gain, and he is in this, as in many other cases, led by an invisible hand to promote an end which was no part of his intention. . . . .By pursuing his own interest he frequently promotes that of the society more effectually than when he really intends to promote it.

My argument on main effects, perverse effects, null effects, and side effects is summarized in the effects tree in figure 4.4, showing which aspects of effects that might be studied in evaluation research.

A more extended real-life example may clarify my line of reasoning. Aside from reduced energy use—the main substantive effect intended—the Swedish 1974–1980 government grant program to energy conservation in industrial buildings and processes might have produced the following main, perverse, and side effects:

FIGURE 4.4
Main Effects, Null Effects, Perverse Effects,
and Side Effects

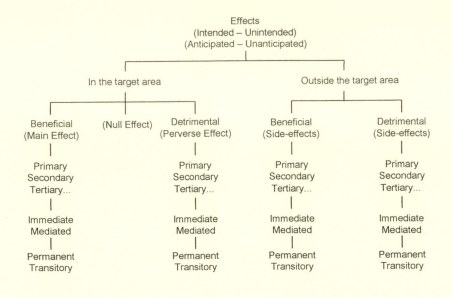

1. Main effect (substantive)	Reduced energy use
2. Null effect	Grants are allocated to actors who would have taken the measures anyway
3. Perverse effect (substantive)	Increased long–range energy use
4. Beneficial side effects	Improved work environment
	Water conservation
	Reduced operation and maintenance costs
	By filling out applications for subsidies, applicants came up with

	other savings and efficiency measures, which have been effectuated.
5. Detrimental side effects	Destruction of capital assets because process equipment is changed earlier than otherwise would have been the case
	Rising prices on energy conservation equipment
	Inconveniences to management and workers in conjunction with rebuilding and installation
6. Other side effects	More power to the National Board of Industry

Undoubtedly, the grants program for energy conservation in industry produced energy savings. The main intended effect was achieved. However, on some occasions the program might have been counterproductive, actually enhancing energy inefficiencies instead of diminishing them. Additional energy-saving equipment might have conserved obsolete technology and counteracted modernization, which could mean that in the long run, more energy instead of less would be used. This would amount to a long–range perverse effect.

A noticeable thing about the grants program is that it produced both beneficial and detrimental side effects. The various beneficial side effects, like the first detrimental one, are quite self–explanatory. The second detrimental side effect could be ascertained only a long time after the initial investment.

There is a great debate among social theorists concerning counterfinality, by–products, and unintended consequences. Karl Popper, among others, in his *Conjectures and Refutations* (1974:124) has forcefully claimed that perverse effects and spillovers constitute the central problem for social scientists:

> It is one of the striking things about social life that *nothing ever comes off exactly as intended*. Things always turn out a little bit differently. We hardly ever produce in social life precisely the effect that we wish to produce, and we usually get things that we do not want into the bargain. Of course, we act with certain aims in mind; but apart from these aims (which we may or may not really achieve) there are

always certain unwanted consequences of our actions; and usually these unwanted consequences cannot be eliminated. To explain why they cannot be eliminated is the major task of social theory.[9]

The importance of noticing perverse effects should be obvious to every evaluator. If the program produces consequences contrary to its main purpose, there must be something wrong with it. But why is it so vital to pay attention to side effects? Because by–products, whether detrimental or beneficial, are crucial factors in every inclusive judgment of the operation of an intervention. Should it turn out that side effects, which have been known, discussed, and positively valued in advance, have not materialized in spite of the fact that the program has been on the books for the intended period of time, this ought to have consequences for any appraisal of the intervention. If the employment effects of economic subsidies to building insulation are much weaker than was calculated with in advance, there will be even less reason than before to keep the program in its present form, even though expectations about energy savings have come true.

Programs may produce spillovers, which in turn constitute or create fresh problems that must be subjected to novel government programs. Solutions to puzzles become puzzles requiring solutions, which in turn become puzzles requiring new solutions, and so on. Aaron Wildavsky writes: "More and more public policy is about coping with consequences of past politics" (1979:4f.,69ff.). Information about side effects is crucial to any comprehensive assessment of government programs.

Unforeseen side effects are of particular interest to evaluators. The actual consequences of a public policy always turn out somewhat differently from what the agent expected before he took action. This is due to the fact that consequences are produced by the application of the program, not by the assumptions originally guiding the decision to adopt the program. Influencing the adoption of the program is entirely different from controlling its outcomes.

By now, we are far removed from the original goals and intentions underlying the intervention. The emphasis would be on global results, planned and unplanned, intended and unintended. The point is, however, that the evaluator still makes a distinction between anticipated and unanticipated results, which presupposes premeditated goals as an organizer. In this limited sense also, the side–effects model is goal based.

Possible sources of suggestions about side effects would be social science theory and the legislative history of the reform. Of particular importance are those apprehensions held by the opponents of the program proposal at the time of its adoption. Other sources would be any public controversy erupting maybe a few years after the adoption of the program, what would come up in government and parliament in conjunction with reassessments of the program, or what the pertinent officials believe about the program when it has been going on for some period of time.

If the totality of effects (positive and negative anticipated consequences, as well as positive and negative unanticipated consequences) of a government intervention were to be investigated, the structure of the evaluation on the outcome side might be as shown in figure 4.5.

Like goal–attainment evaluation, side–effects evaluation is predicated on the normative conviction of the primacy of the parliamentary chain of command. Given this, I strongly prefer side-effects to goal–attainment evaluation. Indeed, the major rationale for doing policy evaluation in the first place is that state actions to some extent are unpredictable and regularly result in side effects not originally foreseen. It is an important duty of evaluation to map and assess the worth of these side effects.

A major challenge to side–effects evaluation is what criteria to apply in judging merit. Ideally, the evaluator would like to trade off the value of the intended main effect of the intervention against the values of the beneficial and deleterious side effects. Negative side effects could then be a grudgingly accepted cost to reach the overall main outcome. Strong positive side effects could also enhance the acceptability of programs with weak goal completion. The performance of this operation requires value criteria for the main effects, for each type of side effect, and for the trade–off between the two.

The descriptive theory of valuing suggested by goal–attainment evaluation—that given policy and program goals should be used as criteria of merit—is clearly insufficient for the following reason. If some effects are not foreseen, the criteria and standards for judging merits and demerits of these effects are not prespecified either. Therefore, goals and other prespecified criteria of merit are insufficient as far as judging each individual unanticipated side effect is concerned. Since the criteria for judging the value of side effects are not stated in advance, the criteria for assessing the trade–offs between the values of

FIGURE 4.5
Side–Effects Evaluation with Specified Side Effects

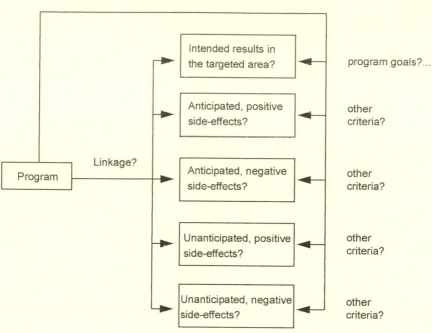

Do the results concur with ...

Intended results in the targeted area? — program goals?...

Anticipated, positive side-effects? — other criteria?

Program — Linkage? — Anticipated, negative side-effects? — other criteria?

Unanticipated, positive side-effects? — other criteria?

Unanticipated, negative side-effects? — other criteria?

the side effects and the main effect are not prespecified either. This will hamper the calculation of the global, aggregated worth of the intervention. To compute the global value, the evaluator must know the value of each side effect individually and add these values to or subtract them from the worth of the main effect.

A feasible solution to this problem involves a different, more creative, descriptive approach to valuing. Aside from mapping the main effect and comparing it with the prespecified goals, she may also chart the side effects but leave it to the commissioners and other users of the evaluation to ascertain their value and carry out the overall, global assessment of the program so to say *ex post facto*. Since the model is predicated on the values of others, it still embraces a descriptive theory of valuing. But the concentration on side effects forces the users of evaluation to consider other values than initially incorporated into the intervention. The evaluator informs the users about a range of effects which makes it necessary for them to produce and use criteria of merit, which were initially overlooked or not articulated.

Goal-Free Evaluation

From the difficulties involved with using premeditated intervention goals as data organizers and criteria of merit, at least one bold evaluation theorist has drawn an even more radical conclusion than those hitherto accounted for. I am referring to the goal-free evaluation model, initially designed by Michael Scriven (1973, 1974, 1980, 1991).

At a first glance, Scriven's contribution seems impudent, almost frivolous. His insistence that evaluations should be goal free must be a *contradictio in adjecto*. How could one possibly *evaluate* if one is prohibited from putting up goals to evaluate against? After all, the purpose of evaluation is to judge the merit, worth, and value of different evaluands.

Several evaluators have testified that Scriven's suggestion in 1972 about the goal–free model was greeted by stunned disbelief. Completely ignoring objectives was shocking indeed. Scriven's perseverance in making his point, however, seems to have had effects upon the theory and practice of American program evaluation (Guba and Lincoln 1981:16ff.).

What Scriven is reacting fiercely against is the evaluators' obsessive attachment to preordained intervention goals. According to the interpretation of goal–free evaluation provided here, the organizer ought to be results, whether planned or unplanned. By not tilting the evaluation toward stated intervention goals, the evaluator can be more open to the total impact of the evaluand.

For the goal-free evaluator wants to concentrate all her efforts on discovering whatever impacts the intervention has produced. She ought to concentrate on what the evaluand is doing without knowing anything about what it is trying to do. Stated or unstated goals ought to be disregarded. As a matter of fact, Scriven recommends the evaluator to take precautions against locating them and their meaning. For the knowledge of preconceived goals and accompanying arguments may turn into a mental corset impeding her from paying attention to side effects, particularly unanticipated side effects. The major task of the evaluator is to take a global view of the intervention and find out about all the effects. Since she must not identify the goals, she will have no basis for distinguishing between intended and unintended effects. She can only ascertain effects.

A skeletal model of goal-free evaluation is displayed in figure 4.6.

Goal–free evaluation is, among other things, an attempt to solve the side–effects problem, the scepter haunting all political planning and goal–based evaluation. It purports to do this by taking a broad view of intervention effects. By consciously avoiding the distinction between main effect and side effects, the model may help the evaluator to trace outcomes that otherwise might have been overlooked. It is argued that goal–based models, whether in the guise of goal–attainment evaluation or side–effects evaluation, tilt the evaluator toward searching for intended effects and overlooking particularly unanticipated and unintended side effects. The goal–free model attempts to remove the negative connotations attached to the discovery of by–products and unanticipated consequences. Scriven maintained that "the whole language of 'side effect' or 'secondary effect' or even 'unanticipated effect' tended to be a put–down of what might well be the crucial achievement, especially in terms of new priorities" (quoted from Patton 1987:36).

In Scriven's own version of the goal–free model, program effects are compared to the needs of the clients, or rather the impacted population. At this point, I have diverted myself from Scriven and ventured

FIGURE 4.6
Goal-Free Evaluation

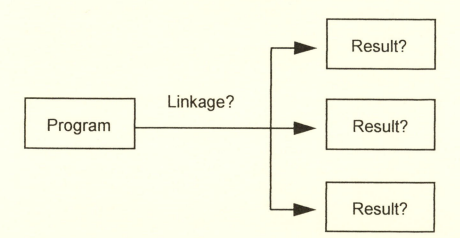

a rendition of my own, excluding also needs from the model. In my consciously idiosyncratic reinterpretation, the goal–free model pays attention to neither pre–stated goals nor client needs. In this version, it is less expensive and easier to handle than side–effects models. The problems involved in determining and weighing program goals or consumer needs are inordinately energy demanding and time consuming. In bypassing the rhetorical bog of goals and needs the evaluator will save precious time that can be expended on more pressing tasks.

The goal–free model, in the interpretation presented here, is apparently related to results–oriented management, a notable public sector steering technique, briefly dwelt upon in chapter 3. Actually, *results analysis* would be an appropriate label. Basically, goal–free evaluation suggests that evaluators should just present the facts; the additional steps of applying criteria of merit to the down–to–earth data, integrating the judgments into an overall value and drawing conclusions for future action are best left to the decision–makers. In this way, my reformed notion of goal–free evaluation might find a place in management–by–results contexts.

From the angle of representative democracy, even the reformed goal–free model suffers from one limitation. The goals that it wants to avoid are not haphazard wishes or incidental desires. Goals of interventions adopted by elected political bodies have an especially elated status, since they have been instigated under due procedure by the representatives of the people. It must be in the interest of the citizenry that these goals are taken seriously in evaluations of intervention output and outcomes. This is a perspective that Scriven, even twenty years after he first came up with the model, seems insensitive to. I have been unable to find any allusion whatsoever to this democratic argument against the goal–free model either in Scriven's contributions or in any other literature on the goal–free model.

That my reformed goal–free model apparently provides no criteria by which to judge the merits of outcomes may be regarded as a weakness. Since valuing must be an inherent property of evaluation, it might be argued that the goal–free model is not evaluation at all. It is effects analysis or results analysis, but not evaluation. A semantic dismissal of this type is too narrow, however. The property of being goal–free might well turn into a strength in an evaluation context: the evaluation recipients may do the assessment. The goal–free model would then point toward an institutional settlement of the value criterion problem in public policy evaluation. The solution would be: find out everything about program results but leave their assessment to the pertinent decision makers and power wielders. This would be the philosophy explicitly undergirding my reinterpretation of the goal–free model.

The lack–of–evaluative–criteria observation does not hit Scriven himself, because he has suggested an expedient. "Merit is determined," he says, "by relating program effects to the relevant *needs* of the *impacted* population, rather than to the *goals* of the program (whether the goals of the agency, the citizenry, the legislature, or the manager) for the target (intended) population. It could equally well be called 'needs–based evaluation' by contrast with goal–based (or 'manager–oriented') evaluation" (Scriven 1991:180).

While interesting, Scriven's claims are not easy to handle. Using needs instead of program goals implies entertaining a prescriptive instead of a descriptive view of valuing. But how do evaluators ascertain needs? It seems methodologically much more difficult to elicit needs than to map results and let recipients do the valuing.

A final weakness that the goal–free model interpreted as results–oriented analysis shares with goal–attainment and side–effects evaluation is the omission of costs.

Comprehensive Evaluations

Comprehensive evaluation models are rooted in the conviction that evaluation should be more extensive than in the all–too narrow goal–attainment model; the process of passing judgments should not be limited to achieved results but include at least implementation, maybe even planning.

It is not the fact that the evaluand[10] is regarded as a constituent of a larger comprehensive whole that is special with comprehensive evaluation models. Specific to comprehensive evaluation is that other component parts of the system than outputs and outcomes are valued, for example, implementation, and feedback.

To clarify the philosophy underlying comprehensive evaluation, I shall use the countenance model, devised by Robert Stake, as a case.[11] Stake identified three stages in the development of an educational program: the antecedent, transaction, and outcome phase. Stake's focus on educational programs has been generalized here to public interventions in general.

Unfortunately, Stake's three phases have no accurate counterparts in public policy or general system language. The antecedent phase consists of events and conditions existing prior to the intervention that may determine, or relate to, its results. In public policy vernacular they may be thought of as "planning" or decision preparation, in systems lingo processes transpiring before inputs are determined. In addition to the program itself, the transaction stage involves processes preceding program delivery as well as program delivery itself. This is covered by "input," "conversion," and "output" in the system model, "public intervention," "administration," and "output" in public policy language. "Outcome" is events and actions immediately succeeding the delivery of the intervention. It might be equated to "outcome" in the general systems scheme and in public policy language.

The major difference between the goal–attainment model and the countenance model is that the former concentrates on the fit between intended and actual results whereas the latter explicitly also involves judging the planning, the decision, and the implementation stages of the intervention.

Roger Kaufman and Susan Thomas (1980:125f.) have provided a pedagogic summary of the countenance model from which the overview in figure 4.7 is slightly adapted and generalized.

Within each of the three major phases of intervention history, a distinction is made between description and judgments. The former category is further divided into intents and observations, the latter into criteria and judgments. This generates the twelve star–marked cells shown in figure 4.7.

In comprehensive evaluation, the first task of the evaluator is to contrast the intended with the actual, the goals with the realities. This confrontation of intents with actual achievements is also typical of the countenance model. Thus, for the antecedent phase, the evaluator would describe the intended preconditions as well as the actual preconditions. What goals were specified concerning antecedent conditions and events? And what actually did take place? For the transaction phase, the intervention as it was planned would be put up against the invention as it was actually carried out. And likewise for the outcome phase: intended impacts would be compared to impacts actually obtained. The three fundamental questions in description would be: Are antecedent events and conditions fulfilled as specified? Is the program carried out as intended? Do the actual impacts conform with those

FIGURE 4.7
Comprehensive Evaluation: The Generic Countenance Model

ANTECEDENT (INPUT) PHASE:
[period of time before the program is adopted and implemented]

Description:
- Intents (what goals are specified, what effects are desired)
- Observations (data concerning the activities and events taking place during this phase; description of existing conditions)

Judgments:
- Criteria (benchmarks of merit to be used as basis of comparison)
- Judgments (the process of comparing the intents, observations, and criteria)

TRANSACTIONAL (CONVERSION) PHASE:
[period of time during which the program is implemented]:

Description:
- Intents (the program as it was planned)
- Observations (the actual implementation and delivery of the program)

Judgments:
- Criteria (benchmarks of merit to be used as the basis of comparison)
- Judgments (the process of comparing the intents, observations, and criteria)

OUTCOME PHASE:
[the period of time immediately following the delivery of the program during which most of the results data are collected]

Description:
- Intents (the intended or predicted results of the program)
- Observations (the data gathered concerning actual results at the end of the program)

Judgments:
- Criteria (benchmarks of merit to be used as the basis of comparison)
- Judgments (the process of comparing the intents, observations, and criteria)

Source: R. Kaufman and S. Thomas, Evaluation Without Fear, 125f.

desired? From this we also see that goals are used as organizers for the evaluative activities.

The judgments aspect of the countenance model is also divided into two separate concerns: criteria and judgments. Criteria refer to the yardsticks to be used as the basis of comparison. Will the worth of the intervention be judged by comparing it to another intervention? Will the program be compared to a set of absolute standards not directly related to it? Will the program be judged from the point of view of its own goals? Will the intervention be assessed by referring to something else? Judgments, on the other hand, refer to the overall process of actually comparing the intents, observations, and criteria of merit. It would constitute some sort of overarching balancing calculus.

Kaufman and Thomas maintained that the countenance model forces the evaluator to describe the events, activities, and conditions that exist before, during and after the adoption and implementation of the intervention. This careful and thorough description will provide a wealth of information about both the intentions of those who develop the intervention and on–site observations of what actually occurred during each of the three stages.

Another distinctive feature of the countenance model is its emphasis on the specification of the criteria to be used in the passing of judgments. In the countenance model, the criteria must not remain implicit but be fully explicated.

An additional prominent attribute of the countenance model is the focus on judgments as a major aspect of evaluation, defining the complete act of evaluation as involving both description and judgment (the two countenances of evaluation, as Stake puts it).

The essence of all comprehensive evaluation models is that value achievement is measured in several stages of the system under investigation.

Comprehensive evaluation models are preferable to the goal–attainment model because of their explicit preoccupation with implementation processes between input decisions and actual outputs. This is a strength on two accounts. It allows the possibility of evaluating against so–called procedural goals, that is, procedural fairness, legality, openness in relation to secrecy laws, or popular participation in decision–making processes. Furthermore, the field is open to explain phenomena in the output and outcome stages by factors in the administration processes. This is of crucial importance if the evaluation is to be able to provide an information base for action. If some outcomes did not materialize because some outputs were not made, which is in turn explained by some factor in the implementation stage, then the decision–maker will get information about which something can be done. The outcomes are influenced by outputs, conversion, or inputs. The general environment of the system can also be scanned for clues to influences on the segment of the system under evaluation. The comprehensive evaluation model can be turned into process evaluation.

In other respects, comprehensive evaluation suffers from the same flaws as the goal–attainment model. Its preoccupation with official substantive goals impedes the discovery of side effects, which is a serious fault. Also, the comprehensive model as construed here pays no attention to costs and disregards clients' viewpoints.

Another drawback with the countenance model is its complexity. According to Guba and Lincoln (1981:14), who have touched upon this criticism, evaluation practitioners have found it difficult to comprehend and operationalize the twelve–cell design of the model. From another point of view, the countenance model is too simplistic, because it makes no clear difference between input, conversion, and output, which are all included in the transaction phase.

Client–Oriented Evaluation

The evaluation models expounded so far have been geared to information wished for by program managers and superior sovereigns. Proceeding from an entirely different point of departure, client–oriented evaluation takes the goals, expectations, concerns, or even needs of the program addressees as its organizing principle and criterion of merit. At the heart of client–oriented evaluation is the question of whether the program satisfies client concerns, desires, or expectations.

Actually, there are two philosophically very divergent points of departure for client–oriented evaluation: client needs and client desires and expectations. Since needs do not necessarily coincide with expressed preferences or demands of the clients, the needs approach involves a prescriptive theory of valuing, that is, the evaluator herself must ascertain which needs are most valid. Establishing needs while retaining a scholarly posture is a thorny issue, which I shall avoid here. Instead, I shall interpret the client–oriented model as based on a descriptive theory of valuing, predicated upon the express desires, expectations, values, assumptions, and objectives of the clients.

There is no common, accepted terminology to denote the targets of public interventions. I have interchangeably referred to them as "addressees," "targets," "clients," and "recipients". As synonyms, I shall use "participants," and, where appropriate, "consumers," and the Janus–like concepts "beneficiaries/maleficiaries."

My extensive experience as an evaluation instructor has taught me to emphasize the difference between program clients (program consumers) and evaluation clients (evaluation consumers). The evaluation client is the person, group, or agency that has commissioned the evaluation of a program, whereas the program client is the intended or actual recipient of the program (Scriven 1991:82). In spite of the fact that expressions like "program users" and "user influence" are very much employed in Scandinavia, I shall avoid it here and reserve the term "users" for evaluation, not program, recipients.

The client–propelled model is justified in two ways. First, it is grounded in political ideologies based on the superiority of the market place over public–sector provision. The belief is that consumer pressures expressed through attitudes toward service provision will lead to the improvement of service delivery and increased consumer satisfaction. In buying a commodity in the store, the consumer pays no attention to producer purposes. Her own assessment of the value of the good is what counts. Client–oriented evaluation is based on the notion that public administration produces goods and services for consumers in the market place. The theory of the market–driven administration is fundamental to client–oriented evaluation.

Second, a democratic, participatory case, is often made for the client–model. According to this argument, the consumer parallel cannot be pushed too far, since the client concept includes a participatory, democratic aspect, which seems to be absent from the consumer concept. The participatory feature suggests that the clients may voice their complaints and desires to the service providers and to some extent influence and take responsibility for service content. The client approach engenders a discursive, reasoning, discussing and, consequently, influencing countenance, which should come to the fore in client–oriented evaluation (Katz and Danet 1973; Goodsell 1981): "the consumer as citizen rather than the consumer as customer" (Jenkins and Gray 1992:296).

The primordial step in the practical application of the client model is to locate the program clients. Since the evaluation normally cannot cover them all, a sample from the target population must be picked. Then the client–driven model points in various directions. The program coverage issue, that is, eventual differences between the intended target population and the actually impacted population, is always important. Is the program covering the whole target population or only parts of it? The crucial activity, however, is to elicit the client's views of the program.

The client model does not tell which program components should be appraised. It allows for a wide variety of assessments. The evaluators may ask clients to pass judgments on some aspect of the service. For instance, clients may be invited to judge program outcome, program output, service availability, service quality, or even service administration. Client–oriented evaluation may also raise the causal issue, that is, the evaluator urges the clients to estimate program impacts. In this case, targets are asked to compare what would have happened had there been no program to what actually has happened with the program in place. Client–oriented evaluation uses the shadow controls design to assessment of program impact (see figure 11.1 and chapter 12).

Another notable feature is that value pluralism is an accepted strand in the client–oriented model. Consumers can disagree in their appraisals. The client approach permits conflicting opinions on public programs and their reception.

It has taken an inordinately long time before the clients were recognized in public administration (Jenkins and Gray 1992:285ff.). The notion of a politics–driven civil service and a parliamentary chain of control—administration as the neutral tool of the elected officials—has exerted a dominant influence over administrative thought. Today, the client–oriented model is employed in numerous evaluative contexts, particularly those concerning public service provision such as urban transit, public utilities, parks and recreation, health services, child care, public housing, and nursing homes for the elderly, where clientele participation is crucial to the operation of the program. The client–oriented model is used to evaluate library services, arts, zoos, and museums. It is a favorite with educators. At universities, students are routinely requested to share their opinions of courses, reading lists, and lectures. They are asked to rate their teachers' abilities to organize the course contents, to stimulate and promote altercation and discussion, to stir student interest, motivation, and critical thinking, and to show concern and enthusiasm for the students. At American universities, these evaluations are occasionally used to rank faculty and courses from a student perspective.

Here are some examples of market research done in the Swedish state sector: the National Audit Bureau (RRV) wanted to know the taxpayers' views on the service level, staff competence, and performance of the taxation authorities; the National Labor Market Board asked how job seekers perceived the services of the local employment offices; the National Board of Public Building wanted to know its clients' (tenants') opinions of how the board manages the provision of premises; the Ministry of Health and Social Affairs asked a large number of parents for their opinions on child care; the National Environmental Protection Agency surveyed the credibility of various environmental agencies in public opinion; and the Patent and Registration Office investigated how inventors perceived queuing time.

In my view, the client–propelled model may complement the previously presented approaches, since it poses another problem for consideration. It can make important contributions to evaluation, but should not be allowed to replace the other models. The exclamation of the Swiss hotel proprietor Cesar Ritz, *"Le client n'a jamais tort"* ("the customer is never wrong"), cannot be the lodestar of all evaluation. The requirement that the civil service must be responsive to client concerns is sound, but only within limits. It can never take precedence over the requisite that the front–line operators should follow the directives of their hierarchical administrative superiors, and indirectly political bodies like Parliament, and the Municipal Council, and ultimately, the citizens. Tax authorities must answer promptly and correctly to inquiries from the general public, but they cannot lower taxpayers' taxes or make haphazard exemptions. As a rule of thumb, I would argue that clients' criteria of merit ought to play a more prominent role in public service assessment than in the assessment of regulatory regimes. But evaluators must be aware of the tendency of the clientele to exaggerate complaints in order to get more service. Greater client involvement in evaluation may surrender power to groups with vested and narrow interests (Jenkins and Gray 1992:296).

The Stakeholder Approach

The organizing principle of the stakeholder model is the concerns and issues of the people who have an interest in or are affected by the intervention. This is quite different from using prefixed objectives as merit criteria, as in goal–attainment evaluation or even side–effects evaluation. Stakeholder evaluation, however, does resemble the client–oriented model, the major difference being one of scope: while the client–driven model is concerned with one group of affected interests, the stakeholder model is geared to all of them.

Stakeholder–based evaluation starts by mapping out the major groups who are involved or have an interest in the emergence, execution, and results of the program. The evaluator identifies the people who hammered out the program, who initiated and funded it, and particularly those who are charged with its implementation. She identifies senior managers, middle managers, lower managers, and front–line operators, who actually deliver program output. She singles out the intervention's primary target group and those who know they have a stake in the program but prefer to keep a low profile. And she identifies those who are unaware of the stake they hold.

An overview of conceivable stakeholders in public interventions (Guba and Lincoln 1989:40f.; Riecken and Boruch 1974:203ff.; Rossi and Freeman 1989:422ff.; Weiss 1972a:18) is presented in figure 4.8.

The fourteen groups listed under "Program Stakeholders" in figure 4.8 represent the major parties interested in or affected by a particular government intervention. The list is compiled with some national reform—decided by parliament—in mind. Naturally, a listing of stakeholders in a smaller agency program or some program at the municipal level would look differently. Actually, the stakeholder model provides no clear answer to the question of who the stakeholders are. It is open–ended in this respect. In figure 4.8 I have also included three potential stakeholders, who may not be interested in the program as such but in its evaluation.

The fourteen major stakeholding audiences are all conceivable participants in an evaluation of the intervention. I shall also assume that all the stakeholders are immersed in the evaluation. The stakeholder model will be interpreted as an holistic approach, directed at the whole spectrum of affected groups and their organized emissaries.

At this point, I shall distinguish between the Swedish and the North American stakeholder model. In the Swedish model, the stakeholders actually execute the evaluation and take responsibility for its findings. In the North American model, by contrast, the evaluation is not performed by the stakeholders but by one particular evaluator or a team of evaluators, who may consist of consultants, employees of the agency in charge, or university researchers. The evaluation team should then unravel and collect stakeholder concerns, expectations, and interests and bring them to bear on the evaluation. While the stakeholders are contacted, provide the problems to be investigated and the criteria and standards to be used as instruments of appraisal, the evaluators—not the stakeholders—carry the full responsibility for the final results.

FIGURE 4.8
Stakeholders in Public Interventions and Their Evaluation

PROGRAM STAKEHOLDERS:

Citizenry:	Citizens who elect representatives to decision–making bodies at all levels in the political system.
Decision–makers:	Political officials responsible for deciding whether an the evaluated intervention is to be instituted, continued, discontinued, expanded, or curtailed.
Political Opposition:	Political opponents of the intervention.
National Agency Managers:	Senior managers in charge of the intervention at the national level.
Program Directors:	Middle managers in the national agency directly in charge of the intervention.
Regional Agency Managers:	Administrative unit at the intermediate level responsible for some aspect of the implementation of the intervention (e.g., regional inspectors).
Private Intermediaries:	Non–governmental institutions charged with some responsibility for the implementation.
Local Agency:	The lowest–level administrative unit responsible for the delivery of the intervention (e.g., a local bureau of a national regulatory agency).
Street–level Bureaucrats:	Front–line operators responsible for program delivery, and who directly communicate with the addressees either face–to–face or via telephone, mail etc.
Clients:	Individuals or collectivities like households, businesses, organizations, municipalities or other units who are the addressees of the public intervention under evaluation.
Neighboring Agencies:	Governmental units in charge of interventions related to the one under evaluation.
Program Competitors:	Organizations or groups who compete for the available resources.
Contextual Stakeholders:	Organizations, groups, individuals, and other units in the immediate environment of an intervention.
Research Community:	Scholars specializing in the substantive issues which the intervention is concerned about.

EVALUATION STAKEHOLDERS:

Evaluators:	Persons responsible for the design, conduct, and findings of the evaluation.
Evaluation Sponsors:	Organizations that initiate and fund the evaluations.
Evaluation Community:	Other evaluators, and teachers of evaluation methodology, who read and judge evaluations for their technical and substantive quality.

Once the major interested parties are discerned, the North American stakeholder model might function in various ways. In their book *Effective Evaluation,* Egon Guba and Yvonna Lincoln (1981:33ff.; also 1989:50ff.) proposed that stakeholder "concerns" and "issues" should be the starting point. A "concern" is "any matter of interest or importance to one or more parties." It may be something that threatens them, something they fear might lead to undesirable consequences for them, or something they are anxious to substantiate. "Virtually any claim, doubt, fear, anticipated difficulty, and the like expressed by anyone with a legitimate basis for making such a representation could be entertained as a concern." An issue, on the other hand, "is any statement, proposition, or focus that allows for the presentation of different points of view; any proposition about which reasonable persons may disagree; or any point of contention."

To build a fitting general design for the study, advocates of the North American stakeholder model nurture a strong penchant for qualitative methodology. The key word is *interactive* search procedure. The evaluator must talk to the stakeholders to elicit their narrative histories and observational data, which in turn should be allowed to affect the evaluator's next step in the search procedure. After a while, she might discover both the purported and the genuine aims of the program, and what concerns various stakeholders nurture regarding evaluand and evaluation. With time, the evaluator gets more involved and can start to determine what concerns and issues should be included in the study. Only then can she take a stand on what the outline of the evaluation should be.

It is typical for the stakeholder model that the evaluator is permitted to search rather extensively for the crucial problems. The goal–attainment and the comprehensive evaluation models point out much more specifically which problems to raise and which questions to ask in the investigation. The North American stakeholder approach is remarkably open in this respect, empty if you like. The idea is that the evaluator must be responsive to the concerns and issues of the affected people and let these govern the next step in the investigatory enterprise. Through interactive communication she is supposed to find out which concerns and issues are to be taken seriously and probed more deeply. The evaluation design will be gradually determined. Stakeholder evaluation is *responsive evaluation* (Stake 1975; Shadish, Jr. et al. 1991:275ff.).

To elicit the final data on stakeholder concerns and issues, advocates of the North American stakeholder model seem to prefer observational and interrogative methods to documentary methods. In many cases, stakeholder evaluators endorse direct or even participant observation. In–depth interviewing is another favored technique. After data are amassed and processed, the reporting of results, which might vary from one stakeholder to another, will commence. The key word seems to be "portrayals," that is, information–rich characterizations using pictures, anecdotes, thick descriptions, and quotes. The comprehensive holistic view mediated through a portrait is important. The evaluator's own value criteria should play no role at all since the selection of measuring rods as well as the measurement proper is supposed to be the task of the stakeholders. Normally, several criteria of merit, standards of performance on these criteria and several comprehensive assessments will be included. In practice, the stakeholder model will become downright pluralist. Finally, it is decided whether the results should be collected into a written report—something that Guba and Lincoln (1981:25f., 39ff.) consider by no means necessary.

The stakeholder model, it is argued, has numerous *advantages*. A knowledge argument, a utilization argument and a goal–management argument may be adduced in its favor.

According to the *knowledge argument,* it would be foolish of the evaluator to avoid the program knowledge, which those involved indubitably have. Stakeholders nurture convictions about side effects, implementation barriers, and outright cheating, which may provide ideas for continued research. Consequently, it is very easy to agree with the recommendation that almost every evaluation ought to begin with the determination of relevant actors and rounds of interviewing.

The knowledge argument, however, is usually accorded less weight than the *utilization argument* in support of stakeholder evaluation. In North American evaluation debate, stakeholder involvement is regarded mainly as a vehicle for increasing the use of the evaluation in upcoming decisions. Findings from traditional goal–attainment evaluations have little impact. The reports are buried in desk drawers and heaped on the bookshelves of the public authorities involved, unread and forgotten. Although the will is there, decision-makers do not avail themselves of the information base in the evaluations to make more rational decisions. The business of evaluation suffers from a malign "desk-drawer syndrome."

This seemingly wildly irrational behavior has puzzled and exercised researchers. Why do decision-makers behave in such an unwise fashion? The allegedly major explanation is that evaluators work in splendid isolation, with too little communication with prospective users. They tend to investigate problems on which there is no pressing demand for information. The stakeholder approach increases the chances that questions of genuine interest to concerned parties will be addressed. It brings to light information that meets the real requirements of the different stakeholders, thereby enhancing the probability that the results actually will be put to use. This is a significant point, since goal-based evaluations often wind up being ignored, without influencing the course of future events.

The *goal–management argument* views the stakeholder model as a strategy to handle situations in which there are no written premeditated goals or where the stated goals are notoriously unclear and difficult to trade off against each other according to accepted scholarly canons. We have already seen that not even the goal–attainment model can fully master the criterion issue, particularly the multiple goals issue so typical of public policies. The stakeholder model, however, provides a practical solution to the problem of eliciting concerns and issues where no written objectives exist or of simultaneously managing several contradictory goals.

Individual implementers may have no clear directives from above concerning what they should do, because with almost no exception, higher–level policy goals are general, contradictory, and muddy. Most importantly, no trade–offs are provided between the several goals that are claimed as lode stars for the policies. This makes it impossible to use given intervention goals as objective yardsticks by means of which the global merits of the policies may be judged. One way out is to regard the choice of overall criteria and standards as an inherently political task. The evaluators should describe the value positions of many different stakeholders, without contesting any of them. The fact that stakeholders disagree is normal and natural in politics, and a sign of health in free nations. Findings should be presented separately on each goal. Actually, it might be advisable to avoid doing a single large evaluation study and conduct several smaller studies instead, geared toward specific stakeholding constituencies. In no case should the evaluator render summative judgments. Overall summation is best left to the stakeholders. The stakeholder model uses a descriptive theory of valuing.

There are also obvious *drawbacks* with the stakeholder model. In most versions, it ignores program costs. In addition, it is inordinately impractical and resource demanding, since every stakeholding constituency must be contacted and nurtured.

The stakeholder model is also fuzzy. It provides no authoritative answer to the question of who the stakeholders are. The range of stakeholders must be decided on a case–by–case basis. There is a need to supplement the stakeholder approach with a political or administrative theory concerning the selection of affected groups. Furthermore, all of the interests concerned, however selected, are treated as equals by the stakeholder model. But in a democratic, constitutional system, elected politicians must carry more weight than administrators or experts on policy instruments and the substantive matters under consideration, just to pick a few. The stakeholder model does not prioritize among the diverse stakeholding audiences. The model is grounded in a modest equilibrium philosophy. There is a risk that the best organized and most committed stakeholders are consulted while vaguely concerned groups are omitted. Even in this regard, the stakeholder approach is in need of a more developed philosophical base.

The most serious objection, however, is the risk that the stakeholder model will embrace a pragmatic theory of truth. Truth can turn into a matter of usefulness, utility, or acceptability to stakeholders. Stakeholders often entertain highly politicized views of program effects. Opponents ascribe everything negative occurring after the program as caused by the program and everything positive as caused by something else. Supporters hold the opposite view. Facts are essentially contested. In these situations the various parties will accept only those findings that fit into their preformed opinions. Too much stress on utility and usefulness can turn evaluators into substituting well–corroborated information to less validated findings that are useful and used by somebody. In my opinion, evaluators must always be on guard against pragmatic leanings. If they start to deliver useful instead of true information, they act as political animals, not as scholars defiantly searching for truth.

In conclusion, while quite controversial, the stakeholder model carries some important merits. The utilization and the goal–management arguments speak in its favor. Another strong reason for it is the knowledge argument. However, stakeholder protagonists, who want to claim they are researchers, must beware of the risks of substituting usefulness to truth.

A Swedish Stakeholder Model: The Ad Hoc Policy Commissions

The definitional difference between the North American and the Swedish stakeholder model is that in the latter the stakeholders perform the evaluation and take responsibility for its results whereas in the former the stakeholders are only consulted and allowed to influence, design, value criteria, and other tenets of the evaluation but the evaluation itself is carried out by some independent evaluators. In the Swedish system of ad hoc policy commissions, evaluation is performed in five partly consecutive, partly parallel, processes: commission work, consultation procedure, public policy debate, government decision, parliamentary decision.

In the Swedish political system, a considerable source of information on past performance and alternatives for future policy action is produced by ad hoc investigative bodies. A highly visible subset of such bodies are the *ad hoc public policy commissions,* in Swedish called *offentlig utredning* or *kommitté,* on rare occasions also *kommission,* or *delegation.*

While the formal initiative may be taken in Parliament, it is always the government *in corpore* that summons ad hoc policy commissions and specifies the problems to be investigated. The written directives, which are made public, indicate what a particular commission should do, determine the economic frames, and designate a completion date for the work. The government also appoints the chairman and other members, experts, and participants.[12]

The policy commissions usually consist of full members, political appointees (*sakkunniga*), experts, and a secretariat. The latter is composed of one full–time administrator, who functions as secretary, and a few part–time secretaries. The format of the commissions and the background of their participants will vary according to the subject under investigation. For highly sensitive matters, such as defence or constitutional reform, the entire commission is frequently made up of full members who are parliamentarians, from parties in office as well as from the opposition. For matters moderately political, full members of all camps in Parliament will be appointed along with representatives of other stakeholding constituencies such as ministries (which are kept amazingly small in the Swedish polity because agencies are rather independent of ministries), national implementing agencies, the Association of Local Authorities, the trade union movement, and organized business. In most cases, people from academia are hired as experts and fact finders. In addition, the commissions themselves are allowed to contract out specific assignments to scholars, who then do their business as independent researchers.

A typical feature of the Swedish commission approach is that *ex post* evaluation is married to prospective policy analysis. Actually, investigations have traditionally focused on alternatives for future action rather than impacts of past policies. Besides an historical account of how the pertinent evaluands as they are codified in the books have evolved over the last decades, the typical commission report includes data on the severity and scope of the problem, substantial prospective assessments of different options or the most promising option for future policy action, and a sometimes clear recommendation of policies. Yet systematic information on the implementation, output, or outcomes of earlier interventions is usually also provided, although to a lesser extent. In the last two decades, however, more emphasis has been placed on the provision of evaluative information. Swedish policy–makers have learnt the same lessons as their counterparts in other countries: implementation according to plan as well as achievement of intended outcomes are problematic. Now, some commissions even have evaluation as their major task (SOU 1981:40–41; the Price Controls Commission).

Sometimes the commissions also perform before–the–fact implementation analyses. They attempt to scrutinize the staff, organizational, and managerial capabilities to determine the degree to which the proposed policy alternative(s) can be specified and brought to street–level execution in a particular bureaucratic setting. This feature is particularly interesting against the backdrop of clamors for *ex ante* implementation analysis as the missing link in public policy analysis.

The conclusive tracts are invariably signed by all full members of the commission. This means that the stakeholders shoulder the complete responsibility for the content, and particularly for the recommended actions. However, members have a right and a duty to register dissenting opinions in so–called reservations (*reservationer*), which are added to the tract. Also, experts may submit dissenting opinions in so–called special utterances (*särskilda yttranden*), which are appended to the report.

The one–, two–, or even three–volume studies (*betänkanden*) are always published, which is a testimony to the comparative openness of the Swedish state policy–making system with its constitutionally regulated presumption against secrecy, the so–called Principle of Publicity. The reports are issued in a series of volumes referred to as Government Official Investigations (*Statens Offentliga Utredningar,* abbreviated SOU). All volumes carry ISBN and ISSN numbers. The tract is primarily addressed to the government. Yet it is also readily accessible to all conceivable stakeholders, citizens and mass media included, since it is available in every municipal and other major library throughout the country. Certainly, the SOU–Series provides worthwhile sources of policy–relevant research into most aspects of Swedish social life.

Commission work constitutes the first stage of policy preparation. In a second stage, the ad hoc commissions are coupled to another well–entrenched Swedish structure of stakeholder evaluation, the *comprehensive consultation procedure*—called *remissväsendet, the remiss procedure*—which is adopted after a commission's proposals are made public. The government sends the published commission studies to numerous interested parties for written reactions. These parties usually include government agencies at the national and regional level, county and municipal governments, universities, institutes of technology, various kinds of interest organizations, trade associations, and professional organizations. The parties must provide their answers within the time limit set by the government. Like the commission reports the consultation answers are also made public.

The remiss procedure can be regarded as metaevaluation in the sense of auditing of a final evaluation. To the extent that the commission reports contain evaluative results, the stakeholders are asked to evaluate an evaluation.

The metaevaluations of the commission reports also take other forms. Since both the commission reports and the consultation answers are open to the public, they might receive wide coverage in the mass media, including front page articles and radio and television news reports. In addition, they may trigger extensive and prolonged public policy debate. Participants in these debates usually include daily newspapers of all political shades from all corners of the ablong country, the national and local television and radio channels, the media of the trade union movement, the business communities, the nonprofit associations. In addition, independent researchers, politicians, representatives of interest organizations, and numerous other categories contribute articles to the newspapers and reveal their opinions in interviews.

The *public policy debate* can be regarded as the third component of the policy formation and evaluation in Sweden. Rather than a separate stage, it should be viewed as a parallel process to the consultation procedure and later stages.

On the basis of the commission proposals, consultation answers, the mass media debate, and probably also other information, a draft proposal *(proposition)* is hammered out in the pertinent ministry, usually in continued close contact with some interested parties. While the elaboration of the *draft bill by the government* may be considered the fourth process in decision preparation, the *parliamentary processing of the bill* may be considered the fifth. When the draft bill is finally submitted to parliament, it is almost routinely approved without major changes. The formal supreme decision–making body, the legislative assembly, exerts minor influence on real decisions. All in all, decision preparation is a very long process with a multitude of actors and widely divergent interests involved where compromises are struck and the issues are decided well before the issues formally enters the parliamentary or even the governmental arena.

Exactly how evaluation–based information is used in the deliberations of the commissions, of the interested consulted parties, in the media debate, in government, and in the diet is difficult to pinpoint. Occasionally, it probably carries some weight in substantive deliberations, albeit far from decisive. In retrospect, however, stakeholders often claim that they make their political judgments, negotiate and strike their political compromises on the basis of the information amassed by the experts. The same goes for the government. Presumably, evaluation is somewhat utilized to render legitimacy to the proposals suggested. Perhaps it also gives some substantive guidance.

Indisputably, the Swedish ad hoc policy commissions are cases of the stakeholder model in action. Yet, the practice deviates in several crucial respects from the stakeholder model expounded in North American literature.

To a much larger extent than the North American stakeholder model, the ad hoc commission institution reflects the view that evaluation is primarily a *political enterprise,* not research work. While a large spectrum of affected interests are consulted and carefully listened to, in the North American stakeholder model it is still the evaluator—that is, a researcher—who is in charge, decides which stakeholder problems to penetrate, how to conduct the evaluation, and also assumes responsibility for the final report and other outcome of the evaluation. The Swedish stakeholder model is more openly political. First, the government establishes the commission, selects the participants, determines the issue agenda, and allocates the funds. By contrast with the North American model, the Swedish stakeholders are full members of the investigation team, execute or at least oversee the execution of the evaluation, and assume complete responsibility for the findings as well as the recommended options for action. Yet, they are mandated to ponder the issues and work within the time and resource constraints specified by the government. Third, performed within a political framework, the commission work is specifically geared to a particular recipient–cum–decision–maker, the national government, and designed to meet a specific pending decision situation before a set deadline.

Another difference concerns the *view of summary statements*. In the North American stakeholder model, there is a tendency toward separate reporting to each stakeholding constituency; assignment of a single global value to an intervention is regarded with suspicion. This is somewhat alien to Swedish official thinking. The philosophy embraced by the commissions strongly suggests that a unanimous final report is something valuable to strive for. Evaluative data should serve the whole spectrum of political interests, not just particular stakeholder concerns, and enable full members to reach unanimous solutions. While minorities have a right and duty to make reservations, the alternative preferred by the reigning political culture is unity.

The accompanying *media attention* seems to be much stronger in the Swedish case, partly because the process is institutionalized since at least a century, and maybe also because of the openness as a consequence of the Principle of Publicity.

Another dissimilarity is that the commission institution is used not only to come up with policy proposals but to effectuate *compromise* on policy implementation as well. Hydroelectric power policy is an excellent case in point. The parties in Parliament already in 1975 set a very clear quantitative goal for hydroelectric construction. But the political parties and other concerned stakeholders have not been able to reach agreement on which particular water courses and river falls should be dammed and exploited, despite numerous attempts with ad hoc policy commissions and consultation procedures. A more clear–cut example of the saying that "implementation is not neutral rule application but the continuation of politics with other means" is difficult to imagine.

A basic similarity between the two models is that results should not be judged against one set of criteria of merit—stated policy goals—but a wide variety of yardsticks, represented by the views of the numerous stakeholding constituencies.

Another commonality concerns the role of research. While the research feature is stronger in the North American approach, it is also in the Swedish case thought that program evaluation, while basically political, ought to be fused with scholarship. The research being executed or collected is discussed in the commissions and the research papers are often presented as annexes to the main report and under the name of each researcher. Parts of the research findings are also included in the major commission text backed by the majority of the full members of the commission.

The remiss procedure bears stronger resemblance to the North American stakeholder model than the commission preceding it, above all because now the stakeholding constituencies are asked individually to react to the commission investigation without being members of any formal appointed body.

The approach taken by the ad hoc public policy commissions is justified somewhat differently compared to the North American stakeholder model. The argument that stakeholder involvement will increase evaluation use is never heard of in Swedish policy communities. Instead, the basic rationale is very Swedish in the sense that the commission model is intended to promote compromises, agreement, support, and forestall bitter political struggle. Commissions are consensus–building mechanisms rather than rational problem–solving institutions. They are vehicles for shaping agreement on the results of earlier efforts, and most importantly, proposals for future action. The appointment of an ad hoc commission marks a political attempt on behalf of the incumbent party or parties to reach accord with the parliamentary opposition, the strong interest organizations, and the public interest associations before the government drafts a bill, and well before the draft bill is submitted to Parliament. Sometimes, commissions are also used to promote accommodations among the dissenting governing parties themselves. Consensus building and the rendition of legitimacy to fundamental decisions are major arguments in favor of the commissions. The underlying assumption is that people will have more confidence in a policy in whose development they were consulted, although in the final analysis it does not agree with their particular preferences.

Finally, a democratic, participatory case can be made for both models. Through the use of the stakeholder approach, affected interests can participate and influence the final outcome, which is of democratic value by itself.

Occasionally, the commission institution is sharply castigated. Commissions are time consuming. The time–consuming argument carries weight because it may take years before the final report(s) are presented to the public. Another critique suggests that commissions tend to erode the authority of the parliament. Once the process reaches the elected officials in parliament, the issue is politically resolved. The role of the parliament will be to rubber stamp what has been decided elsewhere. Also, this stricture carries some weight. A third objection concerns the well–established fact that commissions are also used strategically, as a dilatory procedure, to entomb difficult issues and have them dropped from the public agenda.

"Virtually every important piece of legislation is prepared through the work of specially appointed governmental commissions," Rune Premfors (1983:623) wrote in an article at the beginning of the 1980s. While correct in the past, this statement no longer reveals the whole truth. The sheer number of policy commissions has declined in recent years. In the middle of the 1960s the amount of commissions increased from approximately 250 to 300. During the Center–to–Right coalition period in 1976 through 1982 a peak was reached with 422 commissions in 1980. In the fall of 1983, 206 commissions were at work; in 1987, 195. The average lifetime of a commission used to be three to four years. Lately, efforts have been made to speed up the investigative process. Now, a commission may work only for two years or less. The reports are also supposed to be reduced from 300 to less than 100 pages.

The commissions' influence on state policymaking is probably also less than before. There are moments when time is of the essence and these situations require more rapid modes of decision preparation. For this reason, and maybe also for a political propensity to avoid public debate on sensitive matters, several major settlements are preceded by no public inquiries at all. A blatant case was the decision to apply for membership of the European Community and with several decisions on cross–bloc crisis packages in the fall of 1992. Increasingly, ad hoc commissions of inquiry are also replaced by departmental investigations, commissioned by a minister—not the cabinet as a whole—and produced entirely by officials from within the pertinent department. These studies are published, if at all, in the less accessible Ds–series. Furthermore, it also seems that agency investigations conducted within the appropriate state agency play an increasingly more consequential role.

Economic Models: Productivity

Common to all effectiveness models is their negligence of costs. However resource guzzling a program has been, effectiveness evaluators concentrate on substantive results and disregard costs. Attention to costs, on the other hand, is a typical feature of the economic models of public policy and program evaluation.

Often, private business is held up as an ideal to emulate in the public sector. In private business, profit is the criterion of merit and maximizing profit is the standard of success. In analogy to this, productivity maximization ought to be the standard of good performance for public interventions. Productivity seems to be an unusually clear concept; it is defined as the ratio of outputs to inputs. Or, to quote Wholey and Newcomer (1989:144): "Simply stated, *productivity* is the relationship between output of products and services and input of resources: output divided by input."

Productivity can be expressed through the mathematical algorithm shown in figure 4.9.

Evidently, the ratio formula in figure 4.9 can be operationalized in many ways. Let me provide a Finnish example from the library community. In computing the productivity of Finnish municipal libraries the following measure has been used (Sjöblom 1991:12ff.):

$$\frac{\text{number of books borrowed}}{\text{costs in Finnish Marks}} \quad = \quad \text{cost productivity.}$$

As an alternative to cost productivity people have resorted to work productivity, which can be illustrated by the expression:

$$\frac{\text{number of books borrowed}}{\text{number of hours worked}} \quad = \quad \text{work productivity.}$$

FIGURE 4.9
Productivity

$$\text{Productivity} \quad = \quad \frac{\text{output}}{\text{input}}$$

The difference is that costs in the former case are indicated in monetary terms, in the latter case in the number of hours worked, that is, as physical entities. It should be emphasized, perhaps, that costs can be computed in both ways in productivity measurement. The time unit used could be the fiscal year, the calendar year, or even a monthly period.

Other possibilities would be the ratio of library holdings (number of books kept) to costs, the number of inhabitants in the municipality to costs, or the number of borrowers to costs.

To say something worthwhile about the actual productivity of a public agency, a reference case is needed. That is, evaluators need performance standards on the productivity criterion to tell what high or low productivity means. Several standards are used: comparison with past performance, with similar institutions in the same country, similar institutions in other countries, goals of the political bodies, client goals or stakeholder goals. An overview will be given in chapter 14.

Productivity as a measure of public sector activities carries some technical advantages. Sometimes, costs are not terribly difficult to calculate since they reach the agencies in terms of monetarized funds. However, at other times it may be hard to trace the relevant costs because the funds allocated and spent are often indicated as lump sums on the books. Outputs, on the other hand, may be exacting to catch and compute, even though productivity only presupposes that they are indicated in physical, not monetary, terms.

Let me return to the Finnish municipal libraries to illustrate the difficulties of finding valid output indicators. Is the number of borrowed books really a relevant and exhaustive output measure? Admittedly, it is relevant. To provide the public with an opportunity to borrow books is reasonably the most important task of a public library. But it is certainly not exhaustive. A Finnish report concludes that only 30–50 percent of the library clients borrow books. The other patrons visit the library to read newspapers, magazines, and journals, but this does not show in the borrowing statistics. They frequent the reference library to use dictionaries and encyclopedias or the music department to listen to records, tapes, and discs. Libraries also provide some information services (Sjöblom 1991:18ff.). In the Finnish investigation I am referring to, these problems were noticed and discussed before the researchers decided to choose the number of borrowed books as the indicator of library output. But this does not turn the chosen measure into a fully exhaustive one.

Another intricacy involved in productivity evaluation is that qualities often are overlooked. Books differ in quality. How can that be measured in productivity assessment?

There are other criticisms of productivity as a measure of the virtue of public policies. The most important suggests that productivity is an internal measure, which does not apprehend what we really want to disentangle, namely, the results that the outputs have produced with the end receivers or in society at large, the value of these results, and if the benefits are worth the costs. In the library example, borrowed books are not necessarily significant themselves; people may charge out books from the library, place them in a heap on the desk at home, and after some weeks return them unopened. More important is the reading of the borrowed books. But what really matters are the borrowers' gains from their reading. The gains may be recreational or educational. What the cost–conscious, education–oriented library evaluator really wants to grasp may be:

$$\frac{\text{value of education through books borrowed}}{\text{costs}}$$

But if so, then she has left productivity measurement and entered the field of efficiency evaluation.

Proponents of productivity as a criterion against which to evaluate public policies, programs, and services cannot escape the fact that productivity as a yardstick of output is not an ideal measuring rod for assessing the worth and merit of public sector activities. The public institution may do wrong things, that is, the outputs may not produce the desired outcome.

Economic Models: Efficiency

The second major economic model to be used in modern political and administrative evaluation is the efficiency model. Efficiency can be measured in two ways, as cost—benefit or as cost—effectiveness. "Efficiency assessments (cost—benefit and cost—effectiveness analyses) provide a frame of reference for relating costs to program results," write Rossi and Freeman in their widely used textbook *Evaluation: A Systematic Approach.* "In cost—benefit analyses, both program inputs and outcomes are measured in monetary terms; in cost—effectiveness analyses, inputs are estimated in monetary terms and outcomes in terms of actual impact" (1989:375).

If measured in a cost–benefit analysis, efficiency can be expressed as the ratio of the monetarized value of the outcomes produced by the program to the monetarized costs. If equalized to what is measured in a cost–effectiveness analysis, efficiency pays heed to monetarized costs as in cost—efficiency analysis, but the value of the effects is indicated in physical terms only.

This is expressed in the simple algorithms in figure 4.10.

"Program effects" in figure 4.10 indicate consequences produced by the program. Effects are not identical with all occurrences in the target area after the instigation of the program. These occurrences may have been caused by something other than the program. What we are looking for in efficiency analysis are effects produced by the program, and nothing else. On this account, efficiency assessment (both cost—effectiveness and cost–benefit) uses the same measure as effectiveness analysis. The major difference is that efficiency takes costs into account, which is not the case in effectiveness analysis.

Like all other evaluation models, productivity and efficiency measurement provide partial perspectives. They overlook other requirements normally demanded from public sector activities in contemporary democracies. Examples of such value criteria are legal equity, procedural fairness, representativeness, participatory values, and publicity rules. No productivity and efficiency study or any other evaluation for that matter, however pretentious from a scientific and scholarly point of view, can explain in an objective fashion how a balance should be struck between these values and productivity/efficiency. The trade–off can only be made through public debate, opinion formation, compromise, and eventual majority decisions, that is, through politics.

FIGURE 4.10
Efficiency as Cost–Benefit and Cost–Effectiveness

$$\text{Efficiency (cost--benefit)} \quad = \quad \frac{\text{value of program effects (in SEK, US\$)}}{\text{costs (in SEK, US\$, etc.)}}$$

$$\text{Efficiency (cost--effectiveness)} \quad = \quad \frac{\text{program effects in physical terms}}{\text{costs (in SEK, US\$ etc.)}}$$

Professional Models: Peer Review

Professional models imply that members of a profession are entrusted to evaluate other members' performances with respect to the profession's own criteria of merit and quality standards of performance. The evaluation is conducted by a collegium, which by definition is an assembly of professional equals, so that lawyers evaluate lawyers, professors evaluate professors, surgeons other surgeons, and so on.

The peer review, the most celebrated professional model, has mostly referred to a screening procedure for the selection of contributions to scientific journals. Submitted articles are subjected to peer review to decide whether they ought to be accepted for publication. Peer review is also used to offer guidance to research foundations concerning which projects should get funding. Research proposals are submitted to a group of respected colleagues for screening. On top of that, peer review has also been used to investigate and judge supposed transgressions of rules of ethical conduct and inherited research practices.

However, in this context peer review is a procedure for retrospective assessment of implementation, outputs, and outcomes of public policies. Peer review is particularly aimed at performing an overall quality judgment of the evaluand.

The peer review model is constantly used in *research evaluation*. Renowned scientists of a particular field are assigned to assess the quality and relevance of a research project, a research program, or a university department. And in Sweden, recently, research institutes (Wittrock et al. 1985) as well as disciplines as a whole across the country have been evaluated using international peer groups (Öhman and Öhngren 1991; Engwall 1992). Scientists and their achievements are evaluated by their respected colleagues and equals. Peer review of research usually is—and ought to be—interactive; usually the procedure starts with self–evaluations by the evaluatees; on the basis of these and additional material like documentary evidence and site visits evaluators pass their preliminary judgements; then evaluatees are given opportunity to comment on the evaluators' reports before they are finalized; all in all, the evaluators listen to the evaluatees and solicits their opinions.

Peer review is an institutional model of evaluation. It does not indicate the substantive questions to be asked but how the evaluation is to be organized. The model only tells you that evaluations ought to be carried out by equals. The task of selecting and applying criteria of merit and standards of good performance is left to the professionals themselves.

We might wonder what peer review has to do with public sector evaluation. The model seems miles away from the arena of policymaking and program enactment. The answer is embodied in the principle of the profession–driven public sector. In some areas of public life, goals are so complex and techniques so difficult, that political officials have found it wise to leave the shaping and debating of them to well–educated professionals. Architects, judges, professors, doctors, veterinarians, and engineers would be cases in point. Hence, it is also considered natural to delegate *ex post* evaluation to the professions. But since these professionals work in the public sector, peer review must be regarded as an evaluation model on a par with the other models used in public life.

The evaluation of government–funded basic science and applied research can be thought of as a review of the state's research policies. Research is performed neither by Weberian hierarchies, nor by interest organizations or elected politicians. It is carried out by professional scientists and scholars. Hence, the quality of their work is frequently evaluated in collegiate forms. In research evaluation, experts often work on assignment for somebody, for instance, a research council.

To provide an example, the evaluations sponsored by the Swedish Council of Building Research at the end of the 1980s were assigned to take special interest in:

a. the relevance of problem selection and design of analysis;

b. the suitability of the methods of analysis;
c. the tenability and validity of arguments and conclusions;
d. the work in relation to the discourse in the pertinent area;
e. the practical applicability of research findings;
f. the worth of the research community shaped by the project;
g. agreement between original intentions and findings reached (Nilstun 1988:51).

After the directives had been written, appropriate experts were approached. Preferably, the experts should have more specialist knowledge in the field than the colleagues whose research is to be evaluated. They should also be independent; for instance, they must not have carried out research work in the area under scrutiny in cooperation with the people to be evaluated. There is an important difference between those peer reviews where the evaluatees has suggested and agreed in advance on the choice of experts, and reviews where they have no say in peer selection.

After the expert group, the "peer collegium" as it were, had been chosen, the upcoming work was organized. Invariably, the reviewers and the reviewees interacted with each other during the reviewing process. To the evaluators it was important to take the concerns and arguments of the evaluatees seriously and try to include or at least consider them in the evaluation. On many occasions, the evaluatees were asked to provide relevant publications and other research material in order for the evaluators to become sufficiently informed. The evaluators were then given time to read the material to inform themselves about the evaluees and their products. Then, each researcher and research group was visited for presentations and informal talks. In due time, a preliminary formal report was drafted. An important feature is that the preliminary report was circulated to affected researchers whose written comments were explicitly solicited, and these comments were subsequently paid attention to when the evaluators composed the final report. However, they were not published along with the finished report. In the Scientific Commission of the National Swedish Building Council, the whole procedure took approximately eighteen months.

Collegial evaluation might also be pursued by use of two panels instead of one. These groups might work independently but in the end try to reconcile their findings and judgments. A special form of collegial evaluation is self–evaluation by the affected professionals themselves. Usually this approach is combined with the use of external evaluators.

Peer reviews frequently produce shaky results. Matched panels use widely different merit criteria and performance standards and reach miscellaneous conclusions. However, in technically complex fields, collegial evaluation is probably the finest method available to judge the quality of what is produced.

Final Note

My broad survey of evaluation models has demonstrated that the total agreement that once existed in the early American and European evaluation communities on the appropriateness of the goal–attainment model has been replaced by a situation where several models compete. Internationally, evaluation has evolved from uniformity to pluralism. I greet this development with satisfaction. The danger with all evaluation models is that they are applied too uncritically and that decision–makers wrongly believe that one model can provide comprehensive, final answers. Therefore, it is important to keep in mind they every model provides partial perspectives and answers only. For this reason, combinations of several models is commended.

There is a strong tendency in contemporary evaluation literature to recommend stakeholder and client–oriented evaluation and debase particularly the goal–attainment model. On one important account, I take exception to the tendency of debunking the goal–attainment model. From a democratic point of view—and here I am alluding to representative democracy—the goal–attainment model and particularly the side–effects model are very important, since they are based on the conception of the parliamentary chain of influence. High–level policy goals, set by parliaments and governments are not just any goals whatever. Established through a constitutionally determined procedure, they are institutionalized as the collective goals of the state. Citizens and elected officials have legitimate reasons to ascertain whether policy goals have in fact materialized in the field. Otherwise, they cannot function as principals in the representative system of government.

The democratic argument in favor of the goal–achievement model, however, cannot remedy the fact, that this model runs into difficulties particularly with goal catalogues and is blind to costs. Its major drawback, however, is its lack of focus on side effects. For this reason, I prefer side–effects evaluation to goal–achievement evaluation.

Client–centered evaluation has a role to play, particularly as far as government services are concerned. However, for democratic reasons it cannot replace approaches that take policy goals as their organizer. The strength of peer review lies in its capacity to capture and judge qualities. This is essential in fields dominated by complicated criteria of merit and strong professions. Its paradigm area of application is academic research. The stakeholder model provides the broadest view possible of government interventions, promises to take all involved into consideration, but is impractical to handle. The Swedish version of the stakeholder model entails an interesting combination of social research and political accommodation of various stakeholder interests in order to shape social agreement and render legitimacy to decisions.

Economic models will stay with us forever in public policymaking. It must be kept in mind, however, that like other designs they provide partial perspectives only. The danger with economic models is that decision–makers are fascinated by their mathematical precision and wrongly believe that they provide comprehensive, final answers.

Notes

1. Accounts of evaluation models are provided in Madaus et al. 1983, Guba and Lincoln 1981, and House 1980. In Shadish Jr. et al. 1991, evaluation models developed by Weiss, Wholey, Scriven, Rossi, Cronbach, and Stake are analyzed.
2. Goal–achievement: Scriven 1991:178; goal–based: see House 1980:26ff; goal–attainment model: Kaufman and Thomas 1980:126f.; objectives–oriented: see Guba and Lincoln 1981:x; the Tylerian model: Guba and Lincoln 1981:3ff., House 1980:27; the behavioral objectives approach: House 1980:26ff.
3. For criticism of the goal–attainment model, see Deutscher 1976, and Meyers 1981:110ff. The exposition in Chen 1990:168ff. is very clear and interesting.
4. By focusing on subject–matter goal achievement only, the goal–attainment model pays no attention to procedural goals. Procedural goals include legality and equity of client treatment.
5. Some people use the terms "internal and external effects, where the former accrue directly to the project, for example, elimination of mosquitoes as an internal effect of a mosquito–control project, with opening an area for recreation as an external effect" (Anderson and Ball 1978:26).
6. In Boudon 1982 (5 ff.) the expression "perverse effects" is used, but in the sense of unintended effects, which of course includes side effects as well.
7. Strategic effects cause some problems in my discourse on side effects. The desired main effect with the program could be that the party in government wins the next election. A possible side effect could be that the opposition splits up. In this section, however, I shall only consider substantive effects.
8. Ferguson's memorable phrase "results of human action but not of human design"

seems to have been phrased in the following fashion: "Every step and every movement of the multitude, even in what are termed enlightened ages, are made with equal blindness to the future; and nations stumble upon establishments, which are indeed the result of human action, but not the execution of any human design. If Cromwell said, That a man never mounts higher than when he knows not wither he is going; it may with more reason be affirmed of communities, that they admit of the greatest revolutions where no change is intended, and that the most refined politicians do not always know wither they are leading the state by their projects" (quoted from Hayek 1978:264).

9. Albert Hirschman (1991:35f.) has formulated the same idea in the following fashion: "One of the great insights of the science of society—found already in Vico and Mandeville and elaborated during the Scottish Enlightenment—is the observation that, because of imperfect foresight, human actions are apt to have unintended consequences of considerable scope. Reconnaissance and systematic description of such unintended consequences have ever since been a major assignment, if not the raison d'être, of social science." Also consult Boudon 1982; Vernon 1979; Sieber 1981; Hayek 1979:146ff; Elster 1978:106ff.

10. A neologism in the English language, *evaluand* is a generic term for whatever is evaluated, by analogy with "analysand" and "multiplicand." In this book, I have used "evaluand" only sparingly.

11. Other elaborated models of comprehensive evaluation include the ones elaborated by Fernández–Ballesteros 1992a:205 ff. (figure on 207) and Rossi and Freeman 1989:13f. and passim.

12. The presentation of the SOU–model draws on Söderlind and Petersson 1988; Meijer 1956; SOU 1976:49; Premfors 1983; Andersson and Associates 1978:55ff.; and Johansson 1992. For a short presentation in English, see Vedung 1992:76f.

5

The Eight Problems
Approach to Evaluation

Evaluation is a technique of managing public organizations in which systematic data gathering and other researchlike operations per definition play a considerable role. From this angle, research–infused evaluation differs from other social research not in regard to the research designs and data–collection methods employed, but to the problems to be attacked. Problems, not designs or methods, provide identity to evaluation.

There are eight primary problems of evaluation; they can be phrased as eight questions. Again inspired by Scriven, I shall call this the *Eight Problems Approach to Public Policy Evaluation*.[1] While question one and two concern the evaluation of the intervention, questions three through seven pertain to the intervention proper, and question eight to the feedback process or the utilization aspect of the evaluation. This three–level idea in the battery of questions, illustrated already in figure 2.2, ought to be kept in mind when we proceed.

Evaluators may consider some or all of the following eight problems:

1. The purpose problem: For what overall aims is the evaluation launched?
2. The organization (evaluator) problem: Who should exercise the evaluation and how should it be organized?
3. The intervention analysis problem: How is the evaluand, that is, the government intervention, normally the policy, the program, the components of policies and programs, or the provision of services and goods,

to be characterized and described? Is the evaluand regarded as a means or as a self–contained entity?

4. The conversion problem: What does execution look like between the formal instigation of the intervention and the final outputs?
5. The results problem: What are the outputs and the outcomes—immediate, intermediate, and ultimate—of the intervention?
6. The impact problem: What contingencies (causal factors, operating causal forces)—the intervention included—explain the results?
7. The criterion problem: By what value criteria should the merits of the intervention be assessed? By what standards of performance on the value criteria can success or failure or satisfactory performance be judged? And what are the actual merits of the intervention?
8. The utilization problem: How is the evaluation to be utilized? How is it actually used?

Questions one and two concern the evaluation of the intervention, three through seven the intervention itself, and question eight the feedback process.

Since evaluation is frequently made to order, it is advisable to consider the overall *purposes* of the commissioner. True, the evaluator must find out what policy, program, or program ingredient the sponsor wants to have investigated. Furthermore, the evaluator should also pay attention to the particular problems that the commissioner wants her to illuminate. In talking about evaluation purposes, however, I have something more far–fetched in mind, namely, why the sponsor wants to have these particular things examined. In which decision context will the evaluation be used? Who are the prospective primary users? Is there a hidden agenda behind the evaluation? Is there really a genuine desire with the sponsor to have the program and its outputs and outcomes clarified or does he covet a tranquilizer or some legitimizing evidence?

The purpose problem in the overall sense intimated here is something the basic researcher may circumvent. In the academic community, funds for research are allocated on the grounds of basic–knowledge interests alone. Not so in evaluation. A client commissioning an evaluation also has a political agenda in mind. Hence, the evaluator must pay attention to the commissioner's deeper purposes.

As a second step, it is appropriate to ponder the issue of how evaluation work should be *organized*. Who should conduct the evaluation? The organization problem can be viewed from different angles, which I have touched upon in chapter 4 in conjunction with my discussion of the Swedish policy–commission model and the peer review model. Here, I shall briefly address only the issue of self–evaluation versus external evaluation. Should the evaluation be initiated and produced by the affected people themselves or should some external body commission and conduct the assessment?

At an early stage, the evaluator must make herself familiar with the *intervention*. How should the intervention—policy, reform, plan, program, program component, services, products—be described? What is the nature of the intervention? How should it be depicted? Many interventions are exceedingly diverse, varying substantially from site to site throughout the country.

Occasionally, the issue of describing the intervention can be lightly dealt with. This is true, of course, in self–evaluation conducted by people who already know the program well. Also in externally performed client–centered and stakeholder–oriented evaluation, it is perhaps less essential to dwell upon the nature of the program. In side–effects evaluation, which I prefer to goal–attainment and comprehensive evaluation, the program issue gains in importance. Here, it may be proper to analyze the intervention in terms of ends and means. What goals are laid down in the policy mandate? If several goals are set, how are they ranked? What range of policy instruments are incorporated in the program? Does the program entail regulatory, economic or communication tools of governance? In case several instruments are involved, how are they combined? If only one type of policy instrument is devised —for example, regulations—what kinds of regulations are they?

At this juncture, I must draw a contrast between two cardinal types: explanatory and nonexplanatory evaluations. *Explanatory evaluation* amounts to means–ends evaluation. It sets out to assess programs with respect to something they are supposed to produce or have inadvertently generated. It raises the conversion issue and maybe the impact issue as well, that is, the evaluator attempts to mirror the conversion process, and encircle the outputs and the outcomes of the program; the focus of attention is not put directly and only on the program, but on its implementation and results. *Nonexplanatory evaluation,* on the other hand, assesses the merit, worth, and value of the program through direct appraisal of the program itself, not through assessment of something produced by it. There is no causality issue involved in nonexplanatory evaluation.

For instance, a students' appraisal of a university course is a nonexplanatory evaluation to the extent that the program is the course as it is actually delivered in the classroom, not some higher–level program that might have caused the course. The same goes for book borrowers' appraisals of municipal libraries, hospital patients' appraisals of illness care, prison inmates' appraisals of jail facilities, and research–peers' review of other people's scientific research where the measuring rods are drawn from international principles of high quality in research. What I have called goal–achievement measurement or results–monitoring (chapter 4) is also nonexplanatory, as are legality and equity evaluations, because the problems are whether some actions or processes match some given categories for acceptable behavior or procedure.

Explanatory evaluations have a more complicated structure. Questions four, five, and six in my Eight Problems Approach apply only to them. These questions all presuppose that the program is appraised by looking at something supposedly or actually produced by it.

Question four concerns the *conversion* process between program instigation and program delivery. What does the execution process look like? What orders and directives have been given to the central agency? Has the program reached the eventual intermediaries? Have the intermediaries performed some action? What have the grass–root bureaucrats done in preparation of the final output? Evidently, in this stage evaluators follow the program from its birth up to the point immediately preceding the output.

Then the evaluator may address the *results* problem. In the present book, results are characterized in systems terminology. The evaluator may look for the immediate, intermediate, and ultimate outcomes, or for outputs like number and size of subsidies granted, number and type of patients treated, or number and sort of information brochures disseminated. Outcomes analysis focuses on intended outcomes as well as perverse results, spillovers, or just simply results. Results may thus denote either output and outcomes, outputs only, or outcomes only.

In answering the results question, the evaluator may consult several data sources. She might use appropriate statistical records routinely collected by some governmental agency, scrutinize inherited policy documents, do some interviews, send out a questionnaire, make site visits, or resort to participant observation. A combination of methods is probably advisable. The time perspective is crucial. Extended time series data on results indicators are highly commendable.

It must be underscored that we are interested in "independent" results at this stage. The problem of whether the results are contingent upon the program or not will be attacked at a later stage.

Finally, explanatory evaluators have to disentangle the convoluted matter of intervention *impact*. Has the intervention caused the result? Has it facilitated or counteracted the development? Has it precipitated the outcome, or retarded it, or has it spawned no discernible effect at all?

A fascinating general feature of evaluation from a political science point of view is that the influence of government *on* society really is put in the forefront. The state is not studied as a mere reflection of societal forces, "a committee for the administration of the common affairs of the bourgeoisie," to use Karl Marx' famous phrase (*Communist Manifesto*:19). Neither is it examined as a self–contained entity. Evaluation puts the state's, the government's, and the political system's impact on the surrounding society in focus. Through evaluation, the influence of the public sphere is firmly placed as the central concern of social science. Evaluation, in the words of Theda Skocpol (1985), is "bringing the state back in."

In impact investigation, the intervention constitutes one among numerous possible explanatory factors (or independent variables) to be considered. In philosophy–of–science language, the intervention constitutes part of the feasible explanans to be used in the investigation. What the evaluator takes as results of the intervention on the other hand, makes up the potential dependent variables of the study. Phrased in the jargon of the philosophy of explanation, they form the *explanandum* (*explananda*) of the investigation.

No matter how effective the evaluated intervention has been, it is helpful to pinpoint exactly what the results are contingent upon. Once the contingencies are known, it will be possible to draw conclusions concerning future action from the evaluation. A focus on contingencies also makes the evaluation interesting from an implementation theory point of view. Null effects may occur because the program was not seriously intended to produce any effects in the first place. In addition, the absence of favorable results may depend on implementation barriers, for example, misunderstanding on the part of the implementers due to muddy program goals, faulty communication, lack of funds, inexperienced staff, extended and complex chains of implementation, and agencies and intermediaries pursuing counterproductive self–serving interests. Extraneous confounding factors such as influences from other public interventions—activities, programs, projects, and the like—or changes in surrounding circumstances, may well also explain the results.

To conduct a rich and probing analysis of the impact issue, the evaluator must search for potential explanatory factors operative outside the intervention under evaluation. In particular, I wish to stress the importance of other public interventions. Evaluation should never concentrate entirely on one intervention. Other government activities might impinge upon the measured results as well. Impact analysis actually refers to such a broad explanatory effort.

Impact assessment can be carried out in two steps: as preevaluation, and impact analysis proper. Evaluability assessment is a preevaluation which tries to find out whether the program can be subjected to a full impact analysis.

The seventh issue, the *criterion* problem, is common to all evaluations, explanatory and nonexplanatory alike. What value criteria— yardsticks, measuring rods—should be used in assessing the worth of the intervention? And what measures (standards) on these measuring rods constitute success or failure? From my definition of evaluation, laid down in chapter 1, it follows that evaluators are interested in criteria and standards for retrospectively assessing outcomes, outputs, and conversion. In the chapter on models (chapter 4), we have already seen that public–sector economists recommend outcome criteria, particularly cost–benefit efficiency, and output criteria like productivity. Other models suggest criteria that exclude costs like the achievement of preordained program goals, client satisfaction, and realization of stakeholder goals. Criteria of merit and standards of performance will be discussed in a separate chapter at the end of the book.

Finally, the evaluator must confront the *utilization* problem. An evaluation is supposed to be used in future decision making concerning the evaluated program. How is, then, the evaluation to be utilized in upcoming decision-making processes? Can it be of any other future use? Should the evaluation be organized or designed in a particular way to enhance use and usefulness? Or how has it actually been used by various stakeholding audiences?

The purpose of evaluation is different from the aims of basic research. Basic researchers toil as their own entrepreneurs with no particular practical purpose in view. Evaluators, to the contrary, often work for and report to commissioners, who want to use the evaluation for some imminent practical purpose. This means that timing, feedback, and utilization is crucial to evaluation, but less so to basic academic research; consequently, use is a hotly debated issue in evaluation, but rarely touched upon in pure political science.

The first two questions in the Eight Problems Approach about the evaluative enterprise itself should be raised in every evaluation, but not necessarily included in the final report. Of the remaining five questions about the public intervention, question three, the intervention analysis problem, must be raised in every evaluation. However, it might be accorded more or less weight. Question seven should also be asked in any evaluation. Questions four, five, and six are raised only in explanatory evaluations. Question four is always raised in program monitoring. A major question guiding monitoring is: What are the barriers obstructing the realization of the program? Question eight, about utilization, should be considered in every evaluation.

Note

1.   A list by Scriven is summarized in Shadish, Jr. et al. 1991. Cf. Premfors 1989:140.

6

Evaluation Purposes

Evaluation as qualified monitoring is usually a routinized, continuous feature of public decision–making systems. As impact assessment, evaluation is frequently commissioned on specific occasions. Whether permanent or periodic, monitoring or impact assessing, however, evaluation is performed for either accountability, intervention improvement or basic knowledge advancement.

These three—accountability, improvement, and basic knowledge—are the major overall purposes of evaluation. Actually, accountability and improvement stand out as the most eminent rationales for doing evaluation, since basic knowledge is best regarded as a possible, happy side effect of the former two.

In addition, evaluation always becomes part and parcel of political, administrative, and personal power games. Assessments are ordered to gain time, to show up a front of rationality, or to single–mindedly find traits to defend or destroy the program. These strategic—mostly unacknowledged and hidden—rationales mix with the substantive, acknowledged ones in the context of the same evaluation. Evaluations are established to alleviate several problems at the same time.

My conception of evaluation purposes—problem one in the Eight Problems Approach to Evaluation—differs somewhat from others to be found in the literature. Admittedly, Arvidsson (1986:627) has the three purposes accountability, management, and knowledge, and the same goes for Chelimsky. Joe Hudson, John Mayne, and Ray Thomlison (1992:5), however, have four: increase knowledge, improve program delivery, reconsider program direction, and provide for accountability.

I have merged program delivery and program direction into one and added the strategic purpose.

Let me start with substantive purposes.

The Principal Wants to Hold His Agent Accountable

The key rationale of accountability evaluation is to find out whether agents have exercised their delegated powers and discharged their duties properly so that principals can judge their work. Accountability involves two parties, the principal and her agent. The principal issues orders and directives for the agent to follow; the latter is supposed to carry out the will of the former. While the agent is expected to do the accounting, the principal has authority to pass judgements and make decisions on, for instance, continued allocation of funds. However, the accounting can also be performed by some outside body, commissioned by the principal, or by the principal himself. The essence is that accountability evaluation is intended to serve the needs of an external overseeing body.

Accountability belongs to a wider class of phenomena, intimated by dual concepts like represented—representative, master—servant, superior—subordinate, principal—executive, mistress—maid, farmer—farmhand, employer—employee, and boss—underling. Superiors need illuminations of current or past performance of their subordinates to hold them responsible for what they have accomplished. The mistress must check the accomplishments of her maid and call her to account for her actions. The employer must oversee his employee to control that he is doing the right job, and doing it well. Similarly in the public sector, higher–level principals (like agency managers) want to find out whether their lower–level stewards (like agency staff) are performing their tasks properly in order to hold them accountable.

In accountability assessment, information and evaluative judgments are produced to allow decisions on program continuation, expansion, reduction, and termination. Accountability evaluation assembles an information base on which principals may exercise their judgments on resource allocation. Occasionally, the whole rationale and fundamental direction of the intervention may be reviewed and reconsidered. An evaluation can provide evidence on the extent to which intervention objectives remain relevant, whether program activities still address a pertinent societal problem, or if research in the substantive policy area continues to support the kind of policy instruments employed (Hudson, Mayne, and Thomlison 1992:8). On other occasions, only marginal changes are considered.

Accountability evaluation can focus on various aspects of the evaluand. Rossi and Freeman (1989:157f.) have presented the following list:

Legal Accountability:	Are relevant laws being observed by the program, including those concerning occupational safety and health, community representation on decision–making boards, equity in service provision, informed consent, and privacy of individual records?
Fiscal Accountability:	Are funds being used properly? Are expenditures properly documented? Are funds used within the limits set by the budget?
Delivery Accountability:	Are proper amounts of outputs being delivered? Are the treatments delivered those the program is supposed to be delivering?
Coverage Accountability:	Are the persons served those who are designated as targets? Are there beneficiaries who should not be served?
Impact Accountability:	Is the program producing the intended outcome?
Efficiency Accountability:	What are the impacts in relation to program costs?

The Rossi–Freeman inventory provides some examples of the sorts of information to be amassed in accountability evaluation. I agree with what I take to be their argument that it is impossible and downright unfruitful to state by definition which focus accountability evaluation should have.[1]

Four Accountability Perspectives

"Accountability is the link between bureaucracy and democracy. Modern democracy depends on the accountability of bureaucracies to carry out declared policy and otherwise administer the ongoing structures of governmentally determined opportunity and regulation." These words, issued by Lipsky, contain a deep truth, which ought to be echoed more in public sector evaluation literature.

In accountability evaluation, the *perspective of political officials* is usually held out as fundamental. Elected and appointed politicians require evaluation to hold the administration responsible for its actions. This is what Bo Rothstein (1991) has called "the fundamental dilemma of public administration."

Popularly elected governing bodies like parliaments, and municipal assemblies can only make a tiny portion of all decisions concerning the well–being of citizens that have to be made in postmodern, highly developed societies. The reasons, says Rothstein, are two: the need for situational adaptation and lack of time.

An overwhelming majority of all public–sector resolutions on service distribution and application of regulatory directives concerns individual instances or specific situations. Cases in point are the placement of patients in lines for surgery, teachers' decisions concerning grades for pupils, or decisions on government housing loans to individual building commissioners. More often than not, these decisions have to be made on a continuous basis, for example, by the doctor in her clinic, the teacher in her classes, or the clerk in the local building commission. The resolutions require far more expert knowledge of the specific situation than a popularly elected assembly reasonably can possess. Even if, says Rothstein, we would like all of these decisions on citizen welfare to be justified and made by democratically elected bodies, it is impossible. The requirement of *situational adaptation,* specifically with regard to the quality of addressee information that is needed, is so demanding that elected political bodies cannot exert any detailed influence over these types of decisions.

Likewise, *time* is an exceedingly scarce resource for political assemblies. Usually, they can take fundamental decisions in the same substantive area only every other year, or maybe every three or four years. However, in most functional policy domains, decisions have to be made several times a month, a week, and occasionally even a day, in a continuous manner. The parliamentary resolutions in these cases must therefore be rather general and only contain guidelines. This in turn means that many extremely important decisions for citizens and clients must be made incessantly by bodies, which cannot be considered legitimate by reference to the democratic principle of representation for the simple reason that no democratically elected institution has formally made the decision on these matters.

The necessity of situational adaptation and scarcity of time forces parliamentary assemblies to delegate the right to decide in a number of important areas to other institutions, preferably to the civil service. However, these decisions are political since, in a sense, they directly influence the distribution of values in society, that is, who gets what, when, and how. Along with the relentlessly growing public sector, this delegation of power and influence to the administration has shifted its traditional focus away from program execution to political decision making. The servant is still a servant, but his discretion has increased as his master has assumed more and larger responsibilities (Rothstein 1991).

In this political perspective, evaluation becomes an important tool for political representatives to check that the administration is actually executing the duties assigned to it and to change the funding or the basic subject–matter guidelines for administrative decision making.

Agency management also has a legitimate need to keep an eye on its subordinates. Like politicians, even these principals must delegate influence and power to lower–level underlings. The burden of responsibility is placed at lower levels within the same hierarchy, on autonomous professions such as judges, doctors, and professors, on nongovernmental third parties like large interest organizations, on outside consultants, or on clients. In this *agency–management perspective,* evaluation becomes a tool for agency heads to stay informed about how various subordinates are performing their job.

In overviews of accountability evaluation, these two aspects are usually treated as fundamental, if not the only legitimate ones. However, there are at least two more accountability outlooks that must be brought to the fore.

One is the *citizens' perspective* on evaluation. Despite the fact that citizens are the starting point of the parliamentary chain of control—at national, regional, and municipal levels—and all other political and administrative actors are the executives of the citizens, the citizens' perspective is rarely heard of in evaluation discourse. But the citizenry does in fact need evaluation to assess how elected officials and their agents at different levels are performing their jobs and to hold them responsible in the next election (Hofstee 1992). "All power emanates from the people and Parliament represents the Swedish people." Those are words from the 1974 Swedish Constitution. According to the theory of representative democracy, the politicians are the representatives of the populace. They are elected by the populace to carry out its will, within certain discretionary limits, of course. The populace is the principal and the elected politicians its agents. Political officials, the theory continues, will then make decisions according to the constitution. Information on implementation, output, and outcomes of these decisions must be crucial when in the next election citizens are to assess past policies and exert their power to elect new representatives.

There is also a *client perspective* on evaluation that needs pointing out. Clients constitute a more limited category than citizens. But their interests that the programs produce something more than words, that equal cases are treated equitably, and that the service is satisfactory, are also legitimate. Evaluations from these aspects will become very valuable to them (Jenkins and Gray 1992).

The Problem with Accountability: Principals are Also Agents

Accountability is threatening to executives. They fear unfriendly criticism that, if disseminated, might tarnish their reputation, or even worse, take their jobs away, because the program may be terminated. For obvious reasons, they dawdle, refuse to collaborate, or cooperate through releasing only materials favorable to their cause. They debunk the findings of outside evaluators as unappreciative, parochial, and self–interested attacks on their probity and effectiveness. The evaluator and her commissioner are looked upon as antagonists, if not downright enemies. This fact partly explains why the evaluation function is so weak in public life.

This final strand of thought is absurd, someone might object. Admittedly, executives are negative because evaluation is a threat to them. But the principals must have a keen and real interest in evaluation. They, if any, must be curious about how their assignments are carried out.

This argument disregards two aspects. Most principals in the body politic have dual loyalties; they are at the same time superiors and subordinates, masters and servants. The citizens at the front end of the parliamentary chain of representation have only one role, that of the principal of the national legislators, whom they elect. The national legislators, the government, the national and the regional agencies, on the other hand, have dual roles in the chain of representation. The legislators are the agents of the citizenry, but also the principal of the government, which they elect. Likewise, the government is the agent of the legislature, but at the same time the principal of the national bureaucracy. The national bureaucracy, in turn, is the agent of the government, but also the principal of the regional agencies. And the latter are the agents of the national bureaucracy, but simultaneously the principal of the local administration. The local administration, however, has only one role in the chain of representation, that of an agent. The argument is illustrated in figure 6.1.

FIGURE 6.1
Dual Loyalties in the Chain of Public Representation

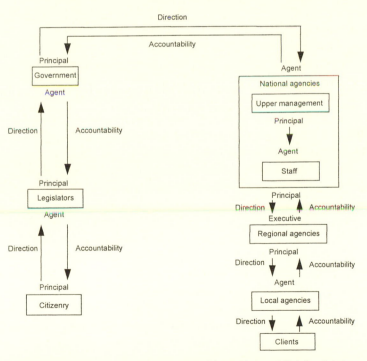

Note. The principal provides direction for the agent and the agent is accountable to the principal.

Actually, the relationships are even more intricate. Elected law makers, for instance, are sometimes appointed by the government on the boards of regulatory commissions, which means that they are supposed to act as the government's executives while also being the government's principal and the citizenry's executive.

Now, back to my general argument on why accountability evaluations are avoided also by principals. Because of their dual roles in the chain of representation, principals might face situations where their own evaluation of subordinates might be used as a check on themselves by their superiors. They perceive the risk that accountability evaluations intended to serve their own information needs could actually become a dagger in their own back. This fear of being unintendedly and unwillingly held accountable, creates a strong drive to avoid evaluation altogether.

The other reason why accountability evaluations are rare in the public sector can be phrased in the following fashion. Too strong an emphasis on accountability can result in the executives' taking a cowardly approach toward crucial initiatives. Knowing his master's every whim and habit, that perfect servant Passepartout in Jules Verne's "Around the World in 80 Days" anticipated Phileas Fogg's wishes to such an extent that the latter did not have to issue one single order. Their relationship appears to have worked as if there had been—to borrow Arthur Okun's memorable phrase—"an invisible handshake" between the two to the effect that the master should offer "a fair day's pay" and the servant "a fair day's work." Too much stress on accountability will replace this penchant for benign anticipation with cowardly servility or obsequiousness.

These mechanisms, each of them in its own way, contribute to the cool or mixed interest toward evaluation in public life.

Executives Want to Improve Their Performance

In the improvement perspective, evaluation aspires to guide program amelioration and refinement. The incremental amelioration and revision of program operations and program direction is basic to the improvement rationale. It is felt that the program will continue its operations in the foreseeable future and that it must operate as smoothly and efficiently as possible. The fundamental question is "How can the program be made better?" The aim is to make the program more streamlined, effective, efficient, service oriented, and adapted to client concerns and needs.

The primary client of improvement evaluation is the personnel responsible for or closely associated with the intervention. It could be front–line program staff, supervisors of front–line personnel, program administrators, or even senior managers. Evaluation is seen as a part of the agency's day–to–day management process with learning and corrective actions as a means toward general system improvement as its primary goal. The program improvement perspective conceives of evaluation as an iterative process whereby evaluation findings are fed back into program planning, management, delivery—and fed back fast enough to enable the modification and improvement of currently operating programs. This objective places the priority on speed, flexibility, and relevance in the evaluation rather than on the development of new knowledge according to rigorous methodological standards. In fact, the need for speed and pertinence *vis–à–vis* a broad range of pressing issues may even obviate the possibility of careful research in the academic sense. On special occasions, for instance, management evaluation may function better if the study is not published.

Accountability evaluation, on the other hand, is not primarily aimed at personnel directly involved with the evaluand, but at the superior principals. Evaluation is designed to be a tool for superiors to check their subordinates and keep them and the program responsible for their actions. This is the crucial difference between improvement and accountability evaluation.

Program improvement, "program modification," or formative evaluation as some authors call this perspective (Anderson and Ball 1978:30ff.), is a worthy and necessary aim for evaluation. Several experts maintain that program improvement (and program direction reconsideration) must be the major purpose. "Accountability emphasizes looking back in order to assign praise or blame; evaluation is better used to understand events and processes for the sake of guiding future activities," Lee Cronbach wrote in one of his ninety-five theses on the reformation of evaluation (Cronbach et al. 1980:4). "In practice," Carol Weiss noted in her textbook (1972a:17), "evaluation is most often called on to help with decisions about improving programs. Go/no–go, live–or–die decisions are relatively rare....It is the search for improvements in strategies and techniques that supports much evaluation activity at present."

Evaluation for Basic Knowledge

The third substantive purpose is *basic knowledge*. Evaluation is now seen as fundamental research that seeks to increase the general understanding of reality. It tests broader theories on the ways agencies function, the coping strategies of front–line service deliverers, or the functioning of particular forms of intervention. It augments the collected body of knowledge in some academic field of study. Theory building and theory testing are important buzzwords in the basic knowledge perspective. Such research may be devoid of practical implications in the immediate future or even in the longer term. It seeks knowledge for knowledge's sake (Rutman and Mowbray 1983:27f.).

Several perceptive methodologists exclude the basic–knowledge purpose (Premfors 1989:140f.). Others accord it the major role, for example, such proponents of theory–oriented evaluation as Franke–Wikberg and Ulf P. Lundgren (1980:129ff.); Chen (1990); and Fitz–Gibbon et al. (1975). A third group regards basic knowledge as a happy side effect in relation to improvement and accountability (Chelimsky 1978; Anderson and Ball 1978:35).

Robert K. Merton, Friedrich A. Hayek, Karl R. Popper, and others have taught us to treat unintended side effects seriously. This is also my attitude toward the basic knowledge outlook on evaluation. The provision of basic knowledge is not the major task of evaluation; basic knowledge is subordinated under accountability and improvement. Basic knowledge is more of a side consideration. The basic knowledge purposes peep out when we stress the importance of disseminating evaluation reports to other prospective stakeholders than the purported primary user, for example, neighboring agencies or university–based researchers. The fundamental knowledge perspective is even more apparent in *metaevaluation,* interpreted as the activity of summarizing the findings of a whole range of single evaluations in some functional area. The point with such summary inventories must be to extract the general ideas from an array of separate studies by integrating them into more general conceptual frameworks (Bernstein and Freeman 1975; Rosenthal 1984; Light and Pillemer 1984; Vedung 1982a).

In my view, the basic–knowledge perspective ought to be more integrated into evaluation. It would be valuable, even in accountability and improvement evaluation, if at least some evaluation viewed the intervention as a case of something more general. While contributing to the growth of a more general body of knowledge, the generalization ambition would stimulate program management and staff to more analogical thinking and deeper self– understanding.

Strategic Purposes

Since evaluation always takes place in action settings, it is usually permeated with game–oriented considerations, *strategic* purposes. Executives use evaluation to hide shortcomings and failures from their principals, to display attractive images of programs, and in general to provide appearances more flattering than reality. Evaluations are commissioned to gain time, to show up a front of rationality, and to disseminate an overly handsome view of the executives' work. These strategic motives for the evaluation are often covert. If disclosed, they would lose their purported beneficial value in the political or administrative power game (Anderson and Ball 1978:34f.).

Often, university evaluators condemn strategic motives and hidden agendas as an abuse of evaluation. Edward Suchman (1967:143, 1972:81), a pioneer in American evaluation methodology, termed studies guided by such concealed motivations "pseudo–evaluations." Suchman has compiled a list of "evaluative abuses" from which the subsequent items are drawn.

One of Suchman's categories, *posture,* engenders attempts to use evaluation as a "gesture" of rationality and to assume the pose of objective, scientific research. Since science and scholarship carry considerable prestige with the general public, a scientific evaluation looks good externally and is regarded as a sign of professional status. The point is to have scholarly evaluations appointed and working. The evaluation is a ritual designed to placate diverse stakeholding audiences.

In *postponement,* the evaluation is used more directly as a tranquilizer. In this case the program is under debate or outright attack. An evaluative study is appointed to delay a pending decision in the hope that the sensitive issue will be defused and public agitation quieted as time goes by. Fact finding is time expending and, hopefully, public opinion will have cooled off and attention diverted to other issues when finally the evaluation reports.

To illustrate this tranquilizer notion, Seidman and Gilmour (1986:24) quoted a poem appearing in *Punch* many years ago:

If you are pestered by critics and hounded by faction
To take some precipitate, positive action
The proper procedure, to take my advice, is
Appoint a commission and stave off the crisis.

In both posture and postponement, the crucial thing is the appointment of an evaluation and the fact that it is working, not the substantive results produced by it. The purpose is to exploit the sheer fact that the program is evaluated as an argument in the struggle for survival or expansion. But whereas the posture aim may be served by an ongoing as well as a terminated evaluation, the postponement idea is basically served only as long as the evaluation is underway.

Suchman's third case, *eye–wash,* involves an attempt to justify a weak program by deliberately selecting for evaluation only those aspects that already beforehand appear successful and avoiding aspects that look faulty. The immediate purpose is, it seems, to have a proper though deliberately partial and biased evaluation conducted for the ulterior purpose of generating support for or deflecting criticism of the program.

The eye–wash case may be expanded to cover all forms of self–glorification or public relations. An official may believe that his program is highly successful and looks for ways to make this wonderful truth known to the world. A well–conducted investigation might do. Copies of the study can be distributed to members of parliamentary committees, interest organizations, top–level agency decision–makers, and the mass media. It is believed that this will bolster the stature of the program and boost the prestige of its managers (Weiss 1972a:11f.).

The eye–wash case differs from posture and postponement because the evaluation is focused on the substantive results, although some biased selection of them. Posture and postment only thrive on the appointment and working of evaluation, not on their findings.

To the Suchman list of purported strategic uses of evaluation, I shall append two additional cases. Both can be subsumed under *ducking responsibility,* a category suggested by Carol Weiss (1972a:11). Evaluations can be appointed to compel opponents to share responsibility for unpopular actions. To achieve this purpose, the evaluation must be organized on a stakeholder basis, where at the least the opposition parties are made members of the evaluation commission. If a compromise is struck in the study group, responsibility will be shared.

Decision–makers may commission evaluation also to completely avoid all responsibility. In contrast with eye–wash, impartial, dispassionate, and unbiased evidence is actually desired. However, the decision–makers want the evaluation to make the decision for them. They may want the evaluation to rally support for a program in order to sustain it or to drum up opposition in order to kill it and divert its funds to other purposes. But they don't want to assume the responsibility themselves; it is more expedient to refer to an evaluation (Anderson and Ball 1978:34; Weiss 1972a:11).

Used strategically, evaluations can be likened to "Potemkin villages." In Swedish, the expression *Potemkinkulisser* ("Potemkin fronts," "Potemkin scenes") stands for devices used by an agent to camouflage bad conditions to his principal. In English and German, the metaphor is "Potemkin villages." The expression refers to Empress Catherine II's visit in 1787 to the Crimea where the governor general of the Ukraine, Prince Potemkin, built artificial house fronts along her route to give her a false impression of good conditions. During the visit, governor Potemkin, the Empress' former favorite and lover, received the title prince of Tauris.

Final Word

However understandable, Suchman's condemnation of studies guided by hidden agendas as pseudoevaluations and evaluative abuses is unrealistic, if it presupposes that we could have entirely clean evaluations, evaluations purged from strategic politicking. This might be possible in scientific laboratories, or in academic field tryouts. But in public policy and public administration, beliefs and judgments concerning the substantive issue under scrutiny will probably always be mixed with strategic motivations. It is impossible to eradicate power struggles in huge organizations, and least of all in the state. And more importantly, it is undesirable to do so. Every society needs an arena for the resolution of real conflicts, and this arena is politics. Actually, as little as evaluation can supplant politics, nor can politics supplant evaluation. Both are needed, and quite often they mix. In addition, the mixture of *bona fide* substantive aims and covert strategic purposes enhances the fascination with evaluation. What we can do is to make evaluators aware of the fact that their endeavor might be involved in some power games. They should find out who initiated the evaluation and why. Then at least they are not caught unaware by the strategic purposes.

Note

1. Accountability evaluation is similar to, but not identical with, summative evaluation in Michael Scriven's terminology (1991:340). The similarity is that both accountability and summative evaluation are conducted for the benefit of some external audience. The difference seems to be that this could be any external audience in the case of summative evaluation, but must be a superordinate audience in accountability evaluation. In my interpretation, accountability evaluation is associated with notions of oversight and administrative hierarchy.

7

Internal or External Evaluation

Who ought to perform public policy evaluation? This second problem in my Eight Problems Approach may seem weird. In free countries, evaluation can and should be conducted by anyone. Parliaments, governments, and agencies can do it. Citizens, media, and clients as well as interest organizations can do it. Here, it will be sufficient to illuminate one limited aspect. Should evaluations be internal or external?

The concepts of external and internal evaluation are complicated, because they may refer to at least three things at the same time: who should arrange, produce, and use the evaluation? While the arranger may be an outside body, the producer and the primary intended user may be the pertinent agency itself. In a similar vein, the arranger may be the agency, but the producer could be an outside body, and the intended user the agency.

Here, an evaluation is considered external if it is *produced* by a body external to the agency legally in charge of the evaluand. Similarly, an evaluation is internal if it is produced by the agency in charge of the evaluand. Figure 7.1 shows the possibilities.

The producers are those responsible for the design, data gathering, data analysis, and the reporting of the evaluation. The arrangers of evaluation include those who decide that an evaluation should be undertaken and pay for its completion. The evaluation user is the person, group, or institution whose information needs about the program is to be met by the evaluation. Evaluation producers, evaluation arrangers, and users could be different groups of people. Yet, one and the same body could also arrange, produce, and be the primary intended user. If

115

FIGURE 7.1 External and Internal Evaluation			
Evaluation Type	Producer	Arranger	User
External Evaluation	External	External	External
	External	Internal	External
	External	External	Internal
Internal Evaluation	Internal	Internal	Internal
	Internal	External	Internal
	Internal	Internal	External

this body is in charge of the evaluand, the evaluation would be internal in a very strong sense of the word.

If some body external to the evaluatee is the producer of an evaluation, the evaluation is external. External evaluations can be arranged and used by insiders, but must per definition be produced by outsiders. When a subordinate body is commissioned by his principal to do an accountability report, and the subordinate chooses to conduct the evaluation in house, the evaluation will be internal according to my terminology. Internal evaluations are self–evaluations. If, on the other hand, the subordinate body contracts with some consulting firm to produce the study, the assessment will be external.

External evaluations can be produced by numerous kinds of external bodies. Figure 7.2 presents an overview of external producers of evaluations.

An important distinguishing line runs between evaluations contracted out to for–profit consultants and to various nonprofit institutions. The latter include public commissions, public auditing agencies, universities and other institutions of higher learning, government–funded public policy institutes, and nonprofit think tanks and foundations.

Should Evaluation be Internal or External?

Now, let us return to our puzzle of whether evaluations should be internal or external. In the first instance, a seemingly strong case might be made for internal evaluation, since ideally every organization ought to be self–evaluating (Wildavsky 1985). "Effective internal evaluation provides an indispensable support for managers," Arnold

FIGURE 7.2
External Producers of Evaluation

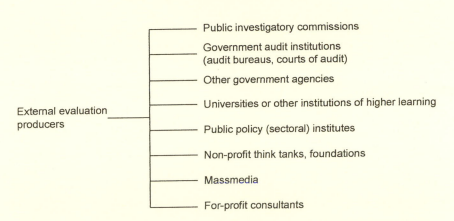

Love argues in his perceptive book *Internal Evaluation*. While this is probably true, internal evaluation cannot solve all evaluation problems, because of the pervasiveness of self–regarding behavior. A better solution than either—or is, simply, both. Generally, evaluations cannot always be performed in house. However, they cannot always be placed outside the agency in charge either. For some purposes, internal evaluation is indubitably appropriate. In other contexts, external evaluation is more suitable. The choice must be made with respect to the major purpose of the study, or more specifically, with respect to who will be the primary user of the information. This means that the three purposes of accountability, improvement, and basic knowledge call for different organizational designs.

Accountability

When the purpose is accountability to outside parties, evaluations should be external. Preferably, they should be conducted by some autonomous body, because objectivity is important. Generally, external evaluations carry greater credibility as objective enterprises than do internal evaluations.

Internal evaluators cannot perform unbiased accountability evaluations for two reasons. If the internal evaluator feels that some program component works well, she will subject this to a painstaking scrutiny. She may keep to the facts and weigh them in a perfect manner. The bias lies therein that dubious or apparently unsuccessful projects are not subjected to the same close scrutiny. The evaluator is personally acquainted with those in charge of the program component and knows that it is ill managed. But she is hesitant to expose this to general knowledge. She may bring together a report, but in a sanguine and haphazard manner in order to have something to refer to. But to avoid the heavy burden of revealing deficiencies, she will not probe the matter very carefully.

In addition, if the agency has expended huge funds on the project, some defense for this must be presented. Therefore, the internal evaluator may balance the criticism with favorable arguments. Merits as well as drawbacks will be presented. However, the internal evaluator may not do a proper weighing of the pros and cons. She may be hesitant to state expressly that the project is a failure. The bias is shown as deceptive balancing.

The external evaluator, on the other hand, can speak more frankly because there is less risk of job loss or personal or dislike. She is probably better at evaluation methods and theories. She has looked closely at other programs and can draw parallels which may be revealing. She may also give the evaluation the hallmark of impartiality and high quality.

However, the mere commissioning of an external evaluator does not safeguard an objective and unbiased evaluation. External evaluators want new contracts. If they are too critical, they run the risk of losing the confidence of the people in the agency. Hence, they may phrase their report more to please their commissioners rather than to provide the truth. External evaluators prostitute their skills (Anderson and Ball 1978:141ff.).

Improvement

Improvement evaluations are best conducted in house. To facilitate rapid use and immediate learning, those who need the information should preferably also amass it.

Consider the case of the National Board of Industry making a preliminary version of an information folder on energy conservation and disseminating it to a selected group of targets for a tryout. The targets will then be asked if the folder has evoked their interest, if the message is comprehensible, if their attitude to energy conservation has changed after reading the information, if their knowledge of energy conservation has increased, if some information is omitted. The evaluation is supposed to yield information that can be used to improve the folder.

Circumstances unequivocally suggest that this evaluation ought to be internal. Actually, those who have authored the folder should both arrange, conduct, and use the evaluation in order to learn from it. Since the folder represents a field trial before the real program will start, the pertinent administrators have nothing to conceal, which means that the objectivity injunction against internal evaluation carries no weight. Moreover, methods considerations are of little importance. Purposive sampling of interesting informants in order to extract valuable insights through in–depth talks is what is called for, not complicated randomized designs and controlled conditions.

Once the program has started wholesale, some monitoring is called for. The purpose is still purely managerial: to improve the workings of the program. The aim is to investigate whether implementation functions well, or if there are barriers and obstacles that must be overcome. Problematic knots are actively searched for in order to facilitate and speed up implementation. All this suggests formative evaluation conducted internally by those immediately in charge.

The internal evaluator understands the program better and can avoid mistakes due to ignorance. She knows the people better and has easier access to them. She will be around once the evaluation is finished and hence can facilitate implementation.

Even in this case, objections to the internal model carry little weight. The evaluation needs to start immediately and produce results as fast as possible. Program staff must learn quickly from mistakes. Objectivity and methods skills are of less importance, because there are no go/no–go decisions within reach.

Basic Knowledge

Evaluations with a basic knowledge outlook should preferably be conducted externally. The primary potential audience of metaevaluations, for instance, is not particular agencies, but government operators, the evaluation community, and academic researchers and teachers in the field of public policy and public administration. Therefore, basic knowledge evaluations might suitably be conducted by universities, research institutes, and other institutions of higher learning. However, basic knowledge evaluations might also be executed in-house. It would be useful for the general culture of an agency, if it brought together and analyzed the knowledge concealed in different evaluations.

8

Characterizing the Public Intervention

Public sector evaluations vary widely in their subject matter. Some are extremely broad in their scope, covering for instance an entire policy area; others exceedingly narrow. Some focus on interventions that may last indefinitely; others on programs that will continue for a few hours only. Some deal with new, innovative programs; others with regular programs that have been going on for decades. Some evaluands are local in their scope; others regional or national, if not international or global in the case of treaties between nations concerning, for instance, pollution reduction. Yet, however wide or narrow, long lasting or short lived, evaluands have to be described.

Seasoned evaluators advise that little energy should be expended on characterizing the intervention, the third item in my Eight Problems Approach. Since intended primary users of the evaluation are already familiar with the evaluand, there is no need to dwell upon it at length. Instead, available time and money should be spent on performance monitoring, impact assessment, dissemination of findings, and other essential things.

There is some truth to this statement. Recently introduced programs require a different evaluation strategy from programs that have existed for a long time. In the monitoring of recently introduced programs for in–house use, the intervention can be taken for granted and all efforts can be directed at what is happening further down in the chain of control. In *impact assessment,* which preferably should be directed at older, more stable interventions, it is important, however, to make a thorough descriptive analysis of the evaluand, since it will be used as one explanatory factor. It is essential, I would argue, that these portrayals do not render the interventions too idiosyncratic and situation bound. The intervention ought to be considered in a rather general light. Regarding it in this way will stimulate various users to analogical and comparative thinking, which may elicit novel insights into the program under evaluation. At the same time, the theoretical merit of the evaluation will be augmented, which may have repercussions on other programs and on the body of general knowledge in the field of public administration. On this account, I strongly agree with Cronbach's argument (1982) that evaluations should permit the extrapolation of findings to other contexts.

While a moderate case can be made for a generalizing approach to the evaluation of a singular program, such a case can be made much stronger with respect to national or international comparative studies of several programs, and national and international metaevaluation. To make cross–program comparisons, general conceptual schemes are needed.

To enhance the generality of evaluative studies, more attention ought to be given to various possibilities of characterizing the evaluand as a case of something wider and more general.

Policy Instruments: Regulations, Economic Means, Information

An option that evaluators have made too little use of is to characterize the intervention in terms of policy instruments. The policy instruments strategy has been identified as "a distinctly new approach to the study of public policy—an approach that identifies a new unit of analysis for policy research" (Salamon 1989:xv). I definitely recommend evaluators to describe their evaluands in policy–instruments language.

Public policy instruments are set of techniques by which public sector authorities wield their power in attempting to effect social change or eliciting support. They are referred to by various names, for example, means of governance, tools of government, modes of implementation, policy techniques, governmental controls, state interventionist techniques, or techniques of statecraft. In the sequel, I shall use these expressions and their derivatives as synonyms and interchangeably.

There are in my opinion three, and only three, basic instruments

that governments have recourse to: the stick, the carrot, and the sermon. Governments can either force us to do what they want, reward us
or charge us materially for doing it, or preach to us that we should do
it. The stick is called regulation, the carrot economic means, and the
sermon might be labelled information.[1] It is my contention that all
other types of policy instruments advanced in the literature can be
reduced to these fundamental three. It is also my contention that this
trichotomy cannot be further reduced; if collapsed into a twofold scheme
the loss of information will be irreparable.[2]

This basic arrangement into regulation, economic means and information is presented in figure 8.1.

Suppose the state wants to reduce the consumption of a foreign
commodity, say, textiles from Korea. The state may impose a ban on
imports of the commodity (regulation), make it more expensive by
levying a special customs duty on it (economic means), or put the
label "Made in Korea" on it in the hope that this piece of information
will reduce the sale of it (information).

While there are three fundamental forms of policy instruments, the
regulatory element is constitutive of public power wielding. "Der
moderne Staat ist diejenige menschliche Gemeinschaft, welche
innerhalb eines bestimmten Gebietes...das Monopol physischer
Gewaltsamkeit für sich (mit Erfolg) beansprucht," Max Weber once
maintained.[3] Regulations are concerned with force and violence. Only
the state has a legitimate right to exert force and violence against its
members. Therefore, regulations are the constitutive element in public

FIGURE 8.1
Policy Instruments: Regulations, Economic Means, Information

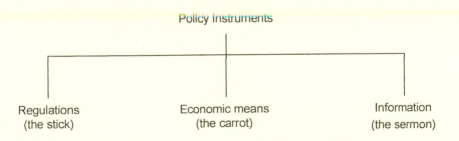

| Regulations
(the stick) | Economic means
(the carrot) | Information
(the sermon) |

power wielding in modern states.

In the regulatory case, the addressees are obligated to do what the government tells them. In the case of economic means, the addressees are free to do what they want, but the government may make action easier or more difficult by adduction or deprivation of material resources in the form of, say, subsidies or taxes. Finally, in the case of information, the relationship is entirely persuasive, to wit, only communication of knowledge, claims, and reasons are involved but no material resources and no obligatory directives. These three types of relationships between governors and governed are the defining properties of regulation, economic instruments, and information.

Let us look somewhat more closely and formally at the differences.

Regulations are measures undertaken by government units to influence people by means of verbally formulated rules and directives, which mandate the receivers to act in accordance with what is ordered in these rules and directives. The decisive characteristic of a regulation is that the purported relationship between the governor and the governed is authoritative in the sense that the latter are thought to be obligated to comply.

To underscore this coercive trait, regulations are associated with threats of negative sanctions such as fines, imprisonment, and other types of punishment. However, this is not always the case. There are regulations intentionally not coupled with threats of negative sanctions. In jurisprudence, there is a classic term for these nonsanctioned rules: *lex imperfecta.*

Thus, negative sanctions are a sufficient but not a necessary characteristic of regulation. The defining property of regulation is that the relationship is authoritative, meaning that the controlled persons or groups are obligated to act in the way stated by the controllers.

Expressions such as "restrictions," "command-and-control devices," or "government directives" are sometimes used as synonyms to regulation.

Economic policy instruments involve either distributing or taking away material resources. They make it cheaper or more expensive to pursue certain actions. However, addressees are not ordered to take the measures involved, a fact that makes economic instruments principally different from regulations. Economic tools always leave subjects of governance a certain leeway within which to choose by themselves whether to take an action or not.

The addressees may decide not to make use of a government incentive—a particular grant—because they hesitate to take the measures required to get it. Or they may apply for a grant because they feel that the strings attached to it are perfectly worthwhile and even in their own interest. The point is that economic incentives neither prescribe nor prohibit the actions involved, but make them less expensive.

The same goes for disincentives. A tax levied on tobacco does not prohibit ingrained smokers from enjoying their Ritmeesters and Camels. Those who continue smoking are not breaking the law. They are fully allowed to indulge in their habit, but the government wants to discourage them by having them pay more.

Yet taxes entail one coercive trait. In performing the action the tax is levied upon, the agent must pay the tax. Now, somebody may wonder what the difference really is between a tax and a regulation. Both seem to involve a measure of authoritative force. The difference is that a regulation proscribes or prescribes the action proper while the obligation in our tax example applies to the payment of the tax, not the action itself. There is an obvious principal difference between banning production, marketing and selling of Ritmeester cigars and levying a tax on the production and provision of them.

Information, or "moral suasion," finally, covers attempts at influencing people through the transfer of knowledge, communication of reasoned argument, and persuasion. The information dispensed may be of many different kinds. It may concern the nature of the problem at hand, how people are actually handling the problem, measures that can be taken to change the prevailing situation, and reasons why these measures ought to be considered and adopted by the addressees. However, no more than the plain transfer of knowledge or persuasive reasoning is offered to pressure people to do what the government deems desirable.

Information is used here as a catch–all term for communication campaigns, diffusion of printed materials like brochures, pamphlets, booklets, folders, fliers, bulletins, handbills, and posters, advertising, labeling, audits, inspections, demonstration programs, counselling, personal advice, training programs, education efforts, and other forms of amassing, packaging, and diffusion of knowledge and recommendations.

In ordinary language as well as in information theory, "informing" is identical with providing objective and correct facts about a state of affairs. Naturally, this basic meaning has been retained in the language of public policy analysis. Yet, in public policy, government can also "inform" the citizenry about what is good or bad, right or wrong. Moreover, government can also "provide information about" what people are allowed to do, or how they should act and behave. The information category covers, in other words, not only objective and correct knowledge, but also judgments about which phenomena and measures are good or bad, and recommendations about how citizens should act and behave. In policy studies literature, information has come to embrace much more than just the transmission of knowledge.

As with the economic tools of statecraft, no government obligation is involved. Under no circumstances are addressees compelled to act in the way outlined in the information. Whether or not to follow the recommendations is entirely up to the targets, because by definition information includes no stronger means of influence than recommendations and concomitant reasoning. This absence of obligation makes information different from regulation, which by definition contains mandatory rules of conduct.

Yet information is also different from economic policy instruments in that no handing out or taking away of material resources is involved. The distributed information may very well include arguments to the effect that addressees will actually benefit materially from taking the measures recommended. However, government neither materially rewards people who take the action, nor materially deprives people who do not. The only thing offered is data, facts, knowledge, arguments, and moral appeals.

All three types of policy instruments may be phrased in the affirmative or the negative. Regulations are divided into prohibitions and prescriptions. Information may persuade a person to perform an action or dissuade him from performing it. In the case of positive economic policy instruments, a material resource is handed over to the person, if he takes the action involved. In the negative case, material resources will be taken away from him, should he prefer to perform the action.

By now, it should be evident that my classification proceeds from the degree of *authoritative force* or *constraint* involved in the governance attempts. In principle, regulation is more constraining for addressees than economic means, and the latter more constraining than information. A ban on the purchasing of Ritmeester cigars puts more restriction on the smokers' freedom of action than a tax levied on the selling of them, which in turn is more restrictive than dissuasive information to the effect that these means of sensual pleasure should be neither bought nor used.

Objections to the Tripartition

The idea of organizing policy instruments according to the degree of constraint can be criticized from several angles. One allegedly damaging objection to this idea of organizing policy instruments according to the degree of constraint would be that, occasionally, *economic means are more constraining than regulation*. Compare the case where a particular line of action is forbidden but the concomitant fines for not complying are very low to the case where an enormous tax is levied on the same line of action. The tax may make the action much more "prohibitive" than the regulation, because the fine for violating it is so low. Consequently, our scheme seems to break down.

This argument is true, of course, but slightly beside the point. I am arguing that in principle regulation is more constraining than taxes, however high, because in the former case you are not allowed to take the action, whereas in the latter case, while allowed, the action will cost a lot of money to perform. If you take action in the former case you are a rule breaker, in the latter case not. It is this cardinal difference that distinguishes regulation from economic means.

Also, the distinction between regulatory and economic instruments seems to run into another difficult borderline instance: *price regulation*. Only the name tells us, according to some people, that price regulation is a regulatory instrument. Since producers, distributors, and sellers are obligated to follow the price directives issued by government, price regulations are regulatory. Not at all, others have retorted. Price regulations are economic instruments, since the purpose underlying their adoption is to influence prices. The right answer depends on who is the major addressee. If the purpose is to influence the consumers, price regulations are economic instruments. They will pay the regulated price that will be lower than the unregulated market price would be. In other words, they are offered a material good in order to be better off. But the method used to accomplish this is through the regulation of producers and distributors. They are mandated to follow the government–issued rules concerning what prices they are allowed to set. To them, price regulations are a mandatory means of government, that is, regulations.

A third seemingly strong objection concerns the *difficulty of drawing a line between information and regulation.* In the contemporary world, mandatory labeling is a widely used technique of government to warn users of some products of accompanying dangers and antidotes (Bardach and Kagan 1982, chap. 9). Susan Hadden, whose *Read the Label: Reducing Risk by Providing Information* is an important contribution to our knowledge of this particular technique, talks interchangeably about "regulation by label" and "consumer information" (1986:1ff).

And she is perfectly right in doing so. For in relation to sellers, who are required by government to provide information labels on their merchandise, labeling is regulation. However, in relation to consumers, who are supposed to read the labels, learn something, and maybe also act in some way or another, labeling is a tool of information. Labeling, and many other strategies of government control, is constructed as a combination of regulation and information, in that intermediaries—in this case sellers—are required to provide something—information—whereas the proper addressees of the particular control system—the consumers—are only supposed to read, learn, and act, should they find it appropriate to do so. Labeling is a kind of mandated disclosure of information.

A fourth important borderline case concerns the difference between *information and threats of* imposing a *regulation.* Wouldn't it be reasonable to view threats of enacting some regulatory measure as a form of information? Because it is not yet enacted, it does not seem to be a regulation. My answer to this is that threats of resorting to regulation should be considered regulatory measures. For the three fundamental means of governance can be *employed* in various ways. They may be employed in the sense of being formally enacted by the proper institution. But they can also be used in this way: that government officials threaten to impose them. During the course of an information campaign, government officials may threaten to resort to unilateral compulsory measures, should information not lead to the desired behavior. Thus, threats of regulation are not a persuasive tool of government, as defined here, but one conceivable way of using the device of regulation.

One may also wonder whether this classification is *truly exhaustive.* Consider, for example, negotiations between public authorities and some private party. Is this not a policy instrument in its own right?

The answer is that while engendering governance, negotiation is not a separate policy instrument. Pursued in calm and civilized forms, negotiations are cases of governing through persuasion. The public authority confines itself to informing, arguing and persuading. At a certain point, however, a threat of regulating the matter may be enunciated. But not even this would constitute a new, separate means of governance but only a threat of regulation.

Summing up, one appropriate way of broadening the horizons of the commissioners of evaluation and other stakeholders is to characterize the intervention in terms of regulation, economic means or information. The intervention under evaluation may of course consist of one, two or all three of these instruments. In addition, evaluators may take one step further and try to indicate what type of regulations, economic means, and information are involved.

Regulations

While being elementary types, the three categories of policy instruments contain numerous internal variations. As shown above, the basis underlying the tripartite division into regulation, economic means, and information is the degree of constraint imposed on the addressees. The general idea of constraint can also be employed to discern and order subcategories within each of the three main types.

Regulation, to start with, engenders numerous varieties. Leaving out prescriptions and concentrating on prohibitions, it is possible to discern four types: absolute prohibitions, prohibitions with exemptions, enabling legislation, and obligations to notify. This line of reasoning is illustrated in figure 8.2.

Unconditional prohibitions are valid without exception. The fundamental idea is that the forbidden activity should not exist at all. There are numerous such absolute proscriptions, for example, against manslaughter, murder, and child abuse. In general, however, regulations are reminiscent of colanders, for they are often perforated by exceptions and exemptions.

Most constraining among these conditional proscriptions are rules combined with exemptions in exceptional cases, *prohibition with exemptions*. In such situations, the proscription is, to be sure, meant to be the normal course followed, but to prevent authorities from ending up in absurd situations, the exemption option is offered as a safety valve.

FIGURE 8.2
Prohibitions Ordered According to the Strength of the Exceptions

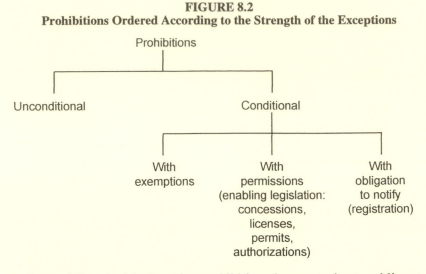

In *enabling legislation,* the prohibition does not aim to obliterate but to control or raise demands on the activity involved. Permits are granted on a regular basis, provided the applicant can show that his activity will satisfy certain specified requirements. The permissions granted can be described as permits, concessions, warrants, quotas, certificates, licenses, or authorizations. A restaurant operator in Sweden must apply for permission to be licensed to serve alcoholic beverages. A fox hunter must have a weapons licence to be allowed to carry a shotgun. A building permit is necessary to build a house.

A third possibility is that proscription is combined with an *obligation to notify.* The planned course of action is plainly forbidden, as long as authorities are not notified about it. Once the proper authority has been informed, however, it can begin. The point with this notification requirement is usually that the notifier under normal circumstances can start his undertaking but that the notification in a few, rare cases triggers a process of investigation, which can lead on to permission or continued prohibition.

Another rationale is to defend customers against fraud. The authorities want the name and the whereabouts of the notifier in case he might deceive some customers. Obviously, this is the rationale for the registration of taxi drivers. They are supposed to be registered and to display sign on their cars carrying a number and a name. In case of deception, the customers can contact the authorities, get the identity of the deceiver, and seek redress.

We can exemplify with an area where the interests of environmental protection conflict sharply with those of agriculture, forestry, and energy extraction. To protect our remaining moors and marshlands against the exploitation of peat for fuel, or drainage for forestry or farming purposes, a national government might introduce a total prohibition against draining and other encroachments; that is, the state could, with its power of coercion, embrace an outright conservationist position. Of course, the proponents of energy, forestry, and farming interests would consider such absolute prohibition an outright absurdity. Their principals, of course, would have to shelf their plans for continued exploitation. One way of avoiding some of the complexities associated with total prohibition would be to link it to an exemption procedure. This transition to conditional procedures would make possible some peat harvesting, some drainage of wetlands for forestry and some for agricultural purposes, but only in exceptional situations. A small part of the wetlands with no unique environmental features might then be released for exploitation.

But we might also weaken the proscription a bit more by switching to the method of enabling legislation. In this case, peat harvesting and wetland drainage would be allowed on certain conditions. The number of permissions granted would depend upon the stringency of the conditions.

A fourth possibility would be to weaken the proscription still more by combining it with an obligation to notify. The prospective user would then be mandated to notify the authorities of his plans. Allowing exploitation then would be the favored option, while continued protection might be chosen in a few cases. In the area of Swedish environmental protection, we have a control system of this type. According to the 1964 Nature Conservancy Act land owners are under an obligation to notify the County Administration when they are ready to start drainage projects to acquire new productive woodland. This notification is the starting point for a consultation procedure according to provision no. 20 of the Nature Conservancy Act. In this way, certain valuable swamplands may be protected while suitable areas for drainage are assigned to the lumber companies.

Economic Instruments

Economic instruments also come in different shapes. An elementary typology is featured in figure 8.3.

An important borderline exists between monetary and nonmonetary economic means. Grants, subsidies, fees, charges, credit guarantees, and interest subsidies are economic means but so are free health care, free medicine, and free day care for children. There has been considerable controversy in Sweden over whether government help to low–income citizens should be in cash or in kind. The cash principle would entail that all people below a certain level would receive actual cash from the state. This would give the receivers the freedom to choose whatever they like to do with their allowance. Personal integrity would not be encroached upon and social stigmatization would be avoided. Against this, some people have argued that social welfare should take the form of government–produced goods and services, offered to the people through publicly owned and operated organizations. In this vein, the state would ensure that the citizens did not waste their resources on less desirable consumption but enjoyed the goods and services decided by authorities in cooperation with scientific expertise.

That economic means, like regulations, can be formulated positively or negatively has already been mentioned. The counterpart to prescriptions would be allowances, to proscriptions levies. Levies imply that material resources are taken away, allowances that material resources are adduced.

Another interesting difference is between taxes and fees. Taxes are

FIGURE 8.3
Some Elementary Types of Economic Tools of Government

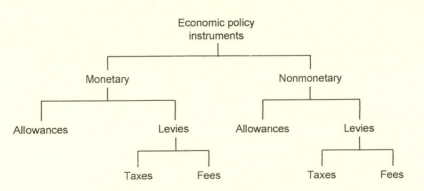

levied without reference to the benefit that the individual receives from the government whereas fees confer such benefits. More formally, a tax is a compulsory payment levied according to law upon a person for the support of government which is levied without reference to the benefit which the individual receives from the government. A fee can be formally defined as a fixed charge to be paid by a person to defray all or part of the expense of some public action that confers a special benefit on the payer and also involves the enforcement of a public policy. An entrance payment to a public art museum would be a fee, since as a counter service, the wonders of the museum are available to the payer of the fee.

Information

Information also comes in many forms. It can be formulated in the negative or in the positive. It can try to persuade the addressees that something ought to be done or to dissuade them from doing something. The recommendation can be tacit or explicitly stated. Here only one distinction will be made, the one between information "on" and information "as."

Information is a necessary condition for the rational functioning of all other government controls. Seriously designed public programs require that intended beneficiaries are informed about the programs' existence and meaning. Such information may be called information *on* policy instruments as opposed to information *as* a policy instrument. In characterizing the input of the evaluation, it might be fruitful to distinguish the policy instruments proper from information about these policy instruments.

If a regulation, for example, a law or a statute, is to be effective, individuals in the target group must be aware of its existence and contents. Otherwise, of course, they cannot rationally abide by it. In many cases, the national government must purvey information to citizens about the meaning and existence of recently imposed regulatory instruments. A good case in point was the campaign in connection with the 1967 transition to driving on the right–hand side in Sweden. Extensive state funds were then allocated to informing motorists about the new, positively coercive legislation (Björkman 1971; Thorslund 1974).

Even economic instruments require concomitant information to function. It seems almost a truism, that prospective addressees must know that there is a grant program and under what conditions economic help might be given in order to be able to apply for subsidies. Often, the dissemination of such knowledge *on* other programs will require specific information measures from the authorities responsible.

Sometimes, government also has to inform people about information programs. After new information material has been developed, the administrative body concerned has to decide whether it should be disseminated immediately to the target population or whether information dispensing tools should be used to tell people about the existence of the material, pointing out how valuable it is as well as encouraging people to order it. In the latter case, the potential users of the information will be informed about the availability of the material, that it is important, and that prospective addressees should order it.

Our three cases underscore the importance of making a sharp distinction between information as an independent policy instrument—information *as*—and information as a meta–policy instrument—information *on*. The making of this distinction will probably enhance the pertinent stakeholders' understanding of the intervention under evaluation.

Conclusion on Policy Instruments

As we have already seen in chapter 5, the third problem in my Eight Problems Approach to Evaluation is concerned with how evaluators should describe the evaluand. Every written evaluation must contain at least a crude description of what is evaluated, and the question is how it should be done. My recommendation is that evaluators should venture to describe their evaluands in terms of policy instruments. This would be illuminating to evaluation commissioners and users. It would also serve as a vehicle toward extrapolation of evaluation findings to other programs and contexts.

Functional Scope

Aside from policy instruments, another seemingly appropriate candidate for raising the theoretical standing of evaluation research would be the functional scope of the intervention. In my mind, however, this approach to evaluand description is less promising than the policy–instruments strategy.

In the Swedish National Audit Bureau (RRV), a distinction between *program–oriented* and *system–oriented evaluation* was formerly highly important. The purpose of the creation in 1967 of a unit for performance auditing in the National Audit Bureau was to put more emphasis on results evaluation as opposed to the traditional focus on financial auditing (Sandahl 1992:115ff.). To begin with, the new unit centered its evaluations on individual programs, which were followed from instigation through the chain of implementation to the results achieved. After a few years, this program–oriented strategy was supplemented by a broader system–oriented approach. The evaluations began to focus on several individual programs directed at the same activity. Some evaluations were macro oriented, attempting to assess a whole functional policy sector, for example, the agricultural policies, the environmental policies, or the land use policies of the national government. The system–oriented approach made it possible to study the simultaneous interplay of several programs, which was regarded as more fruitful and interesting.

There are examples of system–oriented evaluation in the international literature as well. In *Losing Ground,* Charles Murray (1984:13) studied how social policy has affected the American poor and those discriminated against. The author argues:

> By "social policy," I mean a loosely defined conglomeration of government programs, laws, regulations, and court decisions touching on almost every dimension of life. Welfare programs are part of social policy toward the poor, obviously. Jobs programs are part of social policy. So are also federal efforts to foster better health and housing among the disadvantaged. So are also the Miranda decision and Affirmative Action and the Department of Education's regulations about bilingual education.

Charles Murray's study would more than qualify as a system–oriented evaluation.

The other extreme would be *components evaluation,* that is, trying to assess the impact and worth of one special component of a single program. Leonard Rutman (1977:27) has provided an example of components testing of a legal aid clinic. A legal aid clinic might include such component activities as providing legal advice, referral to relevant agencies, consumer education, and representation at court. These elements could be further divided into subelements. Referral, for instance, might include suggesting places where the client can go, sending a letter of introduction, phoning on behalf of the client and making arrangements for a visit, or actually accompanying the client to the place of referral. Having specified referral in these terms, it is then possible to gather data and determine the nature of the consequences from each subelement of a referral activity.

Degree of Centralization

The third way of increasing the general value of single evaluations would be to characterize their evaluands in terms of degree of centralization. Are all major decisions supposed to be made at the national level or is some leeway given to local bodies, like municipalities? While Sweden is a unitary state, the national governing bodies often adopt so–called *optional policy instruments,* which the municipalities may use should they wish to do so. Several land use programs are of this type, for instance, the expropriation law, the law on municipal prepurchasing of land, and the site–leasehold right law. The national parliament has enabled municipalities to expropriate private land for specific purposes, but the expropriation machinery starts only when municipalities decide to use it. Expropriation is optional to the municipalities, not mandatory.

Notes

1. My classification is basically derived from Etzioni (1975:5f.), who talks about coercive, remunerative, and normative power. The term "regulation" carries several meanings. It is used to designate an official *clarification* of a statute or administrative order or ordinance usually by the official charged with its enforcement. It also refers *generally* to the activity of government in controlling the affairs of the community. In my case, it refers to one type of policy instrument that governments may use, not to the general activity of governing.
2. The literature on policy instruments is growing. A classic attempt is Redford 1952. Recent contributions are Hood 1983; Doern and Phidd 1983; Baldwin 1985; Woodside 1986; Gaskell and Joerges 1987; Salamon 1989; Linder and. Peters 1989; and Howlett 1991.
3. "A state is a human community that (successfully) claims the *monopoly of the legitimate use of physical force* within a given territory" [quoted from Weber's *Politik als Beruf (Politics as a Vocation),* Weber 1974:78].

9

Monitoring

Monitoring and impact assessment are two major forms of evaluation. Monitoring keys in on conversion and results—the fourth and the fifth problem in the Eight Problems Approach—while impact assessment covers the sixth problem about intervention consequences. *Monitoring* implies empirical checks of the actual linkages in the chain of implementation, but particularly of the point where the intervention providers encounter the clients, where the government meets society, as it were. Is the intervention being delivered to the clients in ways envisioned in the formal intervention decision? Is the intervention reaching all the prospective participants? These two questions about intervention delivery and intervention coverage are at the center of monitoring.

In addition, monitoring also focuses on processes preceding service delivery. In this case, monitoring is a process evaluation, where the entire implementation process from formal intervention adoption to eventual addressee participation in service delivery is scrutinized.

Actually, monitoring may also concern potential outcomes, whether immediate, intermediate, or ultimate. However, if questions are raised concerning the causes of outcomes, then we are doing *impact assessment*. Yet, also in monitoring, explanations may be proffered, but compared to impact assessment these explanations concern phenomena in the implementation chain through the outputs, but excluding outcomes.

Aiming at incremental improvement, monitoring always focuses on the execution and delivery of existing interventions. The point is to examine whether, for instance, a program decision is carried out according to plan at lower levels of authority in order to correct mistakes and omissions during execution and delivery. While particularly important in the infancy of a program, monitoring is best regarded as a permanent administrative activity.

Starting with a higher–level decision, however, does not prevent the monitor from asking whether a program as delivered corresponds to what the target population actually expects or wants. This client perspective on evaluation may be combined with other stakeholder viewpoints. Monitors may probe how street–level bureaucrats manage and view their work. The point is, however, that the insights gathered ought to produce ameliorations of a program's implementation and delivery within the frame of how they were intended to function.

Intervention Theories

I take exception to the view that monitoring ought to be an atheoretical activity. Monitoring is a practical enterprise that should be grounded in social theory. Monitoring can be construed as a *five–steps activity*. The *first* step entails a reconstruction of the intervention theory, that is, the presuppositions concerning what the intervention was designed to achieve and how this achievement was to come about. The *second* step suggests the selection for empirical checks of some stage in the intervention theory. The *third* step entails collection and analysis of data. The *fourth* step involves the application of criteria of merit and standards of performance to the findings. Somewhat unusual in my approach to monitoring is the *fifth* and final step, involving an analysis of the evaluand, its intended administration and final delivery from a general governance perspective.

Inspiration concerning the *intervention theory* concept has been drawn from the works of the Dutch political scientist Andries Hoogerwerf (1990). Hoogerwerf posits that the "policy theory," which is the term he prefers, contains all the empirical and normative presuppositions and assumptions embodied in the program by its initial framers. He argues that evaluations can be regarded as tests of policy theories.

Intervention theories come in several linguistic guises. According to Hoogerwerf, they are referred to as "the impact model of the program" (Nachmias 1979:9ff.), "the program's theory of action," "the program model" (Patton 1990:107) or "the reasoning underlying the program." I shall use the term "intervention theory" as a general concept and "policy theory," "program theory" (Bickman 1990; Chen 1990) and "reform theory" when interventions might be thought of as a policy, a program or a reform.[1]

Much thought on evaluation assumes that only one theory underlies each undertaking. This is usually wrong. Along with initial framers of an intervention, other stakeholders may also hold presuppositions about an intervention's aims and effects. It is easy to imagine that the political opposition, the implementing agency, the intermediaries and various client groups each entertain assumptions about the outcome of the undertaking. There are many theories undergirding each intervention and each one of them might in principle be taken into account. For this reason, I prefer to talk about "intervention theories" in the plural.

The First Step: Reconstruction of the Intervention Theory

In conjunction with a real-life case, I shall illustrate how the sketched intervention theory method might be applied in monitoring. To highlight the methodological point, I shall deliberately choose a simple program: the Swedish Board for Consumer Policies' (*Statens Konsumentverks*) guidelines for information on gas mileage of new cars, the so-called Fuel Declaration (*Bränsledeklarationen*).

Inaugurated on 1 January 1978 as a two-page document in the Board for Consumer Policies' collection of rules, the Fuel Declaration states that the marketers of new passenger vehicles from 1978 onwards must inform purchasers about fuel use. More specifically, the car dealers must provide information on how much fuel the cars use per each ten kilometers of normal driving. The information must be in a written form and come in three different shapes. Information on fuel mileage economy must be offered as a label on the windshield of each individual car. A poster must be pinned on the wall, displaying the same information concerning all car models sold by the car dealer. Finally, a booklet must be visibly placed somewhere on the premises, supplying the same information on all car models marketed throughout the country. The label, the poster, and the booklet may be considered projects within the program.

The Fuel Declaration's larger program theory is delineated in figure 9.1.

The Fuel Declaration is a supplementary rule (*norm, riktlinje*) to a

FIGURE 9.1
The Fuel Declaration's Envisioned Implementation Chain

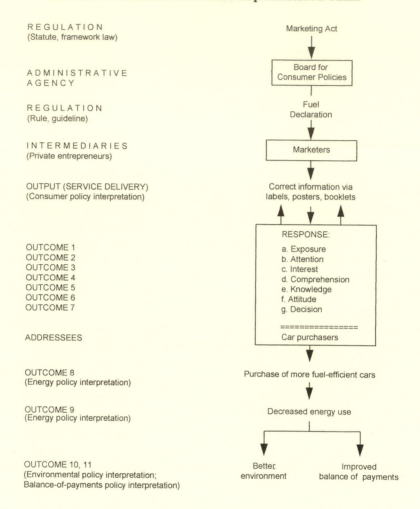

REGULATION
(Statute, framework law)

ADMINISTRATIVE
AGENCY

REGULATION
(Rule, guideline)

INTERMEDIARIES
(Private entrepreneurs)

OUTPUT (SERVICE DELIVERY)
(Consumer policy interpretation)

OUTCOME 1
OUTCOME 2
OUTCOME 3
OUTCOME 4
OUTCOME 5
OUTCOME 6
OUTCOME 7

ADDRESSEES

OUTCOME 8
(Energy policy interpretation)

OUTCOME 9
(Energy policy interpretation)

OUTCOME 10, 11
(Environmental policy interpretation;
Balance-of-payments policy interpretation)

Marketing Act

Board for
Consumer Policies

Fuel
Declaration

Marketers

Correct information via
labels, posters, booklets

RESPONSE:
a. Exposure
b. Attention
c. Interest
d. Comprehension
e. Knowledge
f. Attitude
g. Decision

Car purchasers

Purchase of more fuel-efficient cars

Decreased energy use

Better   Improved
environment   balance of payments

regulatory statute, the 1976 Marketing Act (*marknadsföringslagen*). The latter so–called framework law (*ramlag*) contains a brief requirement stating that in marketing various goods or services, businesses may be required to dispense information of particular importance to consumers.

On the basis of the brief, general outline in the Marketing Act and the preparatory work preceding it, the Board for Consumer Policies in Stockholm—the central agency charged with the implementation of the regulatory statute—has promulgated numerous rules specifying in minute detail what kind of information must be considered of particular importance to consumers and hence disseminated. There are guidelines for a wide variety of goods and services such as diapers, single–family homes, travels, wine, cigarettes, and restaurant services. All the guidelines, the Fuel Declaration included, are cases of "the detailed–package, guiding–hand approach" whereas the Marketing Act is an example of "the broad–direction, unseen–hand alternative," to use Walter Williams's expressive language (1976:276). The Fuel Declaration is one detailed program among many developed under the general Marketing Act.

What is the substantive rationale of the Fuel Declaration? The point where front–end implementers reach program addressees is always of crucial interest in monitoring. I agree with Walter Williams (1980:17) that "the commitment and capacity of the final service delivery organization and concomitantly the individual persons who actually provide services are the central focus of the implementation perspective." In the Fuel Declaration case, obviously, the Board for Consumer Policies wants to act through the sellers of new cars in order to reach out to the purchasers. The points of program delivery are consequently where the prospective car purchasers meet the information with the car dealers. The question now is what the targeted car purchasers are expected to do with the information.

A well–developed program theory would have given us an exact answer to this question. But the written documents produced in the formulation and adoption stages of the Fuel Declaration reveal that the avowed program goals do not provide any unambiguous guidance. Since steps in the intended chain of implementation are tacit, several interpretations are possible.

The program might be interpreted as case of consumer protection policy. According to one construal, the objective would be to offer consumers the possibility to expose themselves to correct information on the fuel economy of new cars, that is, what I have called Output in figure 9.1. The emphasis is on *possibility*. The objective might be to provide accurate and reliable information via the car dealers, period.

A second, more ambitious interpretation, suggests as an additional purpose that the car purchasers should be exposed to the information, attend to it, take an interest in it, comprehend it, and acquire some knowledge from it (outcomes 1–5). But the objective would not be to influence the car purchasers' attitudes, their decisions to buy new cars, their actual purchase of new cars, or to achieve some other ultimate outcome.

The consumer policy construals may seem reasonable. After all, the Fuel Declaration was promulgated by the state board in charge of all national consumer information programs in the country. And the intents of Swedish consumer information programs always stop short of influencing consumers' attitudes and actions. "Give them information but leave the decision to themselves," this is the motto. In this perspective, the Fuel Declaration would be just one among numerous consumer policy programs managed by the Board for Consumer Policies. However, a different interpretation seems more appropriate in this case.

The legislative history of the new program unambiguously suggests that the Fuel Declaration was adopted as an energy conservation intervention. The purpose was to influence car consumers to buy more energy-efficient vehicles than they otherwise would have done (outcome 8). This, in turn, was intended to lead to a decreased fuel use (outcome 9).

But diminished average fuel consumption for new cars was not conceived as the ultimate objective. Rather in was hailed as a means to reach two ulterior goals: a cleaner environment with less obnoxious emissions, and improved national balance of payments due to a decreased importation of expensive foreign oil. Naturally, we may also monitor envisaged results in these stages (outcomes 10 and 11). Since the program was inaugurated in a period of energy shortage, I suspect that improved national balance of payment was the ultimate substantive goal of the Fuel Declaration.

Consequently, the expected main outcome of the program was to ameliorate the balance of payments by encouraging drivers to buy less gas–guzzling cars than before. And the means to achieve this was through unambiguous information on fuel use with the car dealers.

But how would plain information on gas mileage at the car dealers persuade car purchasers to actually buy more energy–efficient cars? How would the messages be adopted by the prospective car purchasers and result in action? On this particular point, the material is tacit. Efforts notwithstanding, I simply cannot produce any empirical evidence for how it was thought this would work. Now, the monitor is faced with two options. If her ambition is to picture the program theory of those who formed the program, she should stop here and admit that she can come no further. However, I shall choose a second option and try to reconstruct the program makers' considerations (Chen 1990:65ff.). From the general context I have simply posited that the gas mileage information was intended to increase the targeted car purchasers' comprehension and knowledge, which in turn was supposed to implant a more negative attitude toward big cars, which in turn would lead to decisions to buy smaller cars, which in turn would be transformed into actual purchases of small cars. In other words, I have assumed that information was intended to influence knowledge, attitudes and action, in that order.

Theoretical arguments may be adduced in favor of the information–knowledge–attitude–action sequence. Learning theory, the dominant model in the field of how persuasive appeals work on the audience, invokes a staircase hierarchy in which the stages come in this particular order.

In conclusion, we do not know for sure what the addressee response stage in the Fuel Declaration's program theory was intended to look like. In the belief that the most widespread theory of persuasion processes is learning theory, I have simply posited that the Fuel Declaration is grounded in that theory.

To sum up, monitoring ought to be theory based. The first step in a follow–up involves the reconstruction of the intervention theory. Ideally, the intervention theory elicited by the evaluator ought to mirror the intervention framers' intentions. It should be a photographic picture of the intervention framers' conceptions of how the intervention would eventually function. In intervention theory construals, the intentional mode should be the favored mode of interpretation (Vedung 1982b:108ff.). On occasion, this ideal is impossible to reach. Parts of the intervention theory may be tacit or wrapped in nebulous language. In that case, a reconstructive interpretation of the intervention framers' preconceptions and presuppositions may supplement the intentional interpretation.[2] The monitor might add something to the intervention theory, on the condition that the intervention framers' would have accepted this addition, if they had the opportunity to familiarize themselves with it.

Although the risk of misunderstanding seems minimal, I wish to emphasize that intervention theories like the one depicted in figure 9.1 do not reflect actual processes of implementation. Ideally, they ought to be representations of intended processes of intervention execution, or, to some extent, reconstructive interpretations of intended implementation activities. And their purpose is instrumental. As instruments of evaluation research, they assist evaluators in finding out how *certain* things—crucial from an evaluative point of view—actually transpire. On the basis of these insights, evaluators may then describe how implementation processes have in fact developed. Secondly, evaluators may also use them as starting points for discussing general governance aspects of the specific intervention case.

The Second Step: Selection of Monitoring Strategy

Having interpreted and reconstructed the intervention theory and made a pictorial representation of it in the form of a chain of implementation, the monitor may turn to the second step in monitoring: using the intervention theory as a base for selecting a monitoring strategy. The intervention theory is supposed to provide guidance when the monitor decides at which stages empirical checks will be performed. The idea is that the intervention is predicated on a number of preconditions that must be met in order that it be effective. It is the task of monitoring to reconstruct these preconditions and investigate whether they have been realized.

Monitoring should preferably start at the point where the governance system meets the addressees, that is, at the cutting edge of the public intervention and the surrounding society. An apparent prerequisite for government information to be effective further down in the chain of persuasion is that it reaches those places where addressees might be exposed to it. In the Fuel Declaration case, the required information must actually be on display with the car dealers.

Parenthetically, I may insert that the Fuel Declaration at the point of delivery is unusually easy to operationalize. Already well defined in documents issued by the Board for Consumer Policies, the program requires all car dealerships to put a label (*etikett*) on the windshield of every new car, to affix a poster (*affisch*) on the wall, and to have a booklet (*broschyr*) placed in a visible place on the premises. The content of the three information media is also very well defined and delimited.

In other cases, the intervention at the delivery point may require forceful operationalization to be tested empirically. In fact, operationalization is one of the intricacies of evaluation. It may be pertinent here to remind the reader of the difficulties involved with the operationalization of, for instance, child care quality, health care quality, or quality in scientific research.

But several other prerequisites must be fulfilled if information efforts are to impact upon a target population. The potential addressees must be exposed to the information. They must attend to it, develop an interest in the message, comprehend it, and gain some insights from it. Although necessary, these conditions are not sufficient. The target individuals must also be influenced in their attitudes by the information and make a decision in line with this attitude. Finally, they must also act in accordance with the decision.

Diffusion of information occurs through a chain of persuasion that is never stronger than its weakest link. If the addressees have not been exposed to the information, the monitor may safely infer that the campaign has been derailed already at this early stage. And if the information has reached the target population, but the recipients have neither attended to it nor gained any insights through it, then the campaign has failed somewhat further down in the persuasion chain but still quite a long distance from the desired outcome.

The three crucial milestones along the road of persuasion in the Fuel Declaration case are information provision, recipient attitude change, and recipient action. The required information be on display at the car dealer premises; otherwise it cannot exert any influence further down in the chain of implementation. In addition, all links in the chain through the action link must function well, if the intended final result is to be attained *as a consequence of the information.*

The full series of assumptions that must be fulfilled for the Fuel Declaration to function according to its intentions are stated in figure 9.2.

There is reason to emphasize the importance of differentiating between prerequisites six and seven, and eight and nine in my listing. Through prerequisite six, the information process is essentially a process of diffusion. Information is disseminated but does not impact upon anything.

Between six and seven—knowledge and yielding—the process turns into an influencing process. And between eight and nine—decision and action—we face the fundamental difficulty with using information as a means of governance: how do we move people from decision to act to actually carrying out the decision in practical behavior?

FIGURE 9.2
Prerequisites to be Fulfilled if the Fuel Declaration is to Work

Prerequisite 1   To have an effect on car purchases and fuel use, the information mandated by the Fuel Declaration must be available in the sales areas

Prerequisite 2   Exposure (the addressees must have been exposed to the information)

Prerequisite 3   Attention (the addressees must have attended to the information)

Prerequisite 4   Interest (the addressees must have become interested in the information)

Prerequisite 5   Comprehension (the addressees must have comprehended the information)

Prerequisite 6   Knowledge (the addressees must have gained or activated some insights through the information)

Prerequisite 7   Yielding (the attitudes of the addressees must have been influenced by the information)

Prerequisite 8   Decision (the addressees must have decided to do what is recommended in the information)

Prerequisite 9   Action (the addressees must have acted according to the previous decision)

Once the requirements underlying the intervention are clarified, the evaluator can choose where to enter and apply some controls. Prerequisite one seems crucial. If the material is not posted with the car dealers the program cannot work. Prerequisites three and five also seem fundamental. The addressees must have noticed and comprehended the information if it is to have some effect. Let us therefore assume that the evaluator chooses to direct her attention to these three requirements.

The prerequisites chosen are, in fact, the criteria of merit to be used in monitoring. If the requirements are met, the result is deemed satisfactory, if not, it is deemed insufficient.

The Third Step: Data Collection, Data Analysis

Now we have reached the third step in monitoring, involving data collection and data analysis.

Investigating the tenability of prerequisite one presupposes a multiple–site design. A number of service delivery points—car dealerships—must be selected, reasonably distributed across the country. The selection must proceed according to some sampling principle. Then data collection can start.

What data sources and data gathering methods we employ depends on what questions we ask. Often, social inquiries draw on one data source and one data collection method only. I commend *triangulation*. Several data sources and data collection methods ought to be used in the same study to illuminate identical problems (Brewer and Hunter 1989; Patton 1987, 1990; Guba and Lincoln 1981, 1989; Kosecoff and Fink 1982; Herman 1987).

There are three broad data gathering methods in the social sciences: documentary, interrogatory, and observation methods (Launsø and Rieper 1993:98ff.).

Documentary methods involve the use of data amassed by others in the form of statistics, and data produced by the process itself such as client records and other written documents, accessible through textual analysis. Documentary methods are unobtrusive, which indicates that the records were not produced primarily for the evaluation but for some other purpose, intrinsic to the organization under evaluation. Documentary methods handle so–called found data, in contrast with interrogatory methods, which produce data tailor made for the investigation. This means that program personnel and target population at the time the documents were assembled were unaware of their future use in evaluation contexts. Unobtrusive methods are immune to reactive measurement effects (see chapter 11).

Statistics collected for other purposes should of course be used in evaluation. In the Fuel Declaration case, however, it is hard to see which statistics that would be.

Text analysis is used for scrutinizing written documents, produced as part of the unfolding of the events themselves. One possibility is to consult the records of the activity to be monitored. Ordinarily, intervention staff collect a fair amount of information about intervention participants. In the Fuel Declaration example, purchase contracts would be cases of program records. Purchase contracts may include information on what previous car model was used and what model has now been bought, which could help in calculating whether the new car is more fuel efficient.

Interrogative methods include interviewing and the use of questionnaires. Interviewing those concerned is indispensable in monitoring.

All in all, evaluators must not be afraid of contacting the people involved and asking them for information. Questionnaires are also useful, particularly to cover a broad area. In the Fuel Declaration case, monitors would like to know whether the prospective car purchasers attend to the information and comprehend the meaning of it. To this end, they must ask the people involved. Talking to people and eliciting people's own reports is very important for evaluators. In this case, they would presumably interview a sample of car purchasers or ask them to fill out questionnaires. I agree with Carol Weiss (1972a:53ff.) that much evaluation research actually relies on interviews and questionnaires, because necessary information about intervention participants is difficult to gather in any other way. The monitor may also interview salespersons or maybe some other category of people within the car dealers on the issue of consumer attention and comprehension.

Interrogatory methods engender data collection through direct solicitation in which intervention staff and intervention clients will be aware that they are being subjected to an investigation. This may create reactive measurement effects.

Observation methods means that the researcher makes site visits to watch for herself what is going on, either secretly from behind a one–way transparent glass, openly as an observer, or as an unacknowledged participant observer. Among the observation methods, direct observation entails that evaluators make their own observations of what is going on in an open manner, that is, it is clear to those concerned that they are dealing with an evaluator. Preferably, the data are amassed in a systematic fashion. The least structured procedure is to take notes of what is observed. A better way, perhaps, is to start from a set of questions that are systematically probed while keeping the mind open to new questions that may come up during the site visit. One problem may give rise to others according to a sort of snowball philosophy.

The strength of direct observation resides in its reliability. In addition, it produces deeper insights than interviews and particularly questionnaires, since observation of the conceptions and actions of those concerned may go on for a longer period of time.

The monitoring of the car dealers' compliance with prerequisite one—affixing the labels to the windshields, pinning the poster to the wall, and deploying the booklets somewhere on the premises—might well be done through site visits and direct observation. The researcher and her collaborators may visit the car dealers, observe, and take notes. It is very important for evaluators to leave their offices and libraries in order to make first–hand observations in the field.

An issue of some controversy is whether site visits should be announced beforehand or not. In monitoring, the best solution is probably to tell affected people that a site visit will take place. The purpose of monitoring is intervention improvement. If preannounced, the site visits will lead to intervention amelioration before they are actually undertaken. This can then be strengthened by monitoring proper and the use of the monitoring results.

Participant observation is different from direct observation, although this distinction is not always made in common textbooks on methodology. In participant observation, the evaluator and her staff are something more than observers making site visits. They make their observations while participating fully in the activity to be monitored. When Günter Wallraff dressed as a Turk to find out how his fellow Germans treated Turkish guest workers, he used participant observation. In the Fuel Declaration case, participant observation would mean that the investigators pretend to be car purchasers or car dealers and register what happens in the purchasing situation. Participant observation of this type is unethical because it presupposes that people are deceived.

Photography, finally, used by the evaluator would be an observation method, whereas the use of photos taken by others must be regarded as a documentary method. In evaluation research, photography is used to make appraisals of complicated policy effects on land use, forests, marshes, city developments, and so on (Collier and Collier 1986; Wagner 1979). It might be used in the Fuel Declaration case to map the information materials with the car dealers, for instance, how posters are hung and booklets are placed.

In evaluations conducted in 1978 and 1980, prerequisite one was checked partly through site visits and partly through interviews with local car dealers. Two general observations were made.

The first was rather trivial. The information requirements were not automatically complied with by the car dealers. Nowhere was compliance perfect. For the labels, the compliance scores were 50 to 60 percent, for the poster between 70 and 90 percent, and as to the folder they rated between 25 and 65 percent.

The second observation was, perhaps, more surprising. Even though compliance was low to begin with, we would expect it to have become more and more extensive during the period. Yet, this assumption did not accord with reality. In some cases, compliance had turned lower. In other instances, it had first improved but then started to go down again. In a third case, it had deteriorated in the beginning but then improved.

Let us pursue the follow–up a step further. To take action to ameliorate the faulty implementation of the Fuel Declaration it is necessary to know what caused the information to not be properly deployed by the car dealerships. To shed some light on this, car dealerships with no information on display ought to be studied. A total investigation could be made, or only some places could be sampled for the investigation.

Insufficient knowledge of the Fuel Declaration provisions may of course have had an impact. It might be the case that some car dealers never heard of the information requirements. This should be examined in the investigation.

The information material required in the guidelines is mostly manufactured by the main offices, as far as Swedish cars are concerned, and by the general agents for foreign makes. These actors are also responsible for the shipment of the materials to the local dealers. This means, for instance, that the Volvo main office in Gothenburg is responsible for the production and distribution across the country of labels concerning all types of Volvo cars. But it is not sufficient that information is dispensed. It must also be posted in its predetermined, proper places.

This may be advanced as two additional prerequisites.

Prerequisite 10   To be available for the car dealers, the information must have been manufactured in the main offices and the general agencies.

Prerequisite 11   To be available to the car dealers, the information must have been dispatched from the main offices and the general agencies.

Turning to the empirical records, it appears that the bottleneck lies with the car dealers, for production and distribution by the main offices and the general agents seems to work quite smoothly.

Why is it that the information materials are not deployed properly with the car dealerships? What causes weak compliance? A feeble knowledge of the requirements may of course play a role. But it could also be grounded in a conflict of interest between the will of the government and that of the car dealers. We may reasonably expect that small–car dealers happily post the information while big–car dealers, who normally would not use gas mileage as a selling argument, avoid posting the material. Weak compliance would then be due to a conflict between the will of the state and the interests of specific car dealers.

In monitoring, the evaluator may also use the stakeholder approach. She may ask car buyers whether the information provided caters to their needs in order to make a rational decision on purchase. In this case, her evaluation takes the goals and expectations of the addressees as its major organizer.

In addition, she may contact another group of stakeholders, the car dealers. What opinions do they have on the information? Should it be shaped in a somewhat different, better way?

To sum up, to acquire monitoring data, the evaluator ought to consult different data sources and employ parallel methods of data collection—triangulation. Of particular importance is direct observation at the point of service delivery where the public sector program operators (car dealers) directly face the addressees (car purchasers), questionnaires to program operators, in–depth interviews with grass–root bureaucrats, and textual analyses of program records and other written primary documents. Obviously, multiple sources of information ought to be tapped to obtain monitoring data: direct observation in connection with site visits, interviews, questionnaires, program records, and case study methodology (Yin 1982:50).

The Fourth Step: Applying Criteria and Standards

The fourth step in monitoring involves the application of criteria and standards of worth to the empirical findings. In the approach to follow–up recommended here, the value criteria underlying the intervention's own prerequisites are the ones that apply. Monitoring subscribes to a descriptive theory of valuing.

To illustrate, I shall chose prerequisite one: To have effect on car purchases and fuel use, the information mandated by the Fuel Declaration must be in the selling places. The criteria dimensions are labels fastened to the windshields, posters affixed to the wall, and booklets visibly displayed with the car dealerships. The standard of acceptable performance on these criteria of merit is 100 percent goal achievement. The Fuel Declaration mandates all car dealers to fasten labels to the windshields, affix the poster to the wall, and display the booklet on the premises. So the actual performance on the three criteria should be compared to the 100 percent set standard of performance.

Another approach to standards selection would be to choose the best record to be found with any car dealer in the study. To illustrate, let us assume that ten car dealerships have been investigated. In six cases the labels were affixed to 80 percent of the cars on display, in one case to 70 percent, in two cases to 60 percent, and in one case to 50 percent of the cars. As standard of performance in this case we might chose the 80–percent rate in light of which the performance of six cases are good, and the four remaining cases less satisfactory.

The scoring could be either global or analytical. In *global scoring,* a single value is allocated to the overall performance of the evaluand, whereas in *analytical scoring* values are allocated to the component parts only. In our Fuel Declaration case, analytical scoring would involve that the labels, the poster, and the booklets would get separate grades. The label prerequisite could be graded satisfactory, the poster requisite reasonable, and the booklet requisite unsatisfactory, for instance, in relation to the selected standard. Usually, in monitoring, analytical scoring is sufficient. The business of piecing the different scores together into a global score might profitably be left to decision–makers.

Even though the prerequisites of the intervention provide the major criteria of merit in monitoring, the perspective could be broadened to include questions to street–level bureaucrats and addressees on their opinions of, for instance, the intervention delivery system. Even such information may help all stakeholders involved think about the ongoing intervention, increase their enlightenment, and enlarge their alternatives about what can and should be done to improve its implementation, all major objectives of monitoring.

The Fifth Step: General Thoughts on the Governance System

An unusual trait in my approach to monitoring is the *fifth* step, involving an analysis of the evaluand, its intended implementation, and final delivery from a general governance perspective. The strategy of embedding the particular intervention into a more general system setting is a highly commendable one in evaluation, because it widens the evaluation users' perspectives and enhances their conceptual understandings of the activities. However, this step might be skipped once monitoring has turned into a more repetitive and institutionalized activity. To illustrate, let me provide some general governance insights concerning the Fuel Declaration.

A whole package of hierarchically ordered governance instruments are involved in the Fuel Declaration system. To begin with, the Fuel Declaration is a case of *mandatory disclosure*. Mandatory disclosure (*märkning*), as we have seen in the previous chapter, is a governance strategy engendering the use of regulation to bring about a flow of information. The ultimate tools of government—labels, posters, and booklets—are informative, because information is supposed to create the effect on the likely targets—the car purchasers. The medium–level tier of regulation—the Fuel Declaration itself—is assumed to fulfill the auxiliary function of propelling the information. The Fuel Declaration mandates the car dealers (regulation) to provide information to the car purchasers (information). And the Fuel Declaration, in turn, is issued under the higher–level Marketing Act (regulations). This shows that public authorities can use multiple hierarchical layers of governance instruments in order to reach the proper targets. Governance instruments come in hierarchical packages.

Another characteristic feature of the governance strategy is that potential purchasers are supposed to encounter actual program delivery through a network of nongovernmental intermediaries: the car dealers. Every car dealership in Sweden is probably owned by some private entrepreneurs. In this case, these private entities have been charged with a public duty. They are, I would argue, mandated to act as street–level bureaucrats, disseminating state–ordered information. The role of the car dealers in the Fuel Declaration system is an example of the growing trend in modern public administration towards *government by proxy*: reliance by government officials on nongovernmental agents or third parties to accomplish public purposes.

Actually, car dealers are not the only private businessmen involved in the service delivery system instigated by the Fuel Declaration. The posters and the labels must be produced by somebody. The production is not carried out locally by the individual car dealers. Instead the local car dealers get some help with this from their national organizations. Every local car dealer is a member of a nationwide organized network, formed around his particular car make. A local Volvo dealer belongs to a nationwide network consisting of all Volvo dealers in Sweden and their common national marketing organization. In a similar vein, every local Volkswagen dealer is served by the national marketing organization for Volkswagen cars, every local Mazda dealer by the national Mazda marketing organization, and so on and so forth. Directed at the marketers of new cars, the Fuel Declaration in practice concerns not only every local car dealer but his national marketing organization and the whole network he belongs to as well. The seemingly tiny Fuel Declaration attempts to activate large networks of private marketing and selling organizations as intermediaries between the national administrative agency and the final addressees.

Third, the Fuel Declaration is an instance of *implementation through corporatist arrangements*. The program emerged through negotiations between the pertinent state agency and the affected corporatist interest networks. The Board for Consumer Policies instigated negotiations with the Association of Car Importers and the Marketing Organization for Swedish Car Producers. The Association of Car Importers organize the national dealerships for each foreign brand of car marketed inside the country, whereas the Marketing Organization for Swedish Car Producers is the top organization for both Volvo and Saab marketing organizations.

Corporatism suggests that the leadership of peak national organizations participate in government decision making. This is exactly what happened in the regulatory history of the Fuel Declaration. And the formation of the Fuel Declaration, in turn, is a case of implementing a higher–level regulatory statute, the Marketing Act. In this sense, the Fuel Declaration constitutes an instance of implementation through corporatist arrangements.

From the above it is also apparent that those who were entrusted with the authority to implement the Fuel Declaration also participated in its formulation. The appearance of the Fuel Declaration is not a case of top–down imposition of the will of the government on the parties concerned. In contrast, it emerged through *negotiations* between the state and the organized affected private business community. On this account, the Fuel Declaration is an instance of another growing tendency in modern public administration, the use of negotiation as a device of policy implementation.

From another perspective, the Fuel Declaration is a case of the implementers participating in the formation of the program they will be charged with executing. The Association of Car Importers and the Marketing Organization for Swedish Car Producers took part in the formation of a program that their members were supposed to act as intermediaries in.

This ends my exposition of the fifth step in monitoring, offering some general observations on the governance situation which the intervention under scrutiny is a part of. Admittedly, this step might be skipped, although it is highly commendable not to do so.

Notes

1. Even the "cognitive map" concept appears to correspond at least partly to an impact model, a parallel underscored by Hoogerwerf (1990). In coining this concept, Axelrod wrote (quoted from Hoogerwerf 1990): "A cognitive map is a specific way of representing a person's assertions about some limited domain, such as a policy problem. It is designed to capture the structure of the person's causal assertions and to generate the consequences that follow from this structure."
2. Reconstructive interpretation is strongly commended in Chen 1990. I for one have tried to develop reconstructive interpretation in *Political Reasoning* 1982, 114ff.

10

Pre–Evaluation

Besides monitoring, impact assessment is the other major form of program evaluation. In impact assessment, problem six in the Eight Problems Approach to Evaluation is addressed. A watertight impact assessment, some evaluation specialists maintain, ought to be preceded by a pre–evaluation. Pre–evaluation involves an early inexpensive peek at an ongoing intervention to determine whether it is in shape for a full–scale, sciencelike evaluation. The evaluator makes a problem inventory and forms a view of the program's susceptibility to full–fledged assessment. The business of assessing impacts of programs currently under way is supposed to be carried out in two steps.

One particular pre–evaluation technique, called *evaluability assessment,* was developed by a group of evaluators, headed by Joseph Wholey at the Urban Institute in Washington D.C., in the middle of the 1970s. Over the years, the technique has been modified and developed (Wholey et al. 1970; Wholey 1977, 1983). It has been taken over by Leonard Rutman and his associates and introduced into a wide variety of federal and state agencies in Canada (Rutman 1977, 1980; Smith 1989).

In Wholey's thinking, evaluability assessment and full–scale evaluation is closely tied to managerialism. Evaluability assessment, according to Wholey, should be seen "not as a rigid set of procedural steps but as a spirit and method directed at results–oriented management and management–oriented evaluation." Evaluability does not tell whether a program can be evaluated—because every program can be evaluated—but whether a program is ready to be managed for results and what changes are needed for results–oriented management. In

157

Wholey's conception of evaluation, results–oriented management is contrasted to process–oriented management. "Results–oriented managers establish realistic, measurable, outcome–oriented program objectives in terms of which they assess and manage their programs and report to higher policy level." In process–oriented management, by contrast, "program objectives are limited to input and process objectives; programs are assessed and managed in terms of input and process objectives; and reports to policy levels are based on input and process data". While realizing that process–oriented management is more typical of government than results–oriented management, Wholey maintains that it should be the other way around (1983:41, 3; Shadish, Jr. et al. 1991).

Wholey and his associates adduced three arguments in favor of evaluability assessment. First, they found it troublesome, sometimes unfeasible, to undertake evaluations of public programs because managers, staff, and other stakeholders procrastinated, were uncooperative, and failed to grasp the purposes of the investigations. In short, there was political resistance to evaluation. Secondly, they had come to realize that programs often could not be evaluated by experimental or quasi–experimental methods, prescribed by the then–reigning positivist methodological orthodoxy. Finally, they had become more and more disturbed by the fact that evaluation results were not used to fine–tune, modify, or otherwise change the program under appraisal. These three observations led the Wholey group to evolve and codify the systematic approach to pre–evaluation interchangeably called evaluability assessment, and exploratory evaluation.

Evaluability assessment as expounded here is applied to ongoing, full–scale interventions. It should be kept apart from preprogram or preformative evaluation, which is oriented toward the planning stage *before* the intervention is launched. Preprogram evaluation typically includes improving program evaluability in the sense of gathering baseline data, and fashioning a program design that facilitates later postprogram evaluation. Preprogram evaluation departs from the conviction that regard for evaluability ought to be present already during the design stage of an intervention, because it can persuade affected stakeholders to accept modification of the planned intervention that will make upcoming *ex–post* evaluations feasible and appropriate. Contrary to evaluability assessment *ex post,* preprogram evaluation is not concerned with ongoing but with not–yet–adopted interventions.

Is the Program Evaluable?

One point with evaluability assessment is to resolve whether current programs in fact are susceptible to rigorous evaluation. It is considered to be a preliminary activity to generate an appropriate technical design for an upcoming, fully mature evaluation. It is the overture to the grand opera performance. I shall call this the *technical design reason* for doing evaluability assessment.

Yet the ambition of evaluability assessors has always extended beyond simply finding out if the ongoing intervention actually can be evaluated through use of radical experimentation. The aim has also been to create a climate among prominent stakeholders favorable for a prospective full–scale evaluation and to pave the way for utilization of this upcoming evaluation in future decision–making. I shall call this second reason the *evaluation politics rationale* for evaluability assessment.

Steps in Evaluability Assessment

Evaluability assessment can be regarded as a successive series of impressionistic data collection waves undertaken to determine what aspects of the current program should be considered for inclusion in a full–scale evaluation. In the first stage, *program analysis,* the nature of the program is determined. In the second stage, *feasibility analysis,* a decision is made on whether a full–scale evaluation should be conducted, and, if so, what aspects of the program ought to be included. A program can be judged infeasible to evaluate on methodological as well as social and political grounds. This means that strong political resistance to evaluation can constitute a reason not to press on with a full–scale evaluation.

On the basis of earlier codifications primarily by Leonard Rutman (1977, 1980) but to some extent also by Rossi and Freeman (1985, 1989), I have summarized the evaluability procedure in a set of steps, presented in the following scheme. The first four steps comprise program analysis, the two last ones feasibility analysis.

Program Analysis (Technical Design Purpose)

Preparing a program documents model. The program documents model should outline the program components, the program goals/

effects, and the causal linkages between them as they are depicted in formal program documents, that is, in funding proposals, published brochures, administrative manuals, annual reports, staff working papers, minutes of policy–making groups, consultants reports, evaluation studies, and other relevant material. Program components are defined as "those activities or sets of activities that directly impact on the clients or the social problems and are expected to produce the stated goals/effects." There are no fixed rules for selecting program components. Rutman emphasizes that the pre-evaluator ought to search for the activities that are most directly linked to the external goals and effects. The purpose is to thrash out a flow model mirroring how the program components are intended to produce program effects according to the documentary evidence. This is similar to my idea of reconstructing the intervention theory (program theory), developed in the previous chapter on monitoring.

Determining key peoples' perceptions of the program. In this stage, the evaluator conducts interviews with important stakeholders in the program to determine their perceptions and views. At the head of the interview list is the principal program manager. Other key people can be interviewed as well, for example, the executives to whom the manager reports, relevant legislators, front–line workers, program clients, critics, technical experts. The purpose is to elicit the different stakeholders' models of how the program works.

"Scouting the program." For some programs, Rutman argues, the analysis of documents and interviews may suffice to determine which aspects of the program should be considered for inclusion in the full–scale evaluation. For others, it might be necessary to collect some data in the field. The aim is not to perform systematic, large–scale data collection, but to get firsthand impressions of how the program actually operates. The methods to be used include interviewing, and direct observation through site visits.

Developing an evaluable program model. Program components and goals/effects that meet the preconditions for evaluability must be determined. Basically, there are three preconditions: (1) program components must be well defined and possible to implement in the prescribed manner; (2) goals and effects must be clearly specified; and (3) causal linkages must be plausible. The evaluable model can be drawn as a flow chart in the way recommended in the previous chapter on monitoring. Its purpose is to serve as the backbone of a full–scale evaluation.

Feasibility Analysis (Evaluation Politics Rationale)

Identifying evaluation users. This step involves an analysis of the feasibility of conducting a full–scale evaluation. The purposes and information needs of the potential stakeholders in the evaluation are examined. The evaluation stakeholders include legislators, the board of directors, budget officials, program administrators, program practitioners, clients, public interest groups, the media, auditors from government watchdog agencies, and the community of evaluators. However, it is impossible to conduct an all–purpose evaluation that satisfies the information needs of all the various stakeholding audiences. Therefore, the evaluation should be conducted for a primary user whose information needs must be explored in order to define the focus, scope, and nature of the study; for Wholey, this primary user is management. The question of how much the program design limits the extent to which evaluation requirements can be met must also be determined. Some program designs may preclude good designs for effectiveness assessment and reliable data collection procedures.

Achieving agreement to proceed. Added to the list by Rossi and Freeman, this final item entails the striking of a formal agreement between the evaluator and the program managers on whether to stop here or continue to a full–scale evaluation. Before the plan is undersigned by the stakeholders, it is important, according to Rossi and Freeman (1985:90), to reach explicit agreement on the following points:

i.   which intervention components to be analyzed, the design of the evaluation, priorities for undertaking the research.
ii.   the commitment of required resources and agreements on necessary cooperation.
iii. a plan for the utilization of evaluation findings.
iv.   a plan for what program managers and program staff should do to strengthen the evaluability potential of intervention components not currently amenable to evaluation, and an approach for subsequently building them into the evaluation effort.

The last subitem in the list is so interesting that I shall discuss it more fully in the next section.

Evaluability Assessment to Create Evaluable Programs

The final item in the negotiated agreement reveals that evaluability assessment does not treat the program only as a given, unalterable structure. On the contrary, evaluability assessment supporters nurture activist hopes. They wish that the assessment will lead to modifications of the program to render it susceptible to a full–blown impact assessment. I shall call this third and last argument for doing evaluability assessment the *program–modification reason*.

Champions of evaluability assessment, in other words, want to use it to restructure the ongoing program to make it susceptible to a strict impact assessment. The program ought to be adapted to the requirements of evaluation research. This is a case, if not a typical one, of a *nonnaturalistic* evaluation strategy. A nonnaturalistic strategy of evaluation engenders that the planned intervention must be accommodated and modified to suit the strict demands of evaluation research. Evaluation considerations should be allowed to influence program design before the program is actually adopted. In the evaluability case, the program is already in place, and evaluability assessment is carried out in the hope that the current program will be modified to satisfy rigorous methodological demands. The opposite, when programs are studied as they are without any ambition of adapting them to evaluation requirements, is called a *naturalistic* evaluation strategy (Patton 1987:13).

Some program components may prove impossible to evaluate rigorously. By communicating this to program managers and policymakers it is hoped that the program in due time will be transformed to become amenable to impact evaluation. Actually, the evaluators should work actively with program managers to increase program evaluability. In this sense, some evaluability assessors perceive their activity as action research and themselves as change agents, not only as outside, neutral, passive observers. To these people, evaluability assessment constitutes a metaintervention which will have a modifying effect on the intervention.[1]

This activist ambition of using evaluability assessment to effect program change to enhance future program evaluability is, however, according to an authority like Rutman, not the major purpose with evaluability assessment. It is more like a hidden agenda, a conceivable and hoped–for side effect. The main stated purpose is to ascertain whether the program in its current shape is politically and technically susceptible to impact evaluation. This philosophy is expressed by Rutman (1980:164) in the following fashion:

> The assessment process is likely to produce changes that facilitate program evaluability. Analyzing the program components and goals/effects may result in program modifications. A feasibility analysis can result in the removal of constraints to permit the implementation of the evaluation requirements. *Such changes that enhance the evaluability of a program should be viewed as a by–product of the evaluability assessment, not its primary purpose.*

Perceptions, Snowballing, and Stakeholder Approach

From a methods point of view, the relationship between pre–evaluation and evaluation proper is slightly paradoxical.

In evaluability assessment, the investigator mainly employs qualitative methods. This seems to mean three things. She attempts to portray and understand the program in terms of the *perceptions,* beliefs, plans, purposes, reasons or intentions of the participants. The program and its inherent and concomitant actions are regarded as meaningful social behavior. She may start with teasing out a picture of the program from written records. Then she successively acquires different pictures through talks with program officers, addressees, and other stakeholders. The actors' own reports of their actions and their monitoring of their actions constitute the material from which the pictures are composed. Finally, she tries to form a picture by herself through site visits and direct observation.

In addition, qualitative methodology also involves a sort of inductive and interactive search procedure, often compared to *snowball rolling.* In evaluability assessment, the findings in one stage of the investigation will determine what to search for in the next. Each new discovery is allowed to lead to the next in order to maximize the possibility of understanding how the program functions *in situ.* Responsiveness to stakeholders' concerns, issues, worries, questions, and perceptions are essential traits in this interactive methodology.

Finally, the *stakeholder approach* (of North American type) is typical of evaluability assessment. All or most stakeholding audiences are contacted by the evaluator for interviews, talks, dialogues, and direct observations.

The methodology of the second step of the total evaluation—the upcoming full–blown impact assessment—is an entirely different story. The proper evaluation is not to be conducted as a step–by–step, inter-active monitoring of the program in its natural setting. On the con-trary, it is supposed to be an impact assessment carried out by quanti-tative methodology in its highest potency: two–group experimentation and statistical analysis of the data. It is assumed that eventual causal links can be properly ascertained only through advanced experimenta-tion with experimentals and controls selected either randomly or through matching, and concomitant strict quantitative, statistical data analysis procedures. Furthermore, in experimental designs people are viewed as reacting to the push and pull of blind forces in the environment, to environmental contingencies as it were. They are not regarded as agents directing and monitoring their own actions while following plans, pur-poses, intentions, or rules.

To sum up, impact assessment of ongoing public interventions is often regarded as a two–step affair. Evaluability assessment, the first step, uses qualitative methodology to investigate whether the interven-tion, in a second step, can be exposed to an impact investigation, carried out through randomized experimentation and statistical analy-ses, predicated upon "quantitative", "positivist" methodology (Wholey et al. 1970; Wholey 1977, and 1983). Herein lies the paradox with evaluability assessment methodology.

Note

1. Policy and program evaluation in general adopts a very clear and specific ap-proach to the famous agency–structure controversy in social science methodol-ogy. Actors influence structures and structures influence actors. The intervention is not taken as a fixed, given structure, impossible to change and improve. On the contrary, an important point with evaluation is that it will be utilized by some actors to transform the intervention so as to make it more effective and efficient in reaching its various goals and avoiding deleterious side effects. The intervention is seen as a structure that can be transformed by purpose–driven actors con-sciously using evaluations as one of their instruments.

11

Impact Assessment as Tryout and
Social Experimentation

> *"Evaluation research is, first and foremost, a process of applying scientific procedures to accumulate reliable and valid evidence on the manner and extent to which specified activities produce particular effects or outcomes."*
> —Leonard Rutman, *Evaluation Research Methods (1977)*

> *"The law of causality, I believe, like much that passes muster among philosophers, is a relic of a bygone age, surviving, like the monarchy, only because it is erroneously supposed to do no harm."*
> —Bertrand Russell, *Mysticism and Logic (1918)*

Evaluation is frequently regarded as primarily a research procedure for testing intervention impact. W. Edwards Deming said, in an oft–quoted remark: "Evaluation is the study of causes"; David Nachmias (1979:7): "At the heart of all policy evaluation research activities is the idea of causality"; and the Swedish philosopher Tore Nilstun: "In the context of evaluation of regulatory reforms causal analysis is a must."

Against this, Scriven (1991:137) has argued: "Evaluation will sometimes uncover the cause of success or failure, of merit or of incompetence —but not always, nor is that its duty, nor should that be its aim. . . . The key task for the evaluator is to evaluate. . . . It is not the evaluator's task to determine the [causation of a condition]."

165

Like Scriven, I do not concur with attempts to equate evaluation to impact assessment. Program monitoring is a portentous evaluation exercise entailing very little, if any, impact analysis. In spite of this, program follow–up is an invaluable tool for organizational management and direction.

Furthermore, in assessment of government services like, for instance, public safety, trash hauling, public utilities, parks and recreation, public transportation, day care for children, services to seniors, libraries and museums, citizens as consumers are asked to evaluate the merit, worth, and value of what they get; usually no causality issue is involved. Monitoring of implementation and service provision is indeed a type of evaluation, but no causal questions concerning program impact are raised. Evaluation without impact assessment is commonplace.

While not equating evaluation with impact assessment, I shall stress the value of it somewhat more than Scriven. Impact assessment is important, particularly for higher level decision–makers in national bodies.

Impact assessment addresses the sixth problem in the Eight Problems Approach to Evaluation. The fundamental intricacy to be faced is to disentangle programmatic from nonprogrammatic effects. Outcomes might be contingent upon nonprogram events, occurring simultaneously or before the program. Generally speaking, this impact problem is extraordinarily difficult to solve. In public policy it may be unsolvable.

Grasping the assumed *modus operandi* of causal analysis is not very demanding. The actual outcomes of the installed program are compared to a *reference alternative* showing what the outcomes would have been if the program not been instituted or if some other program had been adopted. If all other factors were identical in both situations, that is, were the system perfectly closed off from the world, the ensuing difference must be attributed to the program.

From a pedagogical angle, phrasing the impact problem in the *counterfactual* mode is the most illuminating approach. The counterfactual mode is visualized in figure 11.1.

Again, what we want to know is what the result would have been had there been no program, and compare this to the case of having the program. To sort programmatic from nonprogrammatic effects, we would like to contrast the outcome that actually occurred to the out-

FIGURE 11.1
The Impact Problem in Counterfactual Terms

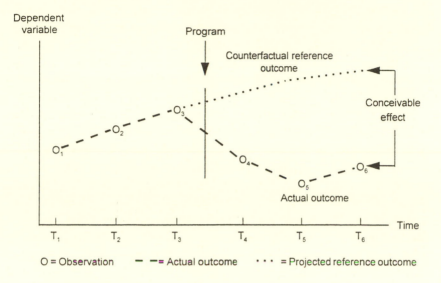

O = Observation   — —= Actual outcome   • • • = Projected reference outcome

Note: The evaluator is supposed to be exercising her evaluation at time T_6.

come that would have occurred in the past if the program had not been instituted. Since the latter outcome never actually occurred, it is counter to facts, or counterfactual. The difference between the factual and the counterfactual outcome would constitute the programmatic effects.

A central prerequisite of impact analysis is to produce a time series of data on the actual outcome. We must know what the outcome variable looked like before the intervention and how it eventually changed afterwards. This historical aspect of the impact issue is crucial and must be strongly emphasized.

It is illuminating to bear in mind that both effects and causes are always "differences." An effect is a difference between the actual outcome and the outcome that would have ensued if there had been a different program or no program at all. The cause is the discrepancy between having and not having a program or between having one program instead of another. Impact assessment always requires some degree of comparison (Nilstun and Hermerén 1984:130ff.).[1]

Neutrally performed impact assessments are important to political life because intervention effects are strongly politicized. Legislators in particular, but also program managers and interest groups in favor of the intervention, seek to capitalize on alleged accomplishments and avoid blame on presumable failures. Everything positive that happens afterwards is credited as programmatic effects, while potentially negative consequences are either ignored or dismissed as caused by something else. Groupings against the program, on the other hand, do exactly the reverse. Public debate on the effects of public interventions tends to be biased, ideological, self–regarding, and determined by strategies of blame avoidance and credit claiming. The so–called *post hoc, ergo propter hoc fallacy* is consciously used as political ammunition in public debate on program impacts.[2] Impact evaluation is hailed as a possible antidote to this overwhelming tendency to politicize the facts.

Elected officials, program managers, and evaluators ought not to jump to hasty conclusions, as does the country boy in the following story. Two country boys travelled to the city for the first time in their life. Prior to embarking the train, they bought themselves two bananas, which they had never seen before. After a little while, when one of them started to eat his banana the compartment went completely dark. The train had entered a tunnel. Horrified, the banana eater exclaimed to his friend: "Don't taste the banana. You will go blind!"

Designs for Impact Assessment

There is no satisfactory, widely recognized solution to the causality problem in the social sciences generally, and even less so in evaluation theory. Enormous efforts notwithstanding, the best minds among Western and Oriental social scientists have not proved capable of providing more than ambitious attempts, however genial, at resolving the issue. "The epistemology of causation, and of the scientific method more generally, is at present in a productive state of near chaos," Cook and Campbell wrote in a major treatise on evaluation (1979:10). Their judgment seems as much to the point today as it was more than fifteen years ago.

The problem is, of course, that past counterfactual states can never be known with certainty. Researchers can never pinpoint beyond doubt what would have happened if Napoleon had won the Battle of Waterloo, if Emperor Francis Joseph had not undersigned the declaration of war against Serbia in 1914, or if Japan had not attacked Pearl Harbor. Or as Bertrand Russell put it in a passage from *The Principles of Mathematics*: "Rational choice depends upon the construction of two causal series, only one of which can be made to exist ... thus all statesmanship, and all rational conduct of life, is based upon the frivolous historical game, in which we discuss what the world would have been if Cleopatra's nose had been half an inch longer."[3] This means we must argue through more or less reliable analogies to sort programmatic from nonprogrammatic effects.

In evaluation, the ideal would be to have a consummate physical copy of the program situation. In the classic experimental design, the control group would constitute such a duplicate of the experimental group. Since the perfect experimental design is almost unattainable in the real world of public policy, approximate approaches must be used. There are several such approximations available to the evaluator. In numerous handbooks on method—written by authorities like Rossi and Freeman (1989), Judd and Kenny (1981), or Nachmias (1979)—it is maintained that the approaches can be rank–ordered according to their capacity of resolving the impact issue in general and the program impact issue in public policy evaluation. This assumed ranking order is shown in figure 11.2.

In the following sections, I shall penetrate a few "research designs"—logical models of proof—that allegedly allow the making of valid, causal inferences (Nachmias 1979:21). While the research designs are approaches to causal analysis in general, I have adapted them here to their purported uses in public intervention evaluation.

There is strong disagreement among evaluation theorists concerning the most appropriate design for assessing impacts of public interventions. There are some robust supporters of a *two–step experimental approach to public policymaking,* engendering that bold, innovative social programs ought to be provisionally tried out under experimental conditions and their permanent enactment made dependent on the results of the experimental evaluation. The reason for their forceful endorsement is that experimentation is regarded as a superior means of obtaining knowledge about program consequences (Campbell and Stanley 1966; Riecken and Boruch 1974; Fairweather and Tornatzky 1977). But their views have been vehemently attacked and largely discarded. Serious doubts have been raised about the appropriateness and usefulness of social science experimentation in general and public policy experimentation in particular. Experimentation is tied to radical program transformation but programs change more through incremental improvement than through all–out replacement. To this end,

---

FIGURE 11.2
Evaluation Research Designs for Illumination of Causal Impact

Experiments with Randomized Controls: In a provisional tryout before the permanent intervention is administered, targets are randomly divided into an experimental group, to whom the intervention is administered, and a control group—randomized controls—from whom the intervention is withheld.

Experiments with Matched Controls: Targets to whom a provisional tryout is given or who has been exposed to the permanent intervention are compared to a theoretically equivalent group, created nonrandomly through matching—matched controls—from which the intervention is withheld or which has been exposed to other intervention(s).

Generic Controls: Effects of the permanent intervention among targets are compared with established norms about typical changes occurring in the larger population not covered by the intervention.

Statistical Controls: Participant and nonparticipant targets of the permanent intervention are compared, statistically holding constant differences between participants and people not covered by the intervention. Statistical controls are also applicable to full coverage programs.

Reflexive Controls: Targets who receive or have received the permanent intervention are compared to themselves, as measured before the intervention.

Shadow Controls: Targets who receive or have received the permanent intervention are compared to the judgments of experts, program managers and staff, and participants on what changes they believe would have happened in the past should there have been no intervention.

Note: A permanent intervention is a "real" intervention by contrast with a provisional tryout intervention.

---

nonexperimentalists support weaker, qualitative, naturalistic designs, which study permanent interventions *in situ.*

Randomized Controls: The Classic Experiment

> *"The Cadillac of program evaluation—controlled, randomized experimentation."*
> —Harry P. Hatry et al., *Practical Program Evaluation for State and Local Governments,* 2nd ed., 1982.

No evaluation design provides a more reliable and elegant scientific solution to the knotty impact problem than controlled, randomized experimentation. Classic, randomized experimentation is characterized by a crystal–clear logic, which is partly captured in figure 11.3.

The classic experimental design requires one *experimental group* and one *control group,* which in principle are equivalent in all conceivable respects. The safest way of establishing two groups with no systematic differences is to select them randomly. A given set of units of analysis—individuals, families, municipalities, car dealerships, and the like—are distributed on two groups according to some method, ensuring that the probability of getting into the one or the other is exactly the same for all units. This procedure—randomization—is marked with "R" in figure 11.3.[4] Once the distribution of the units across the two groups is made, the values of the target variable—also called dependent variable—are measured in both groups. This is marked by O_{mE} and O_{mC} in the figure, where O stands for "observation," E for "experimental" and C for "control group," and "m" for a principally unlimited number of observations. The experimental group is then exposed to the program while the control group is not. The program is indicated by X in figure 11.3. To find out whether the program has had any effects, the values of the dependent variable are registered again in both groups. These measurements are marked with O_{nE} and O_{nC} in the figure. Also "n" stands for what is, in principle, an unlim-

FIGURE 11.3
Classic Experiment with Pre– and Postprogram Measurements

Design	Assign–ment	Preprogram observation	Program	Postprogram observation	Difference
Experimental group (E)	R	O_{mE} (1010)	X	O_{nE} (1080)	$E=O_{nE}-O_{mE}$ (1080–1010=70)
Control group (C)	R	O_{mC} (1015)		O_{nC} (1160)	$C=O_{nC}-O_{mC}$ (1160–1015=145)

R = randomized assignment
O = observation of result variable
X = program (policy, intervention, project, activity, treatment, input)

The net effect of the program is E–C (70–145=–75, that is, 75 units saved) where
O_{mE}, O_{mC} = preprogram scores [O stands for observation(s), measurement(s)]
O_{nE}, O_{nC} = postprogram scores
E, C   = gross outcome for experimental and control group

ited number of observations. Changes that have occurred between the measurements before and after are considered caused by the program.

The logic of randomized experimentation can be illuminated through a contrived example. Let us assume that we want to know the impacts of an innovative government information campaign for energy conservation in multifamily dwellings. In public policy and public administration, classic experimentation implies a two–stage approach to decision making. Prior to permanent enactment, the program ought to be provisionally tried out on a small scale under full experimental conditions. On the basis of the findings produced by the experimental evaluation of the provisional tryout, the decision–makers will decide whether the program should be permanently enacted or not.

The two–step procedure thus engenders that the evaluation must be planned in advance and allowed to influence the design and execution of a pilot campaign. This means that the program must not have been launched prior to the inception of evaluative work. For classic experimentation transformed to the public sector implies that the program must be manipulable by the evaluator; she must be able to turn it on and off. If the necessary precondition of program manipulability is fulfilled, two groups are randomly selected from the total target population. Premeasurements show that the groups used 1010 and 1015 units of energy before the campaign started (the numbers are entered into figure 11.3). The campaign is now administered to the experimental group, but not to the control group. Postmeasurements show that energy use has increased in both groups, but by seventy-five units more in the control group. The conclusion is that the savings campaign has reduced energy use by seventy-five units, since without the campaign energy use would probably have been 1155 in the experimental group instead of 1080.

Classic randomized experiments stress the importance of taking measurements before as well as after the intervention. Thinking in terms of times series or applying an historical perspective is crucial.

The computation of the size of the effect is performed according to the formula E–C, where E is the difference between the measurements after and before in the experimental group and C stands for the corresponding difference in the control group.

Stochastic design effects must also be considered. Randomization can never ensure perfect equation between the two groups; there are always variations between the groups due to imperfections of the randomization procedure. Randomized experimentation can only produce equality of groups within known statistical limits. Therefore, Rossi and Freeman have suggested that the calculation should be performed according to the formula Net effect = E–C+S, where S symbolizes stochastic design effects. The full algorithm is presented in figure 11.4.

How is the reference alternative illuminated in experimentation? This is done by actually producing it under artificial conditions. In studying what is happening within the control group not introduced to the treatment, the evaluator elicits what would have occurred should the program not have been instigated.

How can the experimenter claim that the program has spawned the results? The difference might be due to something else occurring during experimentation. The experimentals might well have been more sensitive than the controls to other forces working simultaneously with the program.

Thanks to the random allocation of units of analysis to the two groups, experimenters can be reasonably assured that no external factor has confounded the results. They have good reasons to believe that *cetera* are *paria,* that is, that the groups *in all other respects* are approximately equivalent. No other circumstance than the fact that only the experimental group has been exposed to the program can have caused the observed changes (Houston 1972:52 ff.; Weiss 1972a:60ff.; Riecken and Boruch 1974:44ff.; Campbell and Stanley 1966.; Suchman 1967.; Wholey et al. 1970). The *ceteris paribus* condition is fulfilled.

FIGURE 11.4
The Rossi and Freeman Algorithm for Effect Calculation
in Randomized Experimentation

When evaluation research was in its infancy in the United States, randomized experimentation was considered to be the outstanding solution to the impact problem in public policy and program evaluation. Its capacity to distinguish programmatic from nonprogrammatic effects was thought to render experimentation a unique strength among available designs for data collection. Randomized experiments, however, raise heavy demands on the framing of government programs. Reforms and other political program packages can never be rapidly and fully initiated across the country, but must first be attempted as small–scale tryouts with experimentals and controls. Assuming for the moment that some provisional tryouts under randomized conditions are possible and desirable in government, even the most ardent supporters of experimentation have to concede that not even this presumable paragon among research designs can unequivocally solve the causality problems of the social world. Human consciousness, our power of self–direction and self–monitoring, is a problem to experimentation.

The Hawthorne Effect

Persons involved in experiments might change their behavior once they become conscious of their role as guinea pigs. The very fact that they are introduced to a pretreatment measuring instrument may affect their posttreatment scores. The subjects may either make special efforts to live up to the expectations of the researchers, or deliberately behave in a way contrary to that expected.

Among specialists, this pretest effect is designated the *Hawthorne effect*. Other labels are the *guinea pig effect,* the *reactive measurement effect* (Webb 1966:13), "reactive effects" (Nachmias 1979:25), or "inadvertent confounding" (Cook and Campbell 1979:38). The first, somewhat strange identification tag is derived from an industrial plant in Hawthorne, Illinois, owned by the Western Electrical Company. In 1924, a series of controlled experiments were launched there centering on the impact of the degree of light in the facility on worker productivity. To everybody's consternation, every change in light conditions, impairments included, increased productivity. Women working exceedingly hard for forty-eight hours a week without breaks still increased their productivity, provided that they realized they were participating in an experiment concerning their work productivity. The researchers concluded: "Any investigation attempting to evaluate definitely the effect of illumination or some such influence must take the greatest of pains to control or eliminate all factors but the one being studied. Many of them can be controlled or eliminated, but the one great stumbling block remaining is the problem of the psychology of the human individual" (Anderson et al. 1974:195ff.).

The Hawthorne effect is related to self-fulfilling prophesies. A self–fulfilling prophesy is a false definition of a situation evoking new behavior, which makes the originally false conception come true.

"If men define situations as real, they are real in their consequences." Robert Merton begins his classic exposition on the self–fulfilling prophesy (1968:476f.) with this quotation from W. I. Thomas. To illustrate the Thomas theorem, Merton tells the tragic story of C. Millingville's flourishing Last National Bank. It started on Black Wednesday 1932, "the last Wednesday, it might be noted of the Last National Bank." The bank was a well–managed institution. A large part of its resources were liquid without being watered. But a rumor of insolvency came about. Once the false rumor was believed by enough depositors, they started frantically to withdraw their money, which soon resulted in the insolvency of the bank. Once the depositors had defined the situation as bad, although in fact it was good, their view of the situation became real in its consequences.

In human affairs, not only "objective conditions," but the meaning ascribed to them by human consciousness plays a role. Merton argues:

> Public definitions of a situation (prophesies or predictions) become an integral part of the situation and thus affects subsequent developments. This is peculiar to human affairs. It is not found in the world of nature, untouched by human hands. Predictions of the return of Halley's comet do not influence its orbit. But the rumored insolvency of Millingville's bank did affect the actual outcome. The prophesy of collapse led to its own fulfillment. (Merton 1968:477)

The Last National Bank failure is a case of a self–fulfilling prophesy. Despite the comparative liquidity of the bank's assets, a rumor of insolvency, once believed by enough depositors, resulted in the real insolvency of the bank.

As an aside, we may note that the Hawthorne effect is related to the Heisenberg Uncertainty Principle, which says that we cannot discover both the momentum and the position of a fundamental particle, because the process of discovery will always affect what is being discovered. It also resembles Bohr's Principle of Complementarity: the observer, far from being independent of his experiment, is inextricably linked with it. The measuring rod inevitably influences what is measured. We can never talk about nature without, at the same time, talking about ourselves (Rasmussen 1987; Vedung 1988).[5]

Five Variants of Randomized Controls

Far from surrendering to the Hawthorne effect, supporters of randomized experiments have thrashed out four methods of neutralizing, if not eliminating, it. All in all, then, there are five types of randomized experimentation, which is shown in figure 11.5.

The first two alternatives to classic, full–information experiments are posited on slight deception. One expedient is *secrecy*. People are simply not told they are guinea pigs in a policy experiment. The second practice to avoid Hawthorne effects, the administration a *placebo,* is outrightly deceptive. In this case, controls are subjected to a dummy treatment, which is said to be identical to the one administered to the experimentals, while in fact it is identical only in certain, superficial, inessential, and nonpotent ways. A placebo gives the aura but not the substance of the treatment.

None of the two slightly deceptive options can be applied regularly on a grand scale in public policy. First, the citizens would probably

FIGURE 11.5
Five Types of Randomized Experimentation

Randomized experiments

Pre- and postprogram measurements   Postprogram measurements only

Full information   Secrecy   Placebo   Solomon
(classic ex-   Four-Group
periment)   Design

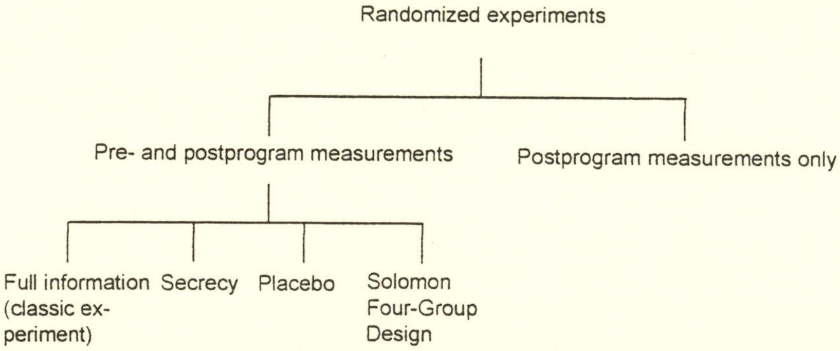

not accept being fooled in this way by their governments and authorities. Second, they contradict the norm of societal openness in a democracy. The question is therefore whether the third and fourth option provide more realistic possibilities for scientific evaluation and science–based policymaking.

The third option for controlling the Hawthorne effect is to work with two pairs of experimental-control group constellations, the so–called *Solomon Four-Group Design*. The Solomon strategy does not eradicate Hawthorne effects, because that is impossible. Rather, it is predicated on the notion that they can be measured, and thus brought under control (Nachmias 1979:30f.).

To illuminate the logic of the Solomon Four-Group Design, let us return to our contrived government information campaign for energy conservation in multifamily dwellings. If the campaign has not yet been launched, the Solomon Design can be used. This means that four groups are randomly selected from the total target population. Premeasurements are taken in the first pair of groups, but not in the second. The program is administered to the experimental groups in both pairs. Postmeasurements are taken in all four groups.

The idea is to experiment not only with the program but with the experimentation of the program as well. Since premeasurements are taken on the first pair of groups, the scores will include eventual Hawthorne effects along with program effects. But the scores of the second group will not include Hawthorne effects, since no premeasurements are taken from them.

The fictive energy use scores for the various groups are shown in figure 11.6.

The gross effect of the campaign, Hawthorne measurement artifact included, seems to be seventy-five units of energy saved. The general computation formula is:

Gross effect of the program, Hawthorne effects included = $(O_{nE1}-O_{mE1})-(O_{nC1}-O_{mC1})$.

The actual numbers are (1080–1010)-(1160–1015)=-75, which means 75 units of energy saved. The lower scores for postprogram energy use in the first pair of groups in comparison to the second indicate that the awareness of being participants in an experiment must have increased propensity to save energy. The net effect of the savings campaign, Hawthorne effects excluded, is 110 units of energy saved, which can be computed from the scores of the second pair of groups (1090–

FIGURE 11.6
The Solomon Four-Group Design Applied to an Energy Campaign

	Assign-ment	Preprogram observation	Program	Postprogram observation	Difference
Experim. group 1 (E_1)	R	1010 (O_{mE1})	X	1080 (O_{nE1})	$E_1 = O_{nE1} - O_{mE1}$
Control group 1 (C_1)	R	1015 (O_{mC1})		1160 (O_{nC1})	$C_1 = O_{nC1} - O_{mC1}$
Experim. group 2 (E_2)	R		X	1090 (O_{nE2})	$E_2 = O_{nE2}$
Control group 2 (C_2)	R			1200 (O_{nC2})	$C_2 = O_{nC2}$

R = randomized assignment
O = observation of result variable
X = program (policy, intervention, project, activity, treatment, input)

The gross effect of the program = $E_1 - C_1$ (70–145=–75, i.e. a 75–units reduction)
where

O_{mE1}, O_{mC1}	=	preprogram scores [O stands for observation(s), measurement(s)] in the first pair of groups
O_{nE1}, O_{nC1}	=	postprogram scores in the first pair of groups
E_1, C_1	=	gross outcome for experimental and control group in the first pair of groups

The net effect of the program= $E_2 - C_2$ (1090–1200=–110, that is, a 110–units reduction) where

O_{nE2}, O_{nC2}	=	postprogram scores in the second pair of groups
E_2, C_2	=	net outcome for experimental and control group in the second pair of groups

1200=–110). The general algorithm is:

Net effect of the program, Hawthorne effects excluded = $O_{nE2} - O_{nC2}$.

The Hawthorne effect is the difference between the net and the gross effect, that is, 35 units of energy saved. The general formula is:

Hawthorne effect = $(O_{nE2} - O_{nC2}) - [(O_{nE1} - O_{mE1}) - (O_{nC1} - O_{mC1})]$.

The digit 35 is obtained by the operation –110–75=–35, which makes 35 units of energy saved.

The Solomon Four–Group Design promises control of Hawthorne effects at the cost of a much more complicated experimental situation. Launching this involved, comprehensive, and probably costly machinery regularly even for major innovative public programs seems out of question. Public policymaking would be too convoluted and time consuming.

The fourth and final way of controlling pre–measurement effects in experimentation seems more realistic, for it implies that *preprogram measurements* are *skipped* altogether. But doesn't the evaluator then have to abstain from essential baseline information on both groups? For how can he decide whether the program has exerted any influence on the dependent variable, if he consciously abstains from collecting materials that shows the values on this variable in both groups *before* the program was enacted?

This question merits attention, but there is a relatively satisfactory answer. The necessary knowledge may be obtained in other ways than through formal pre–measurement. It may be deduced from the fact that the groups are randomly selected. This warrants the conclusion that they are equivalent in all respects. There is a margin of insecurity, of course, but it is known and can be stated. Since the groups are equivalent in every respect, experimenters may infer that the scores on the independent variable must be equal in both groups at the baseline. In this way, all eventual differences in the post–measurement scores can be attributed to the program. The Post–Program–Only Control Group Design is represented in figure 11.7.

The Hawthorne effect is a general deficiency of social experimentation, not an injunction against experimentation in the specific context of public policy evaluation. There are, however, some very strong arguments against the use of experimentation in public policymaking as well. These reasons, specific to the area of public policy, will be discussed in a separate section further on. Here, I only wish to point out that randomized experiments are rarely applicable in the evaluation of public policies. The prerequisite that the evaluator, before the program is permanently enacted, can arrange a small–scale trial run of it with two randomized groups is seldom fulfilled, since public programs as a rule are permanently enacted across the board. There will be no random controls from which the program is withheld. This is connected to a very important characteristic of public policymaking. Political and administrative actors cannot make policies and programs in splendid isolation from what is going on around them. The party in office must consider what measures the opposition will take, if a particular policy is suggested. Elected officials have to consider the opinions and actions of other players, such as the media, the voters, the economic actors in the marketplace, and also foreign powers. The necessity of swift action in combination with the power games of politics makes planned experimentation too stiff and time consuming.

FIGURE 11.7
Experiment Without Formal Preprogram Measurement—
the Postprogram–Only Control Group Design

Design	Assign-ment	Preprogram observation	Program	Postprogram observation
Experimental group (E)	R		X	O_E
Control group (C)	R			O_C

R = randomized assignment
O = observation of result variable
X = program (policy, intervention, project, acticity, treatment, input)

The net effect of the program = $O_E–O_C$
where
O_E, O_C = postprogram scores

The demands of randomized experimentation collide directly with the way public sector decisions are made.

Faced with these difficulties, the advocates of randomized experimentation argue that radical experimentation should concern bold innovative programs only, not modest adjustments of established practices. But even on the rare occasions when brand new interventions are considered or old interventions are entirely replaced, randomized experimentation may prove infeasible. Radical experimentalists may then grudgingly withdraw one step and recommend theoretically matchéd controls, or quasi experiments, as an acceptable back–up. While producing weaker results on program effects, matched controls are somewhat better adjusted to public sector decision making.

Matched Controls: Quasi Experiments

> "More and more I have come to the conclusion that the core of the scientific method is not experimentation per se, but rather the strategy connoted by the phrase "plausible rival hypotheses."
> —Donald T. Campbell, "Preface," Yin: Case Study Method

Even matched controls—quasi experiments—are based on the two–stage approach to public policymaking. First, public policies are introduced on a limited scale on trial and carefully evaluated through the use of two matched groups. Then the findings produced by evaluation of the trial is supposed to provide reasonable guidance to decision–makers when they determine whether the policies will be enacted on a comprehensive scale or not. In matched controls, however, none of the two groups in the pilot test are randomly created by the evaluator. Instead the evaluator tries to select an intact control group resembling the experimental group as closely as possible according to premeditated criteria. Ideally, the other group should be equivalent to the experimental group in all respects deemed relevant. The perfect analogy for equation would be a pair of one–egged twins, raised by the same parents under identical social and natural circumstances.

The inherited professional term for this procedure is *matching*. In India, Korea, and other Asian countries parents devote enormous energy to "matchmaking." They try to match their son or daughter to an appropriate marriage partner. Even quasi experiments, it might be argued, are predicated upon matchmaking.

The decisive, definitional difference between experiments and quasi experiments, consequently, concerns how equation between the two groups is achieved. In experiments, equivalence is established through randomization, in quasi experiments through intelligent matchmaking.

Contrary to what is maintained by several pundits, the manipulability of the input variable—the intervention, the program—does not constitute the borderline between randomized experiments and quasi experiments (Caporaso and Roos 1973:39). True, there are quasi experiments where the evaluator can make important decisions about the content and timing of the program. But there are also quasi experiments where control group selection has to be made after the treatment has occurred (Caporaso and Roos 1973:12ff.). Quasi experiments where the control group is identified after the fact are called *ex post facto* designs. The reasoning is captured in figure 11.8.

The other identical twin raised under equivalent social conditions will probably never be found by the evaluator. She will have to settle for peers, who are only approximately equivalent to the experimentals in certain relevant aspects. And what these aspects are hinges upon theoretical considerations relevant to the evaluative question to be posed.

If the problem is to detect the extent to which a government communication campaign for energy conservation really produces or has

FIGURE 11.8
Two Types of Matched Controls

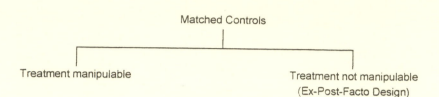

produced a reduction in comprehensive household energy use, the matching should proceed with regard to *all* the contingencies that may conceivably affect this particular result. The evaluator has to form an opinion concerning what factors might impinge upon total household energy consumption. Matching must be guided by a good *theory of the intervention field.*

Obviously, the matching problem cannot be resolved through mechanical application of statistical sampling procedures, however refined. Successful matching presupposes profound insights into the substantive matter under investigation. In other words, it is necessary to work with a pertinent substantive theory, indicating the determinants of the changes in the phenomenon to be scrutinized (Rossi and Freeman 1989:320ff.,196f.).

In our example, we have to form a well-founded opinion of what makes some household units more willing than others to conserve energy. A handful of potential influence factors are listed in figure 11.9.

From earlier investigations we may know that the level of energy consumption is in some way linked to some or all of the above factors. The general attitude toward energy conservation and environmental protection also has some impact.

In the matching, the evaluators have to make sure that the groups are as equivalent as possible in these particular respects. The idea is that by ensuring that these circumstances operate *with equal strength* in both groups, the experimenter is allowed to disregard them. Hereby, some specific explanatory factors constituting potential rivals to the program can be set aside (Houston 1972:60f.; Weiss 1972a:69ff.).

Thus, a properly executed matching is no easy and fast affair. It

FIGURE 11.9
Theory of the Household Energy Conservation Intervention Field

- Energy price
- Dwelling size
- Age of dwelling
- Type of dwelling: single family dwelling, condominium, rental dwelling
- Collective or individual metering
- Household equipment
- Number of people at home during daytime
- Income
- Age of household members
- Attitude toward energy conservation and environment
- Existence of zealots

presupposes theoretical knowledge and technical skills. In general, quasi experiments are held to be weaker than randomized experiments in controlling for potential rival explanations. Another pertinent question to be posed by evaluation theorists is whether the requirements raised by matched controls are more compatible with the preconditions of public sector decision making in modern societies than those demanded by randomized experiments.

The Control Series Design

Most powerful among the quasi-experimental designs with regard to the causality problem is the Control Series Design. Another approach, the Pre–Test-Post–Test Comparison Group Design, can be regarded as an amputated version of the Control Series Design. I shall briefly sketch both designs in figure 11.10, then concentrate my attention on the Control Series Design.

The Control Series strategy involves the collection of target variable data on two groups, selected to resemble each other along as many relevant dimensions as possible. The data concerns a set of points in time and the measurement points are identical for the two groups. Approximately in the middle of the time period, one group has been naturally introduced to the program while the other has not. Since the two groups are matched to control for all factors suspected to exert some influence on the result variable, differences in the postprogram scores might be attributed to the program.

FIGURE 11.10
Two Quasi Experiments

Design	Assign–ment	Preprogram observation			Program observation	Postprogram		
Control Series Design								
Investigation Group	M	O_1	O_2	O_3	X	O_4	O_5	O_6
Comparison Group	M	O_1	O_2	O_3		O_4	O_5	O_6
Pretest-Posttest Comparison Group Design								
Investigation Group	M	O_1			X	O_2		
Comparison Group	M	O_1				O_2		

M = assignment through matching
O = observation (measurement) of the result variable
X = program (policy, intervention, project, activity, treatment, input)

Source: Revision of a figure in Riecken and Boruch 1974:98.

Again, the importance of having a time series of data points must be stressed. The data points should concern the preprogram as well as the postprogram era.

The conclusion is supported by the fact that the groups are approximately equivalent with regard to all contingencies that might influence the results variable—energy use—and are thereby exposed to the *same* external influence from these contingencies. But there is one crucial difference between the two groups: the experimentals have been introduced to a program while the controls have not. This must explain eventual differences in postprogram scores.

However, quasi experimenters readily concede that they cannot be absolutely sure that the program explanation—that is, the conclusion that the program has produced or has not produced the result—is tenable. In technical evaluation vocabulary, they would admit that the program explanation is jeopardized by competing explanatory factors. For this, Campbell and Stanley (1966:5ff.) have coined the phrase "threats to internal validity."

Threats to Internal Validity

Before accepting the program explanation as the most plausible one, the quasi experimenter must systematically consider how the various threats to internal validity might have influenced the result. She must, perhaps, amass data illuminating the size and effect of the threats in order to keep them under control. To ensure that no jeopardy is neglected or played down, the evaluator must draw upon all her theoretical knowledge, critical sense, imagination, and innovative powers.[6]

There are some threats that the Control Series Design is supposed to be immune to, provided pre- and post–measurements have been taken for a sufficiently long period of time.

Firstly, the change cannot be imputed to *random instability*. A long time series of data inexorably reveals random variation on the target variables (Caporaso and Roos 1973:24). Secondly, nor can it be part of a *long-time trend*. The extended time series of data for both groups would tell us if that was the case (Caporaso and Roos 1973:24f.). And third, the change cannot be part of a *periodical* evolution process. A periodical fluctuation is a pattern repeating itself. Seasonal variations are good cases in point. When the data series are sufficiently long for each group, we may easily see if changes in the results are entailed in some cyclical or other periodic pattern (Caporaso and Roos 1973:24f.).

In contrast, the change might depend on *modified data registration procedures*. Changes in data–collection and record–keeping procedures yield idiosyncracies in the measurement series. Of course, the threat can be eliminated, provided no actual adjustments have been made. And should an adjustment actually have been undertaken, it is possible that the new data might be made comparable to the old.

Most importantly, however, changes may result from *substantive factors* besides the program. This point needs elaboration.

The reason why the Control Series Design is open to rival substantive interpretations stems from the possibility that some important causative factor might have been overlooked in the matchmaking. Sustained efforts notwithstanding, the evaluator may have produced an imperfect match. Some substantive contingency outside of the evaluator's control might have impacted upon her target variable scores.

In other words, the solutions to the causality problem provided by the Control Series Design are never better than the theory of the program field actually employed in the matching procedure. Its benefits include the possibility of holding some causative factors constant by matching. Yet, the matching is never exhaustive. To assess substantive threats not eliminated by the matching procedure, the evaluator has to collect data separately on each of them and subject the data to statistical analysis or insightful reasoning in order to decide whether these factors have been influential or not. Such an analysis of supplementary data might help determine the plausibility of the substantive rival explanations.

Should Public Programming Be Social Experimentation?

> *"Before accurate decisions can be made about the effectiveness of any social program, it is quite obvious that there must be a complete scientific evaluation of it. It is . . . important that the evaluation be very sound from a scientific point of view. This essentially means that the evaluation must be an actual experimental one."*
> —G. W. Fairweather and L G Tornatzky, *Experimental Methods for Social Policy Research (1977)*

While the randomized experiment has been espoused as the Cadillac of evaluation, the quasi experiment has been embraced as its Lincoln Continental. Both were once hailed as the best brands that social science methodology can contribute to evaluation.

The strength of the experimental design has been formulated in the following fashion by Riecken and Boruch (1974:5):

We are inclined to emphasize the role of experimentally gathered information in the shaping of social policy because such information is most helpful in learning the causal relationships among program elements and outcomes. If an effect can be demonstrated in a group of units (persons, places, or institutions) chosen at random and subjected to a specified treatment while a similar group that is not treated does not show the effect, one can be reasonably confident that the treatment produced the effect. Such confidence cannot so readily be reposed in nonexperimental evidence, even though sophisticated methods of analysis can be used to reduce the ambiguity of causal inference. The superiority of experimental method lies in the fact that in a true experiment the differences between a treated (experimental) group and an untreated (control) group can be attributed entirely to the effect of the treatment plus an accidental (random) error component which can be accurately estimated and which will be evenhandedly distributed across the control and the experimental groups alike. Furthermore, all the other factors which augment or suppress the outcome variable occur evenhandedly in both the experimental and the control groups.

Yet, not even the Cadillac stands beyond criticism. Hawthorne effects can damage randomized experimentation almost as severely as it damages other designs. Even more serious than the general objections against social experimentation, however, are accusations that experimentation is inappropriate as a *design for public policy evaluation*. Experiments raise such harsh demands on the framing of public intervention and public activities so as to render them almost impossible to use. The preconditions, that the target is initially partitioned—randomly or through matching—into experimentals and controls, and that the former but not the latter is exposed to the program in a pilot tryout before the permanent program is enacted, are very rarely met in the real world of public policy. Novel large reforms as well as novel minor programs are initiated across the board without previous experimentation. In most cases, evaluation is called upon to scrutinize existing programs. The requirements of radical experimentation that interventions be tried out provisionally with random or matched groups prior to full inauguration cannot be met in the real world of public sector programming.

From this dilemma there are two and only two expedients. Either public policymaking must be adapted to radical evaluation research or radical evaluation research to public policymaking.

A few deeply concerned evaluation theorists have chosen the first option. Public officials must straighten themselves up and pursue their trade in a more rational manner. These theorists are not concerned with marginal improvements of current programs but with bold conjectures and large innovative reforms in a future, utopian society. These innovative programs must be adjusted to scholarly demands for the best available scientific designs. Decisions on installing full–scale reforms and programs must be preceded by preliminary pilot tests, designed as randomized or matched experiments. And equally important, decision–makers must pay heed to evaluative knowledge in their framing of the permanent programs. Strict evaluation must be allotted a decisive role in the formation of permanent public interventions.

More than anybody else, perhaps, Donald T. Campbell, the illustrious American evaluation methodologist, has expounded the rationalistic dream of public sector programming as a continual, qualified experimentation under social science direction. In his famous article "Reforms as Experiments" (1969:409), he maintained, among other things, the following:

> The United States and other modern nations should be ready for an experimental approach to social reform, an approach for which we try out new programs designed to cure specific social problems, in which we learn whether or not these programs are effective, and in which we retain, imitate, modify, or discard them on the basis of apparent effectiveness.[7]

Campbell's staunch advocacy of experimental politics belongs to a larger, technocratic or semitechnocratic school of thought according to which politics ought to more sciencelike, if not modelled on the sciences. Kurt Lewin, the eminent social psychologist, held a similar optimistic view of the role of experiments for social betterment. A famous radical exponent of this train of thought was the English physicist John Bernal, who in the 1930s presented grand visionary dreams of public policy conducted according to scientific principles with distinguished scientists occupying leading positions in government. Campbell has never gone that far; in his tentative utopia social scientists are only methodological servants to the decision–makers, not advisors or rulers.

Should public policymaking be pursued as in two steps? Should bold government interventions be provisionally tried out in hardheaded social experiments and their permanent enactment depend on the results of these experiments? At face value, such two–stage view of a rational political system seems sound. Why shouldn't one, using the best methodology available, find out whether purported programs really will achieve what they are supposed to before they are inaugurated across the board?

Yet, experimentation suffers from shortcomings as an instrument of public planning, a fact readily admitted by the experimentalists themselves. Experiments are time consuming, produce narrow knowledge, and weak on external validity.

Laboratory experiments and field trials are *time consuming*. This objection is framed by Cook and Campbell (1979:344) in the following manner:

> Usually a considerable time elapses between planning a randomized experiment and obtaining the results. Major research questions have to be developed and validated, pilot work (or formative research) has to be conducted, the pretest measurements have to be made, the rest of the data collected, cleaned and ordered, the analysis conducted, and the first drafts of reports carefully scrutinized. Thus, it should not be surprising that typically several years pass between the conception of an experiment and the availability of results. When decisions have to be made rapidly, randomized experiments may not be suitable.

Can politicians really wait for years before they act? On some occasion the answer is clearly yes. Take the case of finding a safe final repository for radioactive nuclear waste. Research on this issue has been going for decades and may continue for many years to come. The problem is so serious and the time perspective is so long that the political planning period may be very extended. On most occasions, however, the answer is clearly no. It is obvious that political bodies must react promptly to unpredictable natural catastrophes like earth quakes, floods, droughts, tornadoes, landslides, avalanches, and snow-storms. But the state must also act speedily in response to expectations nurtured or measures taken by other agents. For instance, the incumbent parties often feel that they have to take immediate action because they have promised the electorate to do so. Often, the state must adopt prompt measures due to sudden movements of capital across borders. The standard example is measures to curb currency flight when devaluation rumors start to be believed. Proponents of radical experimentation sustain unrealistic, even naive, views of the long–range, steady nature of public policymaking.

On the other hand, public intervention making not only involves prompt reaction but also meticulous, long–range planning. Since the time–consuming objection seems to carry less weight in these cases, experimentation may have a role to play in future–oriented, long–range planning.

Secondly, experiments produce *narrow knowledge* in several senses. In experimentation, it is difficult to discern effects of more than one treatment, because the administration of an extra treatment involves the cumbersome use of an additional randomly selected group. For the same practical reason, processes between program adoption and program outcomes are rarely adumbrated in experiments. Everything but the program is treated as a black box. This saves the evaluator some precious time and work.[8] To public officials, however, it is a serious drawback, since the implementation phase is of substantial interest to them. Experimentation, it seems, cannot replace the rich and varied knowledge acquired from other sources. An additional narrow–knowledge downside with experiments is their inability to handle unanticipated side effects, because by their very nature they must concentrate on gauging effects that are expected when the experiment starts. This is a serious drawback, since side effects are prevalent.

Finally, experimental results are weak on *external validity,* to use the Campbell–Stanley terminology (1966:5ff.). They may be of limited use in complex field settings, because impact assessors cannot make the wholesale assumption that findings from an artificial experiment will hold true in the field. Real government processes are probably more different from experimental situations in the laboratory than any other social situation to which we may want to apply the findings from experiments. "Even in agriculture, the transition from the controlled experiment at the research station to the average practice on the farm is always problematic. Even if fertilizer A is superior to B in controlled experiments, it may not be superior in the special type of soil found in, say, southeast Georgia" (Cook and Campbell 1979:7). Transferring experimental results to large field settings is very problematic.

Experimentation is certainly an excellent design if applied in the sciences. It may also be of value in some social sciences, particularly psychology and small–group sociology. In government and public administration the situation is different. The case against experimental programming seems to be a strong one indeed.

Still, experiments, provisional field trials, and pilot programs are established (Berk 1985; Hellstern and Wollmann 1983). In the United States, several of Lyndon B. Johnson's famous Great Society programs were initially launched on trial. Some of them were also evaluated through controlled experimentation. According to Charles Murray (1984:149), the inauguration of the Negative Income Tax—a program providing payments to persons whose income fell below a certain floor,

> took the form of the most ambitious social-science experiment in history. No other even comes close to its combination of size, expense, length, and detail of analysis. . . . It began in 1968, ultimately used 8,700 people as subjects, and lasted for ten years. . . . It resulted in a body of literature that, as of 1980, included more than one hundred published titles and countless unpublished reports. Its costs ran far into the millions.

All ambitions notwithstanding, the contribution of the experiment to the program was either tiny or none at all.

Other countries besides the United States use experimentation to a considerable extent. This particularly applies to Denmark and Norway, for instance. There are also historical examples. In the Austro-Hungarian monarchy, reforms used to be introduced on trial in Galicia before they were fully enacted throughout the empire.

An experimental or experimentlike approach is often regarded as typical of Swedish politics. Field trials, demonstrations, and prototypes are commonplace in Swedish political life. The large school reforms of the 1950s, for instance, were tried out on a small scale in a number of communities before being applied throughout the realm.

Yet not even the ample Swedish use of field trials and prototypes can be taken as evidence that this society is a social laboratory in a qualified sense. While frequently referred to as "experiments," most field trials are designed neither as randomized experiments nor quasi experiments. Advanced evaluation methodology requirements are not allowed to influence the designs in any important way. On most occasions, perhaps, the operative motive is not to try out and evaluate in an unprejudiced manner a provisionally adopted program. The real motivations are probably mixed. Sometimes it is symbolic gestures designed to indicate government awareness of problems and sympathetic intentions in order to garner votes and opinion support. Occasionally, the government wants to blaze a trail for the full-scale adoption of the reform, no matter how it works. Having already decided to instigate an all–out reform, decision–makers feel that they do not have the political clout to do it immediately and fully. By having it tried out in an allegedly provisional fashion, the issue will ripen and resistance will soften. In reality, so–called experimental field trials involve little but political consensus–building on the reform. Demonstrations turn into some sort of implementation strategy (Hadenius 1990:80,85f.,117ff.; Premfors 1989).

In addition, preliminary field trials are used to legitimize reforms. For this purpose, it is not necessarily data on implementation and impact that are important but rather the fact that pilot runs have been undertaken. Field trials easily take on an air of rationalistic ritual and tactical maneuvering. One may never overlook the possibility that evaluation can be used to legitimize something already decided or established.

Sweden cannot, then, be characterized as an experimenting society in any qualified sense. Such a society is hardly desirable either. On the other hand, field trials are launched that are experiments in a more watered–down sense. Premfors has pointed out that full–coverage measures, intended to function for a limited period of time only, are often termed experiments or field trials (Premfors 1986:87f.). The term *experiment* is also used to denote field trials, limited in time and space, the effects of which are unknown. If evaluated, the designs to be used are best characterized as naturalistic, qualitative case studies. For the program is studied not under contrived conditions as in randomized experimentation or with matched controls but in its natural surroundings and multifaceted contexts. This type of "experimentation" could even be used to a much larger extent than actually is the case.

In conclusion, it is important to distinguish the case for experimentation in the sciences, in basic social science and in public policy and program evaluation. To the best of my knowledge, in some branches of the sciences, experimentation is widely acclaimed as the design to be applied. The same holds true but to a considerably lesser extent with some basic social sciences like psychology and small–group sociology. In government and public administration the situation is somewhat different. In spite of a very constraining setting, experimentation can play a role, but probably only a marginal one.

Evaluation researchers must adopt a humble stance and learn to live with the insight that public policymaking can never be transformed into science in the way desired by outright technocrats and radical experimentalists. Evaluation methodology must be adjusted to the rules of the political game, not the other way around. This does not imply, however, that evaluation research is entirely futile. There should be a concern for evaluability in the planning stage of a public intervention. However, this concern must not be allowed to become a case of the evaluation driving the project, pushing democratic policymaking into the background. If politically acceptable, preliminary tryouts can and should be arranged. They should also be evaluated, if possible by means of radical experimentation. New innovative interventions and fundamental reconsiderations of existing interventions sometimes occur in public life, and in these situations experimentation may have a role to play. On the other hand, evaluators must accept that even in preliminary field tests of innovations experimentation is often out of the question.

First and foremost, evaluators must acquiesce to the fact that the lion's share of government reforms and programs are already in place and cannot be subjected to field trials. Changes occur but they are incremental. In these cases, evaluators must work on designs that are weaker at establishing equation between two groups and, consequently, causal linkages, but more easily applied to existing political practice. Less emphasis must be placed on randomized and matched controls and more on reflexive, statistical and shadow controls, and above all process evaluations of case–study type. Two-group methods must be discarded in favor of one-group methodologies. To these methods we shall now turn our attention.

Opinions differ sharply on the practical value of radical experimentation in public intervention evaluation. Some theorists have entirely discarded experiments while others have regarded them as the best designs available. I for one have argued that experiments should not be entirely dismissed. Radical experimentation has a role to play, particularly with new public interventions and in local settings. But since most policy change occurs incrementally in existing programs, other methods must be applied. Radical experimentalists will neither succeed nor should they be allowed to succeed in their endeavor to reduce politics and public sector programming into a science.

Notes

1. Nachmias (1979:7) quotes H. M. Blalock: "If X is a cause of Y, we have in mind that a *change* in X produces a *change* in Y and not merely that a *change* in X is followed by or associated with a *change* in Y" (my italics).
2. Fischer 1970:166f., "after this, therefore because of this."
3. Russell's remark goes back to Pascal's Pensées: "Le nez de Cléopatre; s'il eût été plus court, toute la face de la terre aurait changé." Also cf. economic historian Robert W. Fogel's celebrated counterfactual question: "What would have been the rate of American economic growth if the railroads had never existed?" The publication of "Railroads and the American Economic Growth" (1964) marked the arrival of cliometrics or the New Quantitative Economic History. Later, Fogel was awarded the Nobel prize in economics.
4. Randomization must not be mixed up with random sampling. In randomization, the researcher takes a limited set of units and *allocates* each unit to two groups according to some method, which safeguards randomness. Random sampling, on the other hand, concerns *the selection of a sample from a population* in such a way that the sample reflects all important properties in the population. The methods can be combined. First, we may draw a random selection of units from a target population and then allocate each unit to experimental and control groups on a random basis (Rossi and Freeman 1989:278ff.).
5. One of the most famous examples of the influence of methods on research results is probably the American community power research. The positional, reputational, and decision–making methods provide different results.
6. Cook and Campbell 1979: 37ff. provide a systematic, though technical account of various threats. For a simpler presentation, consult Herman 1987, part 3.
7. Also Campbell 1970, 1982; and Campbell and Stanley 1966. This thesis has also been advocated by Suchman 1967; Rivlin 1971; Riecken and Boruch 1974. Campbell's philosophy is analyzed in Shadish, Jr. et al. 1991.
8. Factorial experimental designs that involve more than one program variable are probably too cumbersome to handle in public policy. See Nachmias 1979:32ff.

12

Generic, Reflexive, Statistical, and Shadow Controls

When it is impossible or impractical to form a control group either randomly or according to the principles of matching, radical experimentation is unfeasible. Facing this situation, radical experimentalists are left with two approaches to the impact issue, the sixth problem in the Eight Problems Approach to public sector evaluation.

One is surrender. From this perspective, since impact assessment cannot be performed by the best available methodology, researchers should keep out of the evaluation business and remain in their ivory towers. There is no way that science and scholarship can contribute to ascertaining the impacts of public interventions.

The other is the use of weaker designs. Researchers may continue to insist on sciencelike impact assessments, but with designs more adapted to political realities. This alternative seems to be recommended by a majority of evaluation methodologists. Research may contribute insights on causality in spite of the fact that public policymaking cannot be transformed into radical experimentation.

The designs recommended as alternatives to radical experimentation are *naturalistic*.[1] Focusing on programs as they unfold in real life, no attempt is made to adjust them to the requirements of strictly randomized or matched experiments. Programs are examined in their natural, permanent settings, not in provisional tryout settings. The laboratory spirit disappears because experimentals and controls are neither artificially created (as in randomized experiments) nor matched (as in quasi experiments).

Following Rossi and Freeman, I shall discuss four naturalistic alternatives: generic, statistical, reflexive, and shadow controls. With generic and statistical controls, evaluators still use some reference or comparison case, while reflexive and shadow controls are strict one–group–only designs.

Generic Controls

The generic controls design presupposes partial–coverage programs, that is, permanent interventions adopted by national authorities covering only some part of the nation. In the generic controls design, the results from the smaller group reached by the permanent but partial–coverage program are compared to what would normally or ordinarily happen within the equivalent group in a larger population without the public intervention. The word generic means "relating to or characteristic of a whole group or class." If the program is addressed to children under seven in a specific municipality, the same category of children in the county, or in the nation might be used as the larger reference population. Generic controls uses data on the normal or typical development in a larger population for the same time period as the data from the specific smaller group covered by the program.

In several social and technical fields, public authorities routinely collect and process huge masses of data concerning developments in the whole country, or even broken down by counties and municipalities. Social scientists can rather easily retrieve information on death rates, birth rates, gender distribution, age cohorts, educational achievement, family stability, voting behavior, and the like. Global data is normally also available on, for instance, employment, housing construction, energy supply and use, air pollution, and financial developments. With care, these numbers may be used as generic controls.

A case provided by Rossi and Freeman (1985:279ff.; 1989:339ff.) is fluoridated water programs to reduce the occurrences of dental cavities. The approximately normal distribution of dental cavities in the United States population was well-known. When experiments with fluoridated water were launched in some communities, it was therefore possible to compare the frequency of cavities in these communities with the normal frequency in the population as a whole. Thanks to this, an approximate measure of the effects of the fluoridated water program was achieved, other things being equal.

From this we can see that generic controls implies the use of a comparison or control group. However, the comparison group is neither randomly selected nor matched.

Usually, hard–line evaluators stress that generic controls should be resorted to only under circumstances in which other types of controls are not feasible. They should be used with utmost caution, with intense scrutiny of whether they are equivalent to participants in every critical way.

Statistical Controls

In contrast with generic controls, statistical controls can be applied to full–coverage programs as well. The use of statistical controls is posited on the idea that the units of a single time series should be partitioned into subgroups in an attempt to keep potential external confounding factors under control. Partitioning ought to be done with respect to contingencies assumed to be influential on the outcome.

Let us assume that the Swedes have in fact purchased more energy–efficient cars since 1978. Let us further assume that, in computing this, the evaluators suspect that the increase is larger in some groups than in others. Persons buying cars for their own money are probably more susceptible to fuel use information than people purchasing on behalf of their organization for the purpose of leasing. Since the leasing of cars has increased during the period, the evaluators believe that they have unraveled a factor that has counteracted the Fuel Declaration. To test the leasing hypothesis, they must divide their total sample of persons into two categories, one for private cars and one for leased cars, and then pinpoint the development of automobile purchases in each group. Maybe it turns out that their hypothesis is true. Cars bought for private use are more and more energy efficient, while cars bought for lease have become larger and larger. Thanks to their use of statistical controls, the evaluators have found that the Fuel Declaration might have been particularly persuasive as far as private car buyers are concerned.

The evaluators might continue their efforts to keep extraneous confounding factors constant through the use of statistical controls. Income development might have impacted upon the purchases of cars. People who have raised their incomes might have bought bigger cars, while people who have sustained a decrease of income might have bought smaller cars. Again, the group who has purchased cars for private use is now divided into one subgroup with increased incomes and one with reduced incomes. A statistical analysis may show that both subgroups have bought more energy–efficient cars over the years, but that the subgroup who has sustained some income reduction in the period has been more inclined to do so. Thereby, the evaluators have shown that the Fuel Declaration might have had a particular effect on people who have bought cars for private use and who have sustained an income decrease.

In this fashion, the impact assessors may proceed further and further, dividing their material into smaller and smaller subgroups, until there are so few persons in each subgroup that continued partitioning would be statistically meaningless.

Reflexive Controls

The reflexive controls design differs from generic and statistical controls on the account that no contemporary reference case is used. Reflexive controls is a one–group design where the investigation group is taken to be its own control group. Preprogram scores serve as controls in relation to postprogram scores. The reflexive controls design is typically used when the program has been enacted across the board. There is no way then that evaluators can use a separate, contemporary control group of some kind, because the whole relevant population is in principle affected by the program. The rationale of reflexive controls has been succinctly put by Rossi and Freeman (1985:299):

> The essential justification for using a reflexive control design is that in some circumstances it is reasonable to believe that targets remain identical in relevant ways before and after participation. In other words, in such circumstances one can assume that without the intervention the preintervention and postintervention results scores would have been the same; hence, if any changes show up after the intervention, such changes would be directly attributable to the intervention (that is, net impact would equal gross impact).

Like all other hitherto outlined approaches, the reflexive controls design is a strategy for indicating what data should be collected in order to sustain an analysis of program effects, not a technical method for data collection or a technique for processing data already collected. In reflexive controls design, evaluator attention is singlemindedly focused on *one* group only—the group who is intended to be covered by the program—while variations in the target variable are measured (O=observation) on at least one occasion before and after the adoption of the program (X).

The reflexive controls design may assume several different shapes. Two of them will be somewhat elaborated here: Interrupted Time–Series Design and One–Group–Before–and–After Design. Both might be regarded as stepwise truncations of the Control Series Design, the strongest among the quasi-experimental strategies from a *ceteris paribus* perspective. The amputation idea should be obvious from figure 12.1.

In many cases, the whole group cannot be studied, not even with the One–Group–Before– and–After Design. Because of time or money constraints, for instance, it might be impossible to collect data for all of Sweden in order to illuminate the effects of a particular national regulation. In these cases, some samples must be drawn, or some cases must be selected. However, this does not mean that the evaluator has changed to some other design to solve the causality issue. The design to be used is a reflexive controls design. However, on top of the problems of handling the reflexive controls design proper, the evaluator will now also have some sampling problems.

FIGURE 12.1

Two Reflexive Controls Designs—Interrupted Time–Series and One-Group, Before-and-After—as Amputated Quasi Experiments

Design	Assign–ment	Preprogram observation	Program observation	Postprogram
Control Series Design				
Investigation Group	M	O_1 O_2 O_3	X	O_4 O_5 O_6
Comparison Group	M	O_1 O_2 O_3		O_4 O_5 O_6
Interrupted Time–Series Design				
Investigation Group		O_1 O_2 O_3	X	O_4 O_5 O_6
One-Group Before-and-After Design				
Investigation Group		O_1	X	O_2

M = assignment through matching
O = observation (measurement) of the result variable
X = program (policy, intervention, project, activity, treatment, input)

Source: The scheme is an elaboration of a figure in Riecken and Boruch 1974:98.

Interrupted Time–Series Design,
One–Group–Before–and–After–Design

The Interrupted Time–Series Design embodies repeated periodic measurements (O) on the same group over time. Some measurements must be taken before and some after the intervention. The purpose of the analysis is, of course, to infer whether the intervention (X) had any impact. If it did, we would expect the postprogram measures to be different from preprogram observations. The time series ought to show signs of an "interruption" somewhere after the program is introduced. Hence "Interrupted" in the designation.

The crucial idea is that the line of development observed in the preprogram scores should continue in approximately the same fashion in the postprogram measures, unless the program has intruded and influenced the expected development pattern. On the basis of preprogram measurements, impact assessors form an expectation concerning the probable postprogram scores should the program not have been installed. This counterfactual line of development is compared to the actual development and the difference might be imputed to the program. The longer the time period covered by preprogram measures, the larger the assessors' capacity to predict the general shape of the counterfactual trajectory and thereby our ability to ascertain the impact of the program.

Occasionally, research evaluators can safely predict what would have happened had the government not intervened. An evaluation of the Swedish government grants program to solar energy research maintained that the solar cells, solar collectors, heat storage facilities, and other technical innovations that had been developed must have resulted from the program. The justification of this statement was that the innovations were not competitive on the market in comparison to other methods of producing energy; therefore, they would never have been developed, had the grants program not been in existence (EFN Report 1985:13).

What does the Interrupted Time–Series Design involve in our running example of the Fuel Declaration program? Have the Swedes bought more fuel-efficient cars since the adoption of the program? Available data reveals that this has indeed been the case. While in 1978 the fuel use amounted to an average of 0.91 liters per ten kilometers, in 1979 it dropped to 0.90 and in 1982 to 0.85 liters per ten kilometers. The Declaration seems to have produced the intended effect.

This conclusion, however, is premature. The observed drop might be part of a longer trend toward more fuel-efficient vehicles. This has in fact also been the case. The longer trend seems to have started in 1973. The movement toward smaller cars was clearly discernible well before the guidelines were enacted in 1978. This supports the view that factors other than the Fuel Declaration have been effective. Obviously, the price rises in conjunction with the Arab Oil Embargo and the Ayatollah Khomeini crisis have been causative.

This illustrates the major weakness with reflexive controls. We are far from confident about the role of the public intervention. It might have had an impact. But some other changes—"extraneous confounding factors"-may have produced the deviation from the expected outcome in the postprogram measurements. In the Fuel Declaration case, it might have been a political crisis in the Middle East, a price increase in crude oil, or strong admonitions by political leaders on the importance of economizing on scarce energy resources. The time series on the development of car purchases provide no reliable clues about possible impacts of these extraneous confounding factors.

Yet, the Interrupted Time–Series Design offers certain hints at alternative explanations. Should a break in the trend occur a very long time after the intervention, we may argue that the program has not had any impact. If changes arise well before the institution of the program, the latter cannot be the cause. In addition, if the transformations took place in conjunction with changes in some other factor which we know usually influences the target dimensions, this may lead us to conclude that this other factor is probably the cause.

The reflexive controls designs, then, pinpoint the importance of acquiring a general picture of the nonintervention forces that might influence the result, in other words working with a good *theory of the intervention field*. If the intervention entails enticing consumers through information into buying more energy-efficient cars, then a theory of the intervention field would contain the most important factors influencing people's choice of new cars. It would also indicate how this influence occurs. Such a theory of the relevant intervention field is needed as a supplementary tool to reflexive controls designs.

Car purchases are probably influenced by the general growth of disposable income. The greater the increases in the standard of living and available income that people enjoy, the bigger the cars they will probably buy, at least up to a certain point. Another influential factor is fuel price development. Soaring fuel prices may prompt consumers to buy more energy-efficient cars. Furthermore, car purchasing is probably influenced by certain, very general societal changes. Two cars per family is a more and more common pattern. The second car bought is often smaller than the first, maybe due to the fact that the wives use this particular car more than the husbands and that women tend to prefer smaller and more versatile cars. Still another factor is that increasingly businesses buy cars and lease them to their executives and managers. This can lead to increased purchases of larger cars. These are examples of contingencies to be included in a theory of the program field concerning purchasing of new cars.

In controlling for nonprogrammatic, extraneous confounding factors, we leave the field of design for data collection and enter the area of statistical data processing methods. The Interrupted Time–Series Design is turned into the Statistical Controls Design.

Finally, a warning against exaggerated interpretations of reflexive and statistical controls designs is warranted. Both designs are susceptible to threats.

First, the cause of the change may be the mischievous Hawthorne effect. If the measurement scores are drawn from obtrusive sources like interviews, the interviewees might understand that energy-efficient cars are something important. This insight might induce them to pay greater attention to fuel use than otherwise until the next interview situation. This, in turn, might induce them to change their behavior in ways they otherwise would not have done.

Second, variations may be due to infelicitous modifications of the investigation group. The drop-out rate of individuals may have been greater during postmeasurements than in premeasurements. And it might have been biased. A large or biased drop-out between the first and the last measurement may have resulted in the registered change.

Third, the measuring instrument may have been adjusted during the investigation. If the evaluator discovered and eliminated weaknesses in the original interrogation battery, this calibration may have produced the deviating results. Adjustments may lead to pseudo-changes, difficult to distinguish from real effects (Riecken and Boruch 1974:107).

The Interrupted Time–Series Design is commendable in situations where target variables are highly volatile and prone to change. On the other hand, when target variables are stable over time, and the measures regulated by the programs are relatively dramatic, extended historical perspectives are not necessary. Then, the simpler One–Group–Before–and–After Design with one preprogram and one postprogram measurement can replace the Interrupted Time–Series Design.

An imagined evaluation of the Swedish Deciduous Forest Act may illustrate my contention. This Act proscribes that specific deciduous forests particularly in Scania, Halland, and other Southern provinces, must be saved for the future. While clearfelling is not forbidden, the Act mandates that property owners plant new deciduous trees—like beeches, oaks, and elms—in the area after harvesting. The evaluator may do one measurement before the clearfelling—for instance, by taking photos—and one five years after the clearfelling to check if new trees have been planted.

Neither the Interrupted Time–Series Design, the One–Group–Before–and–After Design, nor any other design for that matter is necessarily connected with specific kinds of data, for instance, statistical social indicators, records on targets served, or subjective measures of people's satisfactions, aspirations, and frustrations. Occasionally, photography might be an appropriate method to capture configurative wholes, qualities, and amenities. In her investigation into the implementation of the environmental clause in the Swedish Forestry Act, Katarina Eckerberg and her colleagues (1987:35) took pictures of forest areas before they were harvested to have some baseline data against which to compare the situation after clearfelling had taken place.

From the controls perspective, both reflexive and statistical designs suffer from obvious weaknesses. Yet, combined with statistical analysis based on a sound theory of the program field, reflexive controls designs produce the most felicitous combination of usefulness to public policy and methodological rigor of all data collection designs hitherto presented. The evaluator can escape from cumbersome technicalities involved in finding an equivalent reference group. There is no need to uphold the enactment of a full-fledged program for years in order to finish the randomized or matched experiments.

Shadow Controls

In shadow controls designs, the net impact of a program is estimated by people with special insights. "Shadow" in this case means "imperfect and faint representation," or "imitation of something." Instead of actually measuring the counterfactual case, the evaluator asks others to estimate it. If preprogram and postprogram target variable data are available, people with special insights are asked to reckon what would have happened had the program not been installed and what the program actually has effected. On some occasions, cognizant people are asked to estimate the preprogram and postprogram scores as well.

Shadow controls may be divided into expert assessments, program–administrator judgments, and participants' judgments. I prefer the expression "expert assessment" to the Rossi and Freeman locution "connoisseurial assessment," because connoisseurs–persons with tastes quite different from the average consumer—are used mostly to appraise the value of some unduly intricate phenomenon, not causal linkages between contingencies. On this account, expert assessments are also different from the peer reviews presented in chapter 3, because the most important contribution of the latter is the application of criteria of merit and standards of performance, not estimates of causal relationships.

Expert assessment involves the use of external authorities to produce the counterfactual case. Those familiar with the field and the typical results of intervention projects in the area are asked to draw on that background to estimate whether a specific actual outcome is greater or less than what is ordinarily the outcome of successful programs in that particular domain.

Clearly, the power of expert judgments depends heavily on the general state of knowledge in the substantive fields relevant to the program. In a field where the knowledge of how to achieve a particular outcome is quite advanced, an expert's appraisal may be relatively accurate. If little is known about an area, an expert's assessment of a project's effectiveness may not be worth more than that of any other person.

Secondly, the quality of the estimates also depends on the choice of experts. An expert ought to be knowledgeable about the area in question and should have demonstrated his knowledge in actual accomplishments. Experts should also be familiar with the findings of other evaluations of similar programs.

Typically, a well–known expert (or a team of experts) in a relevant field is hired as a consultant and sent to visit program sites to examine closely how the program works in order to write a report summarizing her experiences and to render assessments. Visiting experts may examine project records, observe the project in operation, and conduct interviews with participants, talk to project managers, staff, and other officials, conduct interviews with former participants. They may even be participant observers themselves and take part in the program. Expert assessment means the exercise of qualitative social research.

Rossi and Freeman (1989:368f.) have listed a number of data sources and questions to be posed when these data sources are consulted. On the basis of their list, I have constructed the overview in figure 12.2 on data sources and questions that experts ought to consider in order to provide estimates of program impact.

In *program–administrator judgments,* street–level bureaucrats or program managers are solicited for their views of what would have happened in case there had been no program. The merit of this approach is that administrators in general have the deepest knowledge of the program. The problem is whether administrators can take tentative, uncommitted stances toward their programs.

The third possibility, *clients' judgments,* is to ask the addressees to assess what would have happened to them if the program had not existed. For practical reasons, only a select group of addressees will be asked, because all addressees cannot be approached. Impressions of program participants are likely to be grounded in extensive program experience. On the other hand, they have a tendency exaggerate program impacts in order to safeguard their continued existence.

Difference between Shadow Controls and Other Controls

In what way are shadow controls different from other controls, for example, statistical controls in the form of the Interrupted Time–Series Design? I shall briefly delve into this matter, using expert assessment as a case.

Most expositors of expert assessment as a specimen of shadow controls agree that experts ought to collect information and judgments upon which to ground their appraisals. They may contact other knowledgeable people to amass data and listen to verdicts. They may bolster their arguments with statistics. It is difficult to see the difference between, say, the use of reflexive or statistical controls in the hands of an experienced expert evaluator, and the use of shadow controls based

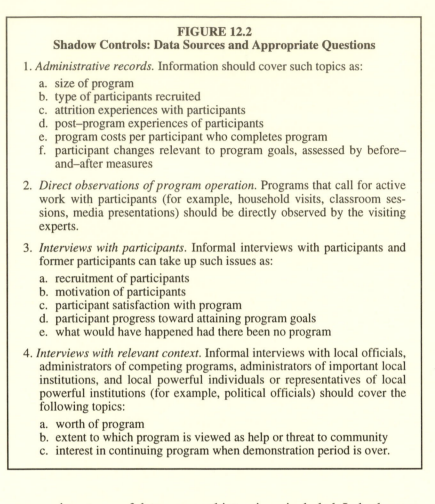

FIGURE 12.2
Shadow Controls: Data Sources and Appropriate Questions

1. *Administrative records.* Information should cover such topics as:
   a. size of program
   b. type of participants recruited
   c. attrition experiences with participants
   d. post–program experiences of participants
   e. program costs per participant who completes program
   f. participant changes relevant to program goals, assessed by before–and–after measures

2. *Direct observations of program operation.* Programs that call for active work with participants (for example, household visits, classroom sessions, media presentations) should be directly observed by the visiting experts.

3. *Interviews with participants.* Informal interviews with participants and former participants can take up such issues as:
   a. recruitment of participants
   b. motivation of participants
   c. participant satisfaction with program
   d. participant progress toward attaining program goals
   e. what would have happened had there been no program

4. *Interviews with relevant context.* Informal interviews with local officials, administrators of competing programs, administrators of important local institutions, and local powerful individuals or representatives of local powerful institutions (for example, political officials) should cover the following topics:
   a. worth of program
   b. extent to which program is viewed as help or threat to community
   c. interest in continuing program when demonstration period is over.

upon various types of data, personal interviews included. In both cases, an expert passes a judgment, based on many sources of information.

The only major difference I can see is that in expert assessment the specialist himself must personally assume responsibility for the correctness of the control case. In generic, statistical, and reflexive controls, it is in principle the data that speaks, not the evaluator.

Shadow Controls are Practically Useful

Advocates of randomized experimentation and statistical analysis have a low opinion of expert assessments, even in public policy evaluation. If not entirely discarded, they are regarded as the absolute last resort, should experimental, generic, statistical and reflexive controls turn out to be unfeasible. They are viewed as the weakest version of randomized experimentation, not offering any additional merits in and of themselves.

This contrasts starkly to the views of qualitatively oriented naturalistic evaluators, who regard stakeholder conceptions, beliefs, reasons, and judgments to be the most important types of data for public policy evaluation.

On many occasions, shadow controls are the only practical alternative available, and not even quantitatively oriented economists abstain from using them. In a Swedish study on the impact of government price regulations on individual businesses, Lars Jonung (1984:149), a noted economist and advisor to the former Liberal–Conservative government headed by Carl Bildt, asked the businesses themselves what their profit level would have been had there been no regulations. The counterfactual alternative was ascertained through the use of shadow controls, obviously in this case, client's judgments.

Supporters of experimentation and statistical controls place little reliance on program–administrator assessments. Naturally, they admit that administrators have the best knowledge of the program, its implementation and its functioning in the field, since they may have worked with the problems for years. However, they do not expect program administrators to apply the appropriate attitude of skepticism toward their own work. Administrators are self–serving and want to put their projects in the best possible light. Rossi and Freeman (1989:371) argue that "properly conducted impact assessment takes as its guiding hypothesis that the project has no effects, a stance that runs exactly counter to the principle that should guide the administration of a project—namely, that the intervention does have important effects on participants. To expect ordinary mortals to hold both hypotheses simultaneously is unrealistic."

In addition, it is also argued that administrators with day–to–day responsibilities for program conduct simply cannot devote the necessary time and care to an impact assessment. They literally have no time to make qualified assessments.

The same views also pertain to clients' judgments. Clients do not have the breadth of experience nor the perceptual competence necessary to pass reasonable judgments concerning the counterfactual case.

There is also an obvious risk that they will be partial in favor of or against the program.

Evaluators of a more qualitative bent, on the other hand, have a marked penchant for program–administrator as well as client judgments. Because evaluation in their opinion is to some extent a political enterprise, it is important that all pertinent stakeholders are offered the opportunity to participate and give their opinions.

Shadow controls cannot ensure watertight results. Yet they should not be discarded. In public policy evaluation, there are often no other options available. Some knowledge of the counterfactual case, however crude and weak, is better than no knowledge at all. Even shadow controls may provide a picture of what an intervention has achieved.

Note

1. Actually, even one type of quasi experiment is a naturalistic design to the extent that it studies what happened to the permanent program and compares this ex post facto to a matched control group.

13

Process Evaluation and Implementation Theory

"A single governmental strategy may involve the complex and interrelated activities of several levels of governmental bureaus and agencies, private organizations, professional associations, interest groups, and clientele populations. How can this profusion of activities be controlled and directed? This question is at the heart of what has come to be known . . . as the "implementation problem."
—Eugene Bardach

The extent to which government interventions contribute to measured results is central to public sector evaluation. Occasionally, evaluations ought to aspire to even higher ambitions. They should try to answer why outcomes do or do not stem from the measures enacted. Following the lead of Urban Dahllöf and several other scholars, I wish to emphasize strongly that the evaluation of at least established interventions should have this extended explanatory ambition. Apart from data on output, outcomes, and general intervention impact on results, evaluations should include more specific information on why installed interventions have succeeded or failed. The evaluation of vintage measures ought to be a theoretical enterprise in the meaning of trying to explain in more detail why the measures have conditioned the impacts or not. I shall call this process evaluation.

General Features of Process Evaluation

Ideally, process evaluation attempts to trace all kinds of intervention consequences, including intended effects, null effects, perverse effects, and side effects whether advertent or inadvertent. Yet the distinguishing feature of process analysis is the emphasis on the diverse explanations of whatever impacts are under focus.

While part of the impact problem—number six in the Eight Problems Approach to Evaluation—the explanatory ambition of process evaluation implies a broader, configurative conception of causative factors than so far discussed. Processes conditioning policy outcomes are complicated networks of interacting causes. Process evaluation seeks to establish a whole pattern of causal interdependencies. It requests, among other things, that effects of processes between intervention instigation and intervention results will be probed and clarified. Furthermore, consequences of intervention surroundings are ascertained, factors operative during the formation of the intervention included.

Process analyses concentrate on evaluands in their natural political, administrative, social, and geographic surroundings, will be executed in close interaction with evaluation commissioners and potential users, and will employ hard statistical data, surveys, and questionnaires, as well as information produced through qualitative data collection techniques like in–depth interviews, textual analysis, and direct observation through site visits (see chapter 9 on monitoring).

In addition, the imaginative process evaluator may use an interactive approach to data collection. Suppose the twentieth interviewee out of a planned sample of fifty comes up with an idea about some unexpected and highly deleterious side effect. On the orthodox survey pattern, one would continue, using the same interview form, through the rest of the sample of respondents. In process evaluation, one may want to alter the form so as to include an explicit question on this point. Of course, one can no longer report the results of the survey as entirely based on a sample of fifty, with respect to the new question. However, one may very well be able to turn up another fifteen people who verify the side effect in question, when explicitly asked about it. In many cases, that result is much more important than salvaging the scientific quality of the survey. It also points to another feature of the evaluation situation, namely, the desirability of time sequencing of interviews. Hence, one should try to avoid using a single mass mailing, a common practice in survey research; by using sequential mailings, one can examine the responses for possible modifications of the instrument.

A second scientific taboo that may be broken in process evaluation concerns preselected samples. If the evaluators discover during interviewing that a distinct unit of analysis is especially interesting because, for instance, in this unit implementation has turned into protracted administrative conflicts between various participating actors, then they may include more of this type of unit in the sample. The design is varied en route as appropriate. This is called cascading, emergent, or rolling designs.

History is crucial to process evaluation. The things to be explained are put within long–range, broad historical explanation perspectives. Process evaluations are geared to eliciting holistic knowledge of intervention formation, intervention implementation and general intervention setting as part of an extensive explanatory approach.

Process evaluations have theoretical import. They can make contributions to theory building on governance. Process evaluation will also be useful in political and administrative action contexts. Because information on outcomes is supplemented with data on how outputs, intervening processes, and the surrounding situation in interaction with each other have effected the outcomes, the evaluation will be of greater practical value for modifying and streamlining the intervention processes. This presupposes, it is often argued, that the explanation concerns variables that can be manipulated, that is, determinants that can feasibly be changed. Structural phenomena deeply imbedded in the fabric of society are of less immediate interest for practical purposes, since they may prove impossible to influence, at least in the short run. The position taken here, however, is that process evaluation should not be viewed in the short time frame of instrumental utility. Process evaluation should contribute also to basic knowledge, and for this purpose broader explanatory approaches will have a given function to fulfill.

Six Broad Factors that Might Influence Intervention Outcomes

The basic issue of explanatory process evaluation can be formulated in two ways: (1) Why is it that actual results—inside and outside the target area—of public interventions may differ from the policy makers' initial expectations?; and (2) Why is it that the desired outcomes are brought about without the aid of the interventions, or even in spite of the interventions? To explicate, what factors is it reasonable to search for in order to explain agreements—or discrepancies—between official intentions and actual results—here limited to outcomes?

Some important factors that may explain outcomes of public interventions are arranged in figure 13.1.

Figure 13.1 enumerates possible contingencies—explanatory factors, independent variables, determinants—that might impinge on policy, program, project, and other intervention outcomes. Influence

---

FIGURE 13.1
Explanatory Factors in Process Evaluation

A. Historical Background of the Intervention
1. Direction of proposed change
2. Political support
3. Size of proposed change
4. Level of attention
5. Symbolic politics
6. Participation of affected interests

B. Intervention Design
1. Clarity (linguistic obscurity, several options for action)
2. Technical complexity
3. Validity of intervention theory

C. Implementation
1. National agencies: comprehension, capability, willingness (public choice, mismatch, capture)
2. Formal intermediaries
3. Street–level bureaucracy: coping strategies, capture, mismatch
4. Addressee participation

D. Addressee Response
1. Comprehension, capability, willingness
2. Formative moments
3. Zealots
4. Camouflage
5. Resistance, free riders

E. Other Government Interventions, Other Government Agencies

F. Issue Networks and Other Environments
1. Support of sovereigns after formal instigation of mandate
2. Support of other actors external to formal administration
3. Mass media
4. Changes in the target area

from one contingency may well occur through interaction with others. Actually, one contingency might become operative only in combination with other facilitative contingencies. For instance, political support in the form of a broad partisan front (A2) may produce a fuzzy reform (B1), which in turn may affect the national agencies' comprehension of it or their willingness to implement it (C1), which in the end will affect the results. For this reason, the resolute process evaluator must conduct complicated configurational analyses. However, these complicated patterns of interaction are not spelled out in figure 13.1.

Finally, readers must be mindful that explanations involving administrative action are circumstantial. Universal explanations, valid for all times and regardless of surroundings, simply do not and cannot exist in the social world.

Now, let me present the various explanatory factors one by one.

Historical Background of the Intervention

Delving into the legislative history of ongoing or terminated interventions may seem superfluous when the purpose is to study their impacts. It would be reasonable, it seems, to start with the intervention as it was at the moment of its instigation and follow up what happened thereafter. Until quite recently, this was also the received wisdom in the research community. As a consequence of the division of labor between the subdisciplines of political studies and policy studies, potential connections between policy formation and implementation— and thus policy outcomes—were never investigated. Political scientists specializing in policymaking and legislative processes rarely showed any interest in what happens after the laws are passed, and policy researchers focusing on implementation and evaluation typically restricted their interests to issues of policy design and policy implementation (Winter 1990:24).

However, as pointed out by Winter (1990:23ff.), Mayntz (Winter 1990:24), Lundqvist (1980), Elmore, et al. (1986) and others, if evaluators really want to understand how interventions and their implementation have an influence on the outcomes, they cannot just start by looking at intervention design. Forces operating in the policy–formation phase may well explain why certain outcomes obtained in the field.

Six subfactors in the legislative history of interventions carry special weight: if the established intervention is in line with or constitutes a clear break with previously pursued policies, particularly in the pertinent functional policy sector; if the reform was adopted with strong political support, under political conflict or consensus and what the partisan and corporatist constellation looked like; if the change was intended to be huge or minute; if the proposed intervention was accorded scanty or extensive attention during its formation; if the intervention was seriously intended or if it entailed traits of symbolic politics; and finally if those central, regional, and local public agencies, private intermediaries, and addressees who would be affected by the intervention actually participated in the framing of it.

The *direction of proposed change* may influence implementation, service delivery, addressee response, and, as a consequence, outcomes. Should the envisaged change point in a direction different from the one public officials and recipients are acquainted with, it will become more difficult to carry out.

If some political ideology dominates the executive and legislative branches of government for a substantial period of time, civil servants will become used to working for certain types of people, who take an interest in certain types of problems. Ingrained patterns of thought and unreflected habits of action will ensue. If then an ideological shift occurs among those in power, for example, through a landslide public election, the new formal power wielders will discover that bureaucrats are not easily swayed in the new direction. Adjustment difficulties may develop into a major obstacle to implementation.

The notion of bureaucratic inertia has played a major role in early socialist thought on the issue of assuming power in the bourgeois state. If the socialists come to power through ordinary elections, civil servants, used to liberal, market-oriented policies, would passively or actively obstruct the new rulers. Socialists would meet great difficulties in implementing their reforms and intentions. In the long run, they might surrender and become prisoners of the bourgeois state.

The inertia hypothesis has also undergone some empirical testing. In their book *The Policy Process in the Modern Capitalist State,* Christopher Ham and Michael Hill mention Seymour M. Lipset's study of the difficulties that the Socialist Party in Saskatchewan found in implementing its policies once it acquired power (1984:56f.). The reason for this was that civil servants had problems in adjusting to markedly different policies, used as they were to serving more conservative governments. Writes Lipset:

Trained in the traditions of a laissez-faire government and belonging to conservative social groups, the civil service contributes significantly to the social inertia which blunts the changes a new radical government can make. Delay in initiating reforms means that the new government becomes absorbed in the process of operating the old institutions. The longer the new government delays in making changes, the more responsible it becomes for the old practices and the harder it is to make the changes it originally desired to institute.

The thesis about the direction of change may be widened to include any new group of political masters who turn their attentions to new issues and problems. Ham and Hill intimate that the comparatively radical Conservative Thatcher government, which captured power in the United Kingdom in 1979, had problems with reorienting the civil servants.

A possible Swedish case might be the Nonsocialist governments that came to power in 1976 after forty-four years of almost uninterrupted Social Democratic rule. Their difficulties in reorienting the bureaucracy is a major theme in analyses of this period between 1976 and 1982 (Rydén 1983).

There are also cases to the contrary. When the Labour party assumed power in Great Britain in 1945, its leaders suspected that the British civil service would sabotage Labour's plans to expand the welfare state and nationalize major industries. For most of its members had been hired by Conservative administrations, and recruited from among the graduates of Oxford and Cambridge universities, thought to be bastions of Tory privilege and seedbeds of Tory opinions. Yet the supposedly reactionary British civil servants faithfully carried out the new policies (Wilson 1989:50f.).

The outcomes will be influenced by the *political support* for the intervention in connection with its instigation or its changes. Programs inaugurated under partisan and corporatist consensus are probably more easily translated into practical results than programs surrounded by conflicts.

There are two important conflict situations. In the first, the intervention is instituted by the majority against the express will of the opposition. The majority may have tried to reach a bargaining solution but failed. It may also just have pushed the intervention through without paying any heed to opposing viewpoints. In the second situation, the intervention is massaged into a compromise between the original supporters and its opponents, whereby a majority is secured.

If adopted under political consensus, a program will probably be implemented more faithfully than if instigated after political conflicts that have not been resolved through compromise. We may assume that the political force behind a program will be weaker if the political parties or the major interest organizations disagreed, and continue to disagree about it. Conflict creates uncertainty about the future of a program, which will probably affect national agencies and other institutions in the implementation stage. Even program addressees may be influenced by political and corporatist disagreement.

Size is important, even in public policy implementation. The greater the change proposed, the more difficult the implementation, *ceteris paribus*. Small, incremental reforms are probably more satisfactorily carried out than revolutionary transformations. Van Meter and Van Horn (1975) suggest: "The probability of effective implementation is inversely related to the extent of envisaged departure from the status quo ante."

The *level of attention* accorded to the intervention by its proponents in the formation process may influence the results. According to Søren Winter (1990:8), who has generated this hypothesis, most actors are only part–time participants in policymaking endeavors since they are constantly haunted by competing claims for attention from other private and public roles. Some participants will disappear entirely and newcomers will enter the stage. Furthermore, their level of attention is affected by the length of the decision–making period, the number of participants, and the amount of competing issues on the agenda. Attention to a program is also affected by the way it is grouped into larger reform packages. In sum, the attention hypothesis suggests that the less the attention, the weaker the implementation and the results.

In a case study of the Danish Disablement Insurance Tribunal, Winter found that limited attention explains why the reform failed to achieve the goals of speeding up decision making and cutting administrative costs, while preserving a uniform decision–making practice. "The decentralization of the Tribunal was not an isolated reform but only a small part of a massive legislative package concerning the entire social welfare system. Other issues in this larger package attracted most of the attention of the many participants in the policy–formation process. Though this process lasted for 13 years, the decision to decentralize the Tribunal was given only a few minutes of debate."

A fifth component of the larger historical background factor to influence results is *symbolic politics*. Symbolic politics means that the intervention is inaugurated for other purposes than to attain substantive results. It might have been enacted primarily to give an impression of being concerned, without necessarily being so (Lundquist 1987:127f.). "In this sense policy may become a substitute for action, to demonstrate that something is being done without actually tackling the real problem . . . governments or policy–makers wish to be seen to be responsive, without necessarily really wanting to take responsibility for the intervention" (Barrett and Fudge 1981:276).

Policymakers may want to be regarded as being firmly in charge of a situation, to satisfy party opinion or strengthen their own party leadership, to keep party membership in line, to secure votes in general elections, or to facilitate government coalitions. The purpose can also be to thwart the morale of the membership of competing parties, to erode their strength in general elections, or to weaken their penchant for forming government coalitions. For these and other reasons, policymakers may find it advantageous to pretend an interest in substantive policy execution. For symbolic purposes are served by the fact that interventions are instigated, and not necessarily that they are actually implemented. Naturally, agency officials, low–level operators, and other official actors may perceive the symbolic content and devote less energy to implementation than they otherwise would have done (Sætren 1983; March and Olsen 1976).

Price controls are often perpetrated by symbolic concerns. According to established economic theory and empirical research, price regulations cannot come to grips with skyrocketing prices in order to reduce inflation. Yet they are resorted to time and again. This is due to the fact that they are cheap to introduce, and very popular with the common man. They can be instantly enacted, which makes the government seem forceful and strong. However, they are often inaugurated for short–term political motives, not for the purpose of long–range reductions in prices and inflation (Jonung 1984:215ff.).

The symbolic politics subfactor is an important one, because it is at the heart of the political power aspect of public sector activities. Actually, one of the fundamental rationales of evaluation in the first place is that substantive interventions are used to strengthen somebody's power base. References to goals, and visions of the future, are used not as lodestars for actual action, but as instruments of legitimizing power. Disclosing the power politics uses of substantive programs is a major task of researchlike evaluation.

Some keen observers have carried the symbolic politics point of view quite far. Donald Campbell, to take one, has stated that "most of what governments want in the name of 'reforms' and 'new programs' are symbolic gestures designated to indicate government awareness of problems and sympathetic intentions rather than serious efforts to achieve social change" (Shadish et al. 1991:147). However, symbolic motives usually do not come in splendid isolation. Policy reforms are often prompted by a mixture of strategic and substantive aims. This could mean that, however strong the symbolic urge, the substantive motivation may be taken seriously by program management, program staff and street–level operators and implemented by the letter.

The intervention–as–symbolism factor may be at work at the agency level as well. Take the Fuel Declaration case again. The Board for Consumer Policies had elaborated on this idea for some time as a piece of consumer information policy. Then the 1973 Oil Crisis came along. The Swedish national government was desperately looking for ideas on how to propel energy conservation. The Board for Consumer Policies jumped on the energy train, as it were, finessing the Fuel Declaration into a piece of energy conservation legislation in order to have it passed. In all of its evaluations, however, the Board for Consumer Policies has acted as though the Fuel Declaration were part of consumer policy, measuring only the content of the information but paying no attention to the eventual energy outcomes. These evaluations in turn might have influenced the way the program was implemented, which in turn may have had some leverage on program outcome.

Participation in the process leading up to intervention adoption may well influence on intervention results. If *affected stakeholders* are allowed to contribute ideas and arguments in the formation of the reform, it will be rendered a legitimacy that in turn will facilitate implementation and compliance. A program formed through a process where the public authority that will later be charged with its implementation has been allowed to participate will probably be more faithfully and effectively implemented than programs adopted above the head of the pertinent authority. The extreme case is when the agency itself has initiated the reform and lobbied for its adoption. Evidently, such reforms will be more easily carried out (Scheirer 1981).

Similarly, the participatory aspect concerns affected parties other than the national agency, such as regional bodies, local implementing agencies, private intermediaries, and clients. It should be noted that intermediaries, local authorities, and clients often are represented by their interest organizations. If for instance client organizations have pushed hard for a program, it will be more acceptable to them than if they had not participated at all in the formation stage. This will probably decrease potential opposition, increase legitimacy, and facilitate compliance.

Now, we will leave the historical background of the public intervention and proceed to the second main component of the implementation theory: intervention design.

Intervention Design

Most important among the intervention design components are clarity, technical complexity, and the validity of the intervention theory.

Clarity is a momentous intervention factor that may account for outcomes. If clarity is the life and blood of science and scholarship, obscurity is at the heart of politics. Lack of clarity often takes the form of obscure goals (Edwards III and Sharkansky 1978:297ff.; Nakamura and Smallwood 1980:35ff.; Van Horn and Van Meter 1977:108ff.). Obscurity makes it difficult for implementing officials and addressees to form a correct picture of what policies are designed to achieve; consequently, they cannot exactly pinpoint discrepancies between objectives and outcomes in order to strengthen execution and compliance. Obscurity allows particularly officials but also addressees the discretion to make additions and subtractions to the intervention as originally conceived.

That policy mandates occasionally contain nothing but bundles of indeterminate and diffuse exhortations is no surprise. But it is one task of public policy evaluation to clarify what such fuzziness is about. It is fruitful to distinguish between *linguistic obscurity* on the one hand and obscurity, which may be linguistically clear but consists of *several options for action.*

Linguistic obscurity, in turn, consists of either indeterminate words or unclear priorities. *Indeterminate words* involve ambiguity and vagueness. *Unclear priorities* imply that two or more goals are provided but without any indication of what the priority among them ought to be.

The Swedish Nuclear Power Stipulation Act offered a couple of

FIGURE 13.2
Policy Obscurity

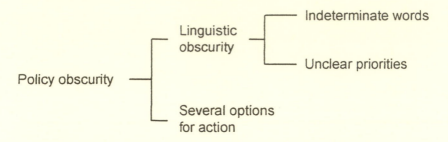

examples of *indeterminate words*. Promulgated by the Liberal–Conservative parliamentary majority in 1977, the central element of the law was the requirement that prior to the fueling of each nuclear power plant not approved for operation before 8 October 1976, the operator must:

> 1. . . . show how and where the final deposition of the highly radioactive waste resulting from reprocessing can be effected with absolute safety, or . . . 2. show how and where the spent but not reprocessed nuclear fuel can be finally stored with absolute safety (Sahr 1985:90).

What was meant by the key formulation "absolute safety"? The so-called Special Statement of Intent in the government bill maintained that the phrase indicated "very strong safety requirements," for which the point of departure must be that the highly radioactive waste from reprocessing and the spent fuel not being reprocessed must be separated from all life. The Parliamentary Committee on Business Affairs also quoted this statement. However, then the Committee advanced an argument that resembles an Indian rope trick. First, the Committee declared that the term "absolute safety" was an adequate expression of the very strict safety requirements that were necessary. But then the Committee denied what it had just said by adding a formulation with classical associations: "that an outright Draconian application of the absolute safety requirement is not intended is obvious from the just presented quotation from the special statement of intent."

The absolute safety requirement was intended to be very strict but it should not be too strictly applied. In a nutshell, this was the content of the Committee's acrobatic reasoning on the radioactive waste issue. The sharply honed formulations were designed to conceal a blatant contradiction. The government did and did not embrace the principle that highly radioactive waste from nuclear reactors must be stored with absolute safety.

The political rationale behind this semantic exercise was to reach a formula enabling the deeply divided three–party government to continue in power. Saving the government was more important than issuing a clear law. One government member, the Center party, wanted to disband nuclear energy, while the other two, the Liberals and the Conservatives, wanted to expand nuclear energy. At the same time, after a forty-four–year-long period of Social Democratic governments, the Nonsocialist parties one year earlier had finally been able to form a government. The new, unique government thought it could not resign after only one year. To save political face, the sole possibility was to cover up the disagreement on nuclear power behind massive linguistic smoke screens. Unclear language permitted the different supporters to attach their own different meanings to the program, while giving the general public a facade of accord (Vedung 1979). Diffuse language was used to conceal disagreement.

Unclear priorities ensue when interventions embody several objectives, occasionally even catalogues of objectives. The program text may suggest that the chief goal must be weighed against several other, potentially conflicting goals, but there is no indication how this counterpoise should occur. Goal catalogues quite often occur within the frame of a single program. However, it is equally common that two or more separate programs contradict each other or that the policies in one functional area counteract policies in another. This latter problem will be dealt with below under the rubric Other Government Interventions, Other Government Agencies. As a result, it becomes impossible to reveal the overall purpose of the intervention. Enforcement officials cannot decide through a neutral act of interpretation which goal should take precedence in competitive situations. This provides them with a broad latitude of discretion.

Catalogues of coveted states of affairs in regulatory mandates constitute a special case. In October, 1985, the simple clause on energy conservation, introduced in 1975 in article 136 of the Swedish Building Act, was framed as follows:

> Creation and allocation of industrial and similar activities of importance to the conservation of energy, wood fiber resources, and the country's collected land and water resources must be approved by the government.

According to documents from the legislative history of the clause, the permit-granting authority must balance energy conservation against economization on wood fiber resources, and conservation of the country's collected land and water supplies. They also indicated that goals other than the three conservation objectives should be taken into consideration such as "societal goals which are important in national land use planning, including conservation of scarce natural resources, high and stable employment, regional balance, and economic growth."[1] Environmental goals should also be considered.

To sum up, conservation of energy, wood resources, and the country's collected land and water resources should be balanced against each other and against other social objectives such as the conservation of scarce resources, high and stable employment, regional balance, economic growth, and environmental values. Yet it is never clarified how to create this counterpoise among the different objectives. This means it is impossible to know exactly what outcome the governing coalition wanted to achieve.

Some goals were probably contradictory. From an energy conservation point of view, the best thing would be to relocate all Swedish industry and, consequently, the entire Swedish population to the southern, warmer part of the country. However, this would be outrageous with respect to regional balance and maybe also conservation of scarce natural resources.

The obscurity that I have called *several options for action* does not manifest itself by definition as impenetrable verbal smokescreens, but emerges at least through a close reading. Often, it is probably the result of a political compromise to the effect that the program will contain at least two options for action for higher or lower implementing agencies. The main alternative may be that the implementers must act in a certain way, but that it is not compulsory to do so but that they can do the other way around. A paradigm case is the so–called land stipulation (*markvillkoret*) in the Swedish Housing Financing Ordinance 1974–1991 (*bostadsfinansieringsförordningen*), which mandated the municipalities to provide the land on which the housing constructors wanted to build residences; at the same time the municipalities were not mandated to do so but were allowed to exempt the housing constructors from the land stipulation (Vedung 1993:100ff.—"the Fox Den Principle," "determinate indeterminateness").

Why is public policy language married to obscurity? One reason is reasons of state. To quote George Orwell (1970:166f): "The great enemy of clear language is insincerity. When there is a gap between one's real and one's declared aims, one turns as it were instinctively to long words and exhausted idioms, like a cuttlefish squirting out ink." Policy obscurity is often intentional and tied to political power games in a democratic system of government. However, obscurity may also ensue because of time restraints or paucity of pertinent knowledge. Some important sources of intentional obscurity and particularly linguistic manipulations are presented in figure 13.3.

Advertent program haziness may stem from power games among leading political actors. Hoping to *conceal discord,* decision–makers rally behind hazy formulations to offer the general public a facade of accord and unity. This may be the case where no clear majority exists for a specific approach or where partners in a coalition government, deeply split on a particular issue, want to get the matter off the agenda for the time being in order to continue governing together.

The second motivation for intentional obscurity or more properly linguistic fuzziness springs from a desire to *conceal accord.* Politics makes strange bedfellows. Sometimes, elected officials want to cloak damaging unanimity. They cannot officially acknowledge agreement with their traditional antagonists, even though full unity on the issues is at hand. Rather they cover agreement with a noise of vague formulations, in order to avoid criticism for guilt by association.

Often, intentional obscurity ensues because some decison–maker wants to *cover up inopportune motivations* and hide real agendas. On occasion, Social Democrats shun to set their action proposals in a Socialist perspective or bolster them with Socialist arguments, because this would scare the voters away. Similarly, Conservatives do not speak with high–pitched voices about ultimate aims of privatizations, but rather emphasize short–term efficiency goals. Obscurity is used as a cover for sinister purposes.

Still another obscurity may result from *lack of time* and *paucity of*

FIGURE 13.3
Motives for Public Policy Obscurity

I	Obscurity to Conceal Discord (Disunity)
II	Obscurity to Conceal Accord (Unity)
III	Obscurity to Conceal Inopportune Motivations
IV	Obscurity Due to Lack of Time and Knowledge

knowledge. Political officials cannot muster enough time, energy, and skills to penetrate carefully all the many issues that simultaneously compete for their attention. In addition, decision–makers usually come and go; particular persons may be involved only for shorter periods of time. It is impossible for them to collect and master the technical knowledge necessary to frame directives providing unequivocal recommendations for action in each singular, future situation. Realizing this, formal decision–makers may issue general policy mandates— regulatory statutes, framework laws—providing broad discretionary powers to the regulatory agencies to issue specific rules and norms. Often, the decisions on rules in these agencies are preceded by negotiations between the regulators and the trade associations most closely affected by a prospective norm. This is the prevalent regulatory procedure in advanced Western democracies in matters concerning public health, work environment, land use, housing construction, and consumer protection. In these cases, policy indeterminateness shifts the responsibility for issuing specific rules from formal decision–makers to formal implementers and affected interest organizations (West 1985).

Apparently, administration in these cases must be considered a creative activity, an innovative enterprise, an exercise in continuous problem solving. It must be regarded as extended policy formation, not machinelike execution of preestablished goals and decisions.

The program's *technical complexity* may influence its outcomes. The complexity-simplicity dimension, the second component of the program design contingency, is a property of the set of norms that always accompany policy instruments. A highly technical program will be more difficult to understand and consequently more difficult to implement than a nontechnical, simple one. Technical complexity is different from obscurity, since a program may be very clear but still very complex.

The third and last constituent of the intervention design determinant is *validity of the intervention theory*. Although it is perfectly clear what the intervention instigators want to achieve and how it should be done, the intervention may founder because it is based on wrong presuppositions. A deficient intervention theory may spoil the whole effort.

Implicitly at least, every public intervention is predicated upon a conception of, on the one hand, the determinants of the negatively valued problematic behavior (or situational circumstances) to be changed and, on the other hand, the linkage between the intervention and these determinants (Pressman and Wildavsky 1984; Mazmanian and Sabatier 1981, 1983; Sieber 1981:68ff.). To illustrate I shall use the vocational training program for released prisoners discussed in the Rossi and Freeman textbook (1985:72f.). From their account I have made a reconstruction of my own, presented in figure 13.4.

Intervention theories thus consist of three parts. At the heart of any intervention theory is a causal hypothesis about the influence of one or more determinants (general social processes) on the behavior (or con-

FIGURE 13.4
An Intervention Theory

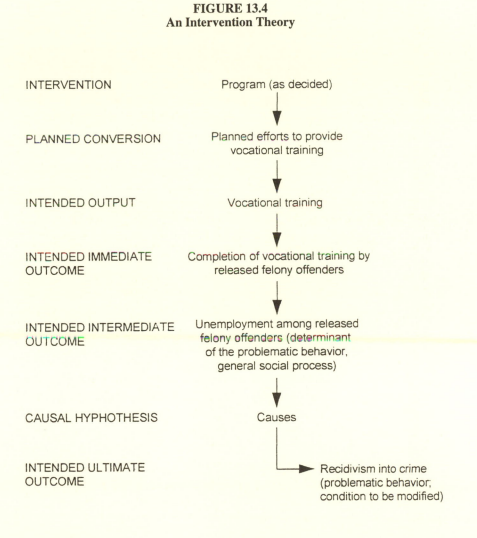

INTERVENTION	Program (as decided)
PLANNED CONVERSION	Planned efforts to provide vocational training
INTENDED OUTPUT	Vocational training
INTENDED IMMEDIATE OUTCOME	Completion of vocational training by released felony offenders
INTENDED INTERMEDIATE OUTCOME	Unemployment among released felony offenders (determinant of the problematic behavior, general social process)
CAUSAL HYPHOTHESIS	Causes
INTENDED ULTIMATE OUTCOME	Recidivism into crime (problematic behavior; condition to be modified)

dition) that the program seeks to modify. According to Rossi and Freeman, many social scientists believe that lack of employment (process, determinant) among released felony offenders results in recidivism, that is, they relapse into crime (problematic behavior, condition to be modified). A number of investigators maintain that if released prisoners are unable to find legitimate employment, they will probably seek out illegal means of obtaining an income. In this case, the first part of the program theory would be the causal hypothesis that unemployment (determinant, process) causes recidivism (problematic behavior, condition to be changed).

The second ingredient of the intervention theory specifies the relationship between the intervention and the determinant cited in the first part as associated with the behavior or condition to be ameliorated or changed. In the recidivism case, the intervention (program) concerns education, or more specifically, a certain amount of vocational training immediately after release from prison. The training program decided upon is thought to be prepared and actually carried out. The idea embodied in this vocational training program for ex–prisoners is that completion of it (actual implementation) will reduce unemployment (determinant) and therefore indirectly recidivism (problematic behavior).

The third part of the intervention theory is normative; in the actual case it is the positive value affixed to reducing the problematic behavior, that is, recidivism.

In talking about a valid intervention theory I rather mean the so–called causal hypothesis part of it. While a valid intervention theory in this respect by no means guarantees goal achievement, a faulty one may lead the reform astray and cause outcome failure.

Implementation

Apart from intervention history and intervention design, the third major group of determinants that might condition results occur during implementation. That implementation has an independent impact on intervention outcomes was a great discovery some decades ago. Implementation is divided into four major problem areas: national agencies, intermediaries or interorganizational networks, street–level bureaucrats, and addressee participation in low–level intervention refinement and intervention delivery. According to Lennart Lundquist (1987:76ff.), implementation involves three types of properties, which can be applied to each of the four problem areas: comprehension, capability, and willingness. People in the national agencies, intermediaries, street–level bureaucrats, and addressee implementers must comprehend the intervention, be capable of executing it, and be willing to do it. The reasoning can be summarized as follows:

National agencies:	Comprehension?	Capability?	Willingness?
Intermediaries:	Comprehension?	Capability?	Willingness?
Street–level bureaucrats:	Comprehension?	Capability?	Willingness?
Addressee implementers:	Comprehension?	Capability?	Willingness?

Deficient administrator *comprehension* of intervention content may cause execution problems. No matter how clearly and consistently formulated, a government subsidy program that potential applicants do not know of cannot contribute to achieve the goals it was instituted to reach. The comprehension ingredient is important in all four problem areas of implementation. For simplicity reasons, I shall mention it only at the national agency level. Deficient comprehension of the intervention by the implementers may influence both the implementation and, hence, the results.

The second subfactor to foster results is the *administrative capabilities* of the actors involved in implementation. Again, let me adumbrate this from the point of view of the central agency. If execution of a program requires appropriations, personnel, talent, time, energy, and equipment unavailable to administrators, the probability of achieving successful results will be weakened.

Perhaps the most common situation is *lack of financial resources*. With insufficient funds, administrative authorities cannot hire enough staff to conduct the technical analyses involved in the development of rules and regulations, to process applications for economic support, to collect and distribute information, or to effectively monitor regulatory compliance.

A sufficient number of *personnel* positions and ability to hire qualified people to hold these positions is necessary to accomplish administration tasks. Regulatory programs require skilled inspectors to provide the information by which the regulators can judge the level of regulatory compliance and, hence, regulatory efficacy. The personnel must possess specified technical know–how, adapted to the program's character and to recipient needs. Nuclear reactor inspectors in the

Nuclear Power Inspectorates around the world are probably required to have at least an M.A. degree and some past nuclear experience. The search for people with proper educational background may take time. Sometimes the staff must be enrolled in introductory and on–the–job training programs. All this means that time elapses and implementation is delayed.

And, even though inspectors and other personnel have the proper education, they may lack appropriate capital *equipment* to discover infractions of the rules (Hemenway 1985:11).

Lack of resources may stem from the vicissitudes of legislative processes in Western countries, which produce mandates for action without providing the appropriations necessary for their effective realization. Political officers propose policies to garner votes in elections. Covering the expenses for these reforms is not equally popular, so programs are instigated without the necessary economic backup. In addition, tax researchers have shown that citizens accord a high value to public services but are less prone to pay for these services via taxes. Neither ordinary citizens nor clients see the connection between tax–paying and service level (Hadenius 1986:122ff.).

Outcomes are influenced by *administrative willingness*. In this area, there are three major theories: the theory of the bureaucracy's self–regarding behavior, the attitudinal mismatch theory, and the regulatory capture theory.

Public bureaucracies have agendas of their own, which may conflict with the faithful implementation of the principal's directives and recommendations. To pursue its own interests, a government agency may try to twist the policy mandate to fit its own purposes. A specifically influential view in this area is the conception of bureaucrats as budget maximizers. To enhance their personal reputation, salaries, fields of influence, and other self-serving goals, bureaucrats tend to expand their budgets. The urge to maintain the organizational status quo or to grow takes precedence over concern with the faithful implementation of actual substantive policies. Public officials cease to be civil servants and turn into uncivil masters. From this assumption, researchers in the so–called *public choice tradition* have been deducing hypotheses about utility–maximizing bureaucratic behavior (Niskanen 1971; Lewin 1988).

These self-serving interests are most salient, perhaps, when political parties and the general public want to trim the governmental machinery. All the bodies concerned routinely respond by standing up and complaining loudly that every cutback of funds and personnel will reduce services to catastrophic levels (Jørgensen 1981).

Usually, the theory of the bureaucracy's self–regarding behavior is applied to agency managers and other individual civil servants. But self–serving goals might also be pursued by employee unions. Trade unions may safeguard the interests of staff and management at the expense of the tax payers and the public interest.

A somewhat milder variation on the administrative–willingness theme is that civil servants may harbor doubts about the appropriateness of the policy itself, which may hamper their oversight (Sabatier and Mazmanian 1980:153, 489; Downs 1967; Elmore 1978:191ff.; Van Horn and Van Meter 1977:113). Some scholars argue that the attitudes of top–level management are particularly important for implementation. Here, this notion is called the *attitudinal mismatch theory*. Noncompliant agency actions stemming from attitudinal mismatch are of two basic kinds: ends based and means based. In ends-based noncompliance, enforcement officials disapprove of the objectives of the policy, or at least accord those objectives a low priority in the competition for scarce resources. Ends–based noncompliance usually stems from political convictions. Means-based noncompliance on the other hand, involves doubts about the effectiveness of the recommended action to reach the stated goal. Means–based noncompliance questions the technical solutions chosen by the government.

Both objections question the merits of the intervention, but they have quite different implications. Whereas in ends-based noncompliance, the goals and values are at issue, in means–based noncompliance the beliefs about the probable effects are contested. Since the latter concerns statements of fact, not statements of value, they presuppose a different kind of remedial action and are in theory easier to overcome.

On occasion, the state attempts to change or promote action patterns that the addressees do not want to alter. They may try to resist the intervention or to capture it. The capture concept belongs to a well–known theory of bureaucracy, the *regulatory capture theory*. The notion of capture has been developed particularly in relation to regulatory programs. The regulatory capture theory suggests that whole agencies may be seduced to act in a manner favorable to the addressees, or that the single street–level bureaucrat may be seduced to do so. Here, the subject will be limited to agency capture.

The regulatory capture hypothesis was given its most influential expression by Gabriel Kolko in the early 1960s. Kolko, addressing the formation of regulations and regulatory agencies, suggested that regulation was little more than an elaborate hoax perpetrated on the American people by big business. Where traditional theorists had maintained that regulatory agencies were created to curb the abuses of big business, Kolko argued that in reality regulation served the opposite purpose: big business had actively sought regulation to help to stabilize its industries and protect itself from competition.

The skill and forcefulness with which Kolko developed his ideas gave them widespread currency. "Indeed, he fueled what became a virtual cottage industry for New Left historians—discerning the malevolent hand of big business behind policies that had previously been considered popularly inspired Progressive and New Deal reforms" (Lamoreaux 1984).

Another influential formulation of the regulatory capture concept was given by the Chicago economist George Stigler, who later was awarded the Nobel Prize in economics. Like Kolko, Stigler (1971) directed his attention to the capture of a whole regulatory system and to the front–end stages of the regulatory cycle. He speculated that most regulation was actively sought by industry in order to control competition, especially in the entry of new arrivals. Stigler assumed that the losses to society from regulation outweighed the gains to the regulated group—in other words, that regulation entailed net economic costs that would be levied on society by politically powerful interest groups (Mitnick 1980:111ff., 158ff.).

Of more interest in the present context, however, are authors who have argued that capture may occur in the administration stage of a regulatory system, which may affect the outcomes. Foremost among these theories is the life–cycle view of regulatory action, developed by Marver H. Bernstein (1955:74ff.). Bernstein posited that regulatory agencies generally progress through four stages over time, which he designated as gestation, youth, maturity, and old age. Often lasting twenty years or more, the gestation period begins when a problem develops in an industry, causing social or economic distress. If the distress is sufficiently acute and sustained, reform efforts will increase in intensity until elected officials pass legislation that creates a regulatory agency. During its period of youth, the agency works out an identity. At this stage, it still "lacks administrative experience, its policy and objectives are vague or unformed, its legal powers are unclear and untested, and its relations with Congress are uncertain" (1955:79). By contrast, the interests it was created to regulate are typically well organized and effective. But compensating somewhat for this imbalance is the crusading zeal of the newly appointed administrators.

In maturity, however, begins what Bernstein calls "the process of devitalization." Public interest in regulation recedes, and with it the commissioners' initial fervor. Officials grow less concerned with articulating regulatory policy and more involved in routine adjudication. It is at this point, Bernstein argues, that the regulatory agency becomes particularly susceptible to capture (1955:90):

> Politically isolated, lacking a firm basis of public support, lethargic in attitude and approach, bowed down by precedent and backlogs, unsupported in its demands for more staff and money, the commission finally becomes a captive of the regulated groups.

The agency's primary goal becomes the maintenance of the status quo and its own position, which is now more the servant than the master of industry.

There is a time dimension in the regulatory agency capture theory as expounded by Bernstein. Governmental intervention often occurs as a result of a broad political coalition that succeeds in breaking down the resistance and instituting a reform designed to serve the public interest. From its inception, the new regulatory agency is met with popular enthusiasm. After some time, however, public opinion languishes and shifts its attention to other functional areas. In these kinds of situations, the regulatees and their interest organizations may actually impose their will on the regulatory body and distort the regulation so that it favors themselves (Lamoreaux 1984).

The capture risk seems greater in cases of agencies regulating one single industry. At least partly, this results from the agency's need to maintain political support, when the only logical source of backing is the regulated industry itself. The general public is too amorphous to offer the specific patronage that the agency may need in defending its budget, or its very existence, before the executive and the legislative branches of government (Mitnick 1980:46f., 95f.,132ff., 206ff.; Selznick 1980; Kaufman 1967:75ff., 217ff.; Peters 1982:79; Kelman 1981:80ff., 184ff.). This means that the agency capture theory is less relevant to agencies with broad and complex jurisdictions-such as the Swedish Board for Consumer Policies-than to single-business regulatory bodies, like the Private Insurance Supervisory Service or the War Materials Inspectorate.[2]

The second subcomponent of the implementation determinant suggests that the comprehension, capabilities, and willingness of *formal intermediaries* may positively or negatively direct the outcomes (Salamon 1981; Hood 1986; Modeen and Rosas 1988, 1990; Friberg 1973; Dunsire 1978).

To an ever-increasing extent, governments strive to realize their intentions by means of nonstate agents and parties. The nongovernmental organizations, NGO's for short, enter the stage as middlemen or hidden bureaucrats between national administrative agencies and target groups (Berger and Neuhaus 1977; Hjern and Porter 1981; Hjern and Hull 1982). This may prove highly advantageous to effective implementation. It might boost outreach and enhance the legitimacy of the policy in the eyes of the targets. However, the premeditated implementation process may also be diverted into completely different directions. The middlemen may appropriate the intervention and twist it to fit their private interests.

It is worthwhile to outline some general principles according to which the implementation of public policies might be organized. Governments have several types of models from which to choose.[3]

At the one extreme, public services are delivered by government–owned and government–operated public businesses. Like their private counterparts, they are expected to cover their costs from sales and make a return on their investments. The Swedish State Power Board, which operates as a public company in producing and distributing electricity, is a case in point.

Public enterprises may avoid the rigidities usually associated with public bureaucracies and function more efficiently. However, they may also exploit their peculiar governmental status to escape competitive pressures and thereby decline into public liabilities.

The classic idea is to use neutral civil servants. In this case, public administrators are appointed on the basis of formal merits and expertise, not political considerations. They should work impartially, honestly, sincerely, and trustworthy, in short according to Tacitus' principle *sine ira et studio*. Public officials should obey their superiors and subordinate their personal interests to those of the state and the public.

The cadre principle is third concept. In this model, public servants are appointed according to political conviction. Socialist governments hire socialist civil servants, conservative governments appoint conservative civil servants. In the former Socialist countries of Eastern Europe and in North Korea under Kim Il–sung the cadre principle reigned supreme. To a much lesser extent, the spoils system in the United States works in this fashion.

Intergovernmental arrangements are often used for the grass–roots delivery of national public interventions. In federal systems, federal agencies delegate to regional and local governments to deliver public services in their areas of jurisdiction. In unitary systems, municipalities are often called upon to serve as lieutenants in the implementation of national policies. Governing bodies at the same regional or local level enter into all forms of compacts among themselves to share in delivery and economize on overheads.

The political majorities of middle– and lower–level governments are often different from those of principals of the national programs they are supposed to implement. Being elected by the people local citizens, the municipal government may feel that policies imposed from above work against the best interest of the local community. This conflict of interest may make them unwilling to act.

A fifth possibility would be to use corporatist arrangements, in which the top leadership of nationwide interest organizations are used in the implementation process. It might be trade union associations, business organizations, housing associations, tenants associations, building associations, and so on and so forth. Often this starts with negotiations between the national administrative agency and representatives of an association, and ends up with a formal agreement that the association will manage the implementation of the program.

A sixth option would be to use professions. Professions are occupational groups that have the power to define and control their own work. They have obtained from the state special privileges, such as a system of licensing and self–government, and a protected market. Possession of a skill based on theoretical or even scientific knowledge is another alleged property of professionals. Military officers, medical doctors, university professors, computer technicians, and maybe even librarians are examples of professionals. Governmental research policies are implemented by university professors, health policy by the medical profession, and defense policy by the military officers. Government funds to stage actors, musicians, poets, novelists, and painters where decisions about distribution are made by groups of prominent members of these groups are maybe also cases of administration through professions.

Still another possibility is to negotiate deals with nonprofit local associations to supply public goods and services. The use of voluntary local home–owners' associations, sports clubs, or tenants associations, would be cases in point. This is different from corporatist arrangements in that leaders of the national organizations are not involved.

Governments may use private business contractors to carry out programs. They avoid the headaches of direct delivery by contracting with private business firms. This may increase cost effectiveness and avoid the build–up of large bureaucracies. However, accountability and evaluation may be difficult. Excessive profits may be made at public expense. The program may be diverted in directions not conforming with the original intentions in the program.

Our standard case, the Swedish Fuel Declaration, contains cases of nonpublic intermediaries. Information to the customers is disseminated by the car dealers. All car dealers in Sweden are private entrepreneurs, so private businesses are here functioning as street–level bureaucrats.

Comprehension, resources, and the attitudes of intermediaries may facilitate as well as impede results achievement. Comprehension of and attitudes to the intervention to be implemented are probably decisive. If their fundamental attitude is positive, private intermediaries may contribute substantially to a satisfactory outcome. There are several reasons for this.

Nonstate institutions representing the targets or staying in closer contact with them than national government agencies are more aware of the problems that members of the target group have and a deeper knowledge of how to reach out to them. They may thus in a more lighthearted manner deliver the program to the target group and carefully have them act in ways that the government deems desirable. A reasonable balance is struck between central control and adaptation to local needs.

The chances of reaching out are further strengthened because the private associations may offer to use their highly specialized organizational network. Organizations regularly have congresses and meetings, where information can be exchanged and decisions made. Through membership newsletters, face–to–face discussion, speeches, and other communication, the organization leadership may reach out to local decision–makers and individual members. All this will enhance the interface between the program and its intended beneficiaries and addressees.

Another important aspect is that the use of nongovernmental intermediaries may increase the program's legitimacy in the eyes of the recipients and the general public. For people are most susceptible to ideas and conceptions emanating from sources they like, respect, and have confidence in.

The use of private intermediaries may also impede result development. Intermediaries may have negative feelings about the program and thus act inefficiently. Outcome may be hampered because the coordination of various program elements is made more difficult if private middlemen enter the scene between government and clients.

Implementation research must be credited for the discovery of the influence on program results of the third subcomponent of the larger administration factor: *street–level bureaucracy*. Michael Lipsky's famous book *Street–Level Bureaucracy* has been particularly influential in this respect. According to Lipsky (1980:3), street–level bureaucrats are "public service workers who interact directly with citizens in the course of their jobs, and who have substantial discretion in the execution of their work." Typical street–level bureaucrats are teachers, police officers, social workers, judges, public lawyers, health workers, and many other public employees who grant access to government programs and provide services within them.[4]

According to Lipsky, street–level bureaucrats actually create policy through the multitude of decisions they make in interacting with the clients. They possess discretion that cannot be completely controlled because there are never enough resources to provide close, frequent, and direct supervision of them, and also because they are physically separated from their superiors. There are no precise performance criteria in existence that specify exactly how an engineer, public health nurse, social worker, or teacher should do their job. In sum, argues Lipsky, policies are formed in implementation by program operators developing routines and shortcuts for coping with their everyday jobs.

Obviously, the street–level bureaucracy's comprehension of the program influences their work and thus program output and outcome. The comprehension aspect was treated above in the section on central agencies. The capabilities of the street–level bureaucrats will also impinge on program results. A seemingly universal problem is that front–end personnel feel that their resources are too scarce. A lack of educated

personnel and technical equipment impedes the discovery of regulatory violations and their prosecution in court, and decreases the quality
and quantity of the services provided.

For some inspections, the magnitude of the legislative charge makes
it virtually impossible to have enough inspectors to keep an eye on
violators. Occupational safety and health standards apply to more than
20,000 workplaces, yet the U.S. Board of Occupational Safety and
Health (OSHA) can only inspect a tiny fraction of them every year.

Time constraints generally limit the ability of inspectors to discover
many of the infractions of norms and regulations. They are too hurried
to do a thorough job. Hemenway has pointed out that OSHA inspectors spend only about one–third of their available time in the field. The
rest is used to prepare for travelling and reporting the site visits. Regional inspectors for the American Nuclear Regulatory Commission
spend only about 25 percent of a typical working week at the power
plant. Much valuable time is tied up doing clerical and other mundane
work (Hemenway 1985:11; also Bardach and Kagan 1982:123ff.).

In adjustment to the resource problem, program operators adopt
various *coping strategies*. To avoid caseload, they limit the information about their services, ask clients and inspectees to wait, make
themselves unavailable to contacts or make ample use of referrals of
clients to other authorities.

A second coping strategy is creaming. Front–line operators concentrate attention to a limited number of select clients, program types, and
solutions. They prefer easy, well–defined cases to difficult, amorphous,
and time–consuming ones. They attend to cases that promise to be
successful and play down the most difficult ones. Some implementation researchers argue, that coping strategies are so common that they
bias implementation in systematic fashions, which in turn impinges
upon the final outcome (Lipsky 1980).

An alternative explanation can be predicated upon the above–mentioned *regulatory capture theory*. Capture—or cooptation—may occur
at several levels: the agency level, the intermediary level, and the
individual inspector level (Hemenway 1985).

As pointed out by Hemenway and other scholars, regulatory inspection is inherently adversarial. Normally, the inspector's principal task
is to discover violations of the agency's prescriptions. The inspectee,
on the other hand, generally prefers that few infractions be either
found or reported. The inspected company may want to devote less

resources to preventing the regulated problems than society deems justified. In this way, the inspector and the inspectee often have opposing goals.

However, the relationship between inspector and inspectee is not one of pure conflict. They are not involved in a zero–sum game. In many facets of their interaction, cooperation can make both better off. Both, for example, want to see some problems corrected. No one wants a nuclear catastrophe, a plane crash, or food poisoning. The inspector can be obnoxious, obdurate, and impose great costs on the regulated firm, but he gains little from acting in this manner. Indeed, he will be made worse off, for the regulated firm can retaliate in a variety of ways, imposing costs on him. Most of the time both parties benefit by acting civilly and reasonably, displaying some respect and regard for the other (Hemenway 1985:13).

The primary beneficiaries of the regulations, and thus the inspections, are generally dispersed and unorganized interests–elevator riders, pedestrians, apple eaters, swimmers, nursing home residents, and the like. Many of these never see the inspector, nor do they understand his work. Rarely will they reward him for doing a god job, or punish him for a bad one.

By contrast, the inspector knows the inspectee. Face–to–face meetings are common. Often, there is continuing interaction. The inspector has the power to impose large costs on the inspectee. The inspectee thus has the motive and the opportunity to influence the inspector's behavior.

The inspector is more prone to cooptation when he meets the inspectee face–to–face, when examinations are long, and when there are repeat encounters. He is more easily captured when he monitors only one industry, and most particularly, only one firm. Hemenway (1985:52) quotes one meat and poultry inspector:

> [We] go out among the regulated to do our job. We don't just visit them periodically, we just about marry them. Day after day, night after night, we are in the lion's den alone with the lion. How are we supposed to get along? USDA doesn't tell us. How are we supposed to resist the barrage of threats and temptations the packers constantly direct at us? USDA doesn't tell us. USDA does tell us to use our ingenuity to do our job, to use our common sense–but that's not very helpful when you're in the lion's den.

The inspector may be swayed to the inspectee's viewpoint by psychical inducements or by tangible material rewards. Regular bribes are of course the paradigm case, but often more sophisticated methods are used. Prospects of future well–paid jobs are a reward for some inspectors. If inspectors plan to seek employment with the regulated industry, it behooves them to maintain a friendly rather than an adversarial relationship. All this is conducive to capture.

The personal career motive shows that the capture theory is connected to the *theory of the market–driven public administration.* The administration is not entirely controlled from the top as in the hierarchical theory, but also by the career expectations of individual staff. Staff members who plan to quit have a personal interest in building a fund of goodwill with prospective potential employers.

Finally, attitudinal *mismatch* between central program intentions and local executors can also affect the results. The mismatch theory was dealt with above under agency level and will not be discussed further here. Suffice it to say that street–level inspectors may also develop coping strategies because they believe regulations are unjustified. They may, for instance, hide infractions simply out of resentment.

Occasionally, addressees participate in intervention implementation, usually at the grass–root level. In these cases, the comprehension, capability, and willingness of the participating addressees may affect performance and outcomes.

Addressee Response

The fourth major determinant, which may impinge upon the results of public interventions, concerns the addressees. Their comprehension, capability, willingness, organizational belongingness, and general predicament may influence compliance with regulations and other regulatory outcomes.

Clients' *comprehension* of the intervention may influence their behavior. However unequivocally formulated, a grants program unknown to prospective applicants will not contribute to the results it was instituted to achieve. A government health campaign that does not reach the targets cannot work according to intentions.

On many occasions, the program reaches out to the addressees without difficulties. The Norwegian researcher Torstein Eckhoff, among others, has pointed out that some large addressees, such as huge companies and trade associations, have designed sensitive receptor devices, facilitating the task of acquiring information about government regulations affecting them. Many business firms have hired staff with the express purpose of gathering information about public policies that might concern them. Since the units in this target group are large and relatively few, the national government is also able to make sure that they get the right kind of information.

With respect to regulations aimed at the general public, communication deficiencies are more pervasive and therefore a stronger explanatory force. Official publications such as the Swedish *Book of Statutes* and the *Parliamentary and Ministry Records* have a limited readership. They are often supplemented with press releases, advertisements, brochures, and, in some cases, radio and television programs. Yet, even using all of these channels, it is not possible to reach all the targets. In addition, the information is often incomplete. For example, according to Eckhoff, studies have shown that people have a rather scant acquaintance with the regulations which give them rights and duties.

Whether addressees are *individuals or collective actors* will have consequences for the process analysis. Collective addressees like communes and business companies are both easier and more difficult to influence. They are easier in the sense that they are fewer, but more difficult because collective decisions are needed for compliance to occur and results to be achieved. Individual members of the collectivity may be reached by the program, but this may be insufficient because it will never be brought to the attention of the board for a collectively binding decision.

The program's time adaption to the decision situation of the addressee is a *capability* factor that may explain the outcome. If the program arrives in a *formative moment,* it may produce immediate results, otherwise not. Assume that the state is disseminating information to industrial firms suggesting that they should save electricity and that this should be done through the use of modern energy–conserving equipment. If the message arrives when the firm is on the verge of changing its machinery, it might be effectuated immediately. If the firm on the other hand has just changed its machine equipment, it may take several years before the issue of new machinery will be raised again. The formative moment is not present and the propaganda will remain unnoticed.

The *willingness* of individual recipients may play a role. The program may be more efficiently implemented among some actors be-cause of the existence of *zealots,* people who are strongly committed to the cause and who are willing and capable to commit their time and energy to it. The exchange of people in a collective entity thus can be of importance. If the zealots disappear to other activities, the desirable results may peter out; if zealots enter the organization, the program may suddenly give effect.

The state often attempts to alter behavior that the addressees do not want to change or to effect some action that addressees have little interest in taking. For instance, the program may try to affect things that are only of secondary importance for the targeted addressee. Gov-ernmental requirements of environment–friendly equipment or a good working environment may be examples of this, because they might conflict with the desires of the business to show good productivity and large profits.

Regulatees, presumptive beneficiaries, or other types of addressees may, of course, dutifully comply with regulatory instructions and di-rectives or willingly participate in programs. On some occasions, how-ever, they may try to *capture* the agency officials, a theory that has been treated above. At times, they may camouflage the infractions, or their severity, or attempt to prevent them from being reported.

Through *camouflage,* regulatees attempt to circumvent regulatory requirements by hiding infractions from government inspectors. The ability of the inspectee to conceal violations largely depends on the nature of the inspected items. Some problems are more difficult to cover up than others. It is easier to camouflage faults with conduct and behavior than with pieces of capital equipment. Hemenway (1985:15) argues:

> It is easy for the fire marshal to insure that the sprinkler system is properly in-stalled, or the housing inspector to determine if the boiler is functional or the sink works (or indeed whether the bathroom has a sink), or for the restaurant inspector to observe whether the thermometer in the walk–in refrigerator gives accurate readings. It is more difficult to monitor behavior. It is hard for the field marshal to know whether exit doors are occasionally obstructed, or for the housing inspector to notice if garbage is sometimes left in the halls, or for the restaurant inspector to guarantee that employees always wash their hands, place their long hair in a net, and keep the can–opener free from dirt.

Regulatees may also simply *resist* obeying regulations. Civil dis-obedience, as probably invented and certainly popularized by Ma-hatma Gandhi, would be a case in point. The idea is to urge large numbers of protesters very publicly to break some specific law. Civil disobedience campaigns are usually nonviolent, and should be as law–abiding as possible in every way except with regard to the specific law or policy that is the focus of attention.

It is important not to confuse a civil disobedience campaign with a general peaceful protest against a policy in a fully law–abiding way. The latter may also explain, partly or entirely, the results.

An entirely different possibility is that the addressees on their own initiative have planned to implement the measures that the government wants them to do, but that they participate in the program anyway, for example, by applying for and getting economic support. Then the addressees are *free riders* on the government program. To elicit programmatic effects, free rider participation must be subtracted, because their measures would have been taken even without the program.

Obviously, the reactions of the addressees are crucial for the outcomes of any policy.

Other Government Interventions, Other Government Agencies

The fifth broad group of contingencies that may condition the policy results is other government interventions.

Several evaluation researchers have warned against the risks associated with concentrating the evaluation on one particular intervention. I entirely concur with these warnings. Also in this respect, it is important to adopt a systemic approach to evaluation in order to paint a configurative picture of the whole. Outcomes may stem from programs in other policy sectors, or programs in other sectors may interact in complicated ways with the program under evaluation to produce the outcome. Similarly, other programs in the same sector may condition the outcome or strengthen or weaken the program under evaluation. The measured outcomes thus may have been influenced by the actions of other agencies and actors at the national, regional and local level during the implementation. Networks of nongovernmental actors linked to different government agencies may also influence the results. This thesis of implementation as conflict has been strongly emphasized by, among others, Hjern, Winter, Elmore, and Hanf.[5]

The systemic–centered and conflict–oriented notion is nourished by the institutional theory of administration. The public administration of a country is not a unitary actor with one and only one clearly expressed will, for the simple reason that the collectivity of politicians is in disagreement on most issues. The national government wants many different things at the same time in a way that necessitates a balancing of these different desires. To safeguard various interests and wishes on a continuous and routinized basis, the government has founded different institutions, agencies. This means that the government as a whole will consist of different organizations with highly divergent and even contradictory desires. The body of administration may be considered an additive system consisting of layer upon layer of institutions and bodies, which have been established at different points in time to safeguard and solve problems that once upon a time entered the government agenda. Far from being homogenous and united, the civil service is characterized by fragmentation and conflict between agencies and bodies which defend their own assignments and administrative domains.

The institutional theory of public administration further asserts that management and staff will be socialized into agency cultures, which enables the institutions to resist pressures for change and to lead lives of their own. They will be relatively robust against short–sighted attempts of change and adjust only over time to new conflicts and assignments in the political system. All in all, governments have had difficulties with finding methods to discard activities which have stiffened into fossils.

Let me use hydro–electric power exploitation as an illustration. The Swedish state has taken a strong interest in the transformation of wild rivers into sources of hydro–electric power. As early as 1909, a government body, the State Power Board, was founded to safeguard the public interest in this respect. The government also pursues regional policies to ensure that the population is reasonably spread across the whole country and labor market policies to fight unemployment. Since most wild rivers are in the northern part of the country, regional policy motives strongly supports exploitation. Labor market policies point to the same direction. The national, regional and local agencies in charge of these two policy areas also tend to support the policy of harnessing these rivers.

Simultaneously, the national government wants to save some water courses for environmental, scenic, tourist, historical and other reasons. The national boards for the environment and for cultural affairs thus tend to disapprove of exploitation. Dams will drown state–owned forests. The agency in charge of government–owned and government–

operated forestry may become pitted against the State Power Board. Water–power exploitation may damage the reindeer industry of the Laplanders. The Chamber Collegium, which manages Laplander policies, therefore tends to go against further hydro exploitation. Far from being united behind a common clear goal, public sector actors evidently direct contradictory requirements toward the wild rivers. This makes the implementation of hydro–electric power exploitation policies highly controversial and conflict–oriented, which influences their outcomes.

Consequently, the success and failure of public policies may be explained by reference to the institutional theory of public administration.

Issue Networks and Other Environments

The last major factor in my general implementation theory is called issue networks and other environments. The degree of support in the immediate and distant environment of the intervention may account for its results.

Administration, output and outcome may be debilitated because legislative and executive *sovereigns* may not be persistent enough in their support of a program once it has been instigated. This point is made by Nakamura and Smallwood in their *The Politics of Policy Implementation.* Sovereign demonstrations of stakeholding in statutes and other programs include monitoring to back up a particular interpretation of their content, public statements during the implementation phase to reinforce a particular interpretation of a policy, and the claiming of credit for the program during its implementation phase.

Support or resistance from *other stakeholders,* that is, actors who are neither policymakers nor formally involved in the administration, may influence the results. Statements and actions by affected interest organizations or nonprofit associations provide encouragement to agencies, in spite of the fact that these institutions have no official role to play in the administration. Torstein Eckhoff (1983:36ff.) has shown that farmers', fishermen's, and forestry associations have performed the role of disseminators of information on the regulatory regimes affecting these businesses. The trade union movement has played a similar role with respect to legislation on work environment.

One example provided by Eckhoff concerns the differences between the Norwegian Maid Law and the Swedish law on working hours for farmhands. The Swedish law was much better known and compliance was much higher due to the fact that the Swedish farm-hand association disseminated information on it among its members and intervened in cases of violations.

Another good case concerns the Swedish Weapons Exportation Act, which prohibits the sale of arms manufactured in Sweden to countries currently at war. However, it was not the War Materials Inspectorate, the official overseer of the Act, which found out that the Swedish arms industry, particularly Bofors, had sold weapons to Iran during its war with Iraq, using persons in Singapore as the middlemen. The viola-tions were discovered and made public by the non–profit, voluntary Swedish Peace and Arbitration Association. In this case, a nonprofit, nongovernment organization, with no formal role in the administration of the Act, came to influence the outcome.

In her study of the environmental clauses of the Swedish Forestry Act, Katarina Eckerberg (1987:20) noted that environmental groups and individual environmental fighters influence the outcomes.

A special case is whistle blowing. In monitoring regulations, for instance, inspectors may get some help from anonymous tipsters and whistle blowers. Customs authorities may receive help from anony-mous and even paid tipsters. Disgruntled current and former employ-ees can offer tips and expose company infractions. This was actually the case in the above-mentioned Bofors affair.

Still another important subcomponent of the environment factor is the *mass media*. A strong positive opinion in the mass media for a specific program will psychologically strengthen the management and staff of overseeing agencies and make them act more strongly and persistently to discover infractions.

The larger environment impacts on the outcomes. A program may be inherently clear, perfectly communicated to implementers, meticu-lously executed according to plan, and yet basically ineffective be-cause of changes in the larger policy environment that upset the initial prerequisites for implementation. Events can take place within as well as outside the country: a war may break out, prices may soar, or opinions may change.

A concrete example will illustrate this train of thought. In Sweden, the main reason for the decline in energy consumption from the begin-ning of the 1970s well into the 1980s was probably the substantial price rises on oil between 1973 and 1979. These price hikes were produced in the international system. The Swedish government's energy conservation policies precipitated and facilitated the development but in the main did not produce it.

This ends my configurative survey of factors and theories that may contribute to explaining the outcomes of public interventions. It is my hope that it will provide guidance in the execution of process evaluations.

Notes

1. Govt. bill no. P 1972:111, appendix. 2:363. See also govt. bill no. P 1975:30, app. 2:41.
2. Swedish cases of regulatory capture are discussed in Jonung 1984:170 and Grip 1987.
3. Interesting insights into this problem can be found in the works by my former Uppsala colleague Bo Rothstein, in Rothstein 1986; and in a chapter in Rothstein 1991.
4. Kaufman 1967; Wilson 1978; Pressman and Wildavsky 1984; and Stjernquist 1973 are examples of empirical case studies of implementation processes; also Kelman 1981:180ff. By "implementation analysis" is often meant the analysis of conceivable alternative courses of program execution before a formal program decision is made. It is such *ex ante* activity that Allison (1980:237) is referring to when he characterizes implementation as "the 'Missing Chapter' in conventional Analysis," and Hargrove (1975) when he speaks about "the missing link." Also expressions like "backward mapping" and "forward mapping" refer to *ex ante* analyses, not studies of actual implementation processes (Williams and Elmore in Williams 1982).
5. See References and the chapters in Hanf and Toonen 1985.

14

Merit Criteria and Performance
Standards

> *"It is the reader's task (in digesting the report) to 'evaluate' in the literal sense of the concept, and the evaluator's task to provide the reader with the information which he may wish to take into account in forming his judgment."*
> —Lee J. Cronbach

> *"Bad is bad and good is good and it is the job of evaluation to decide which is which."*
> —Michael Scriven

One key process in evaluation is to determine the merit, worth, or quality of the public intervention under appraisal. But what constitutes a valuable public intervention and how can it be appraised? For analytical reasons, this quandary—the seventh in my Eight Problems Approach to Evaluation—may be divided into the following parts:

1. Identification of appropriate criteria of merit to be used in the assessment.
2. On the chosen criteria, selection of performance standards that constitute success or failure.
3. Ascertaining the actual performance of the evaluand on each criterion and comparing it to each standard.
4. Integration of the judgments into a single, overall appraisal of worth of the intervention.

Descriptive and Prescriptive Valuing

On several occasions throughout this book, I have acknowledged my intellectual debt to Shadish, Cook, and Leviton's formidable treatise *Foundations of Program Evaluation* (1991:46ff.). I find their account of the valuing component of evaluation particularly illuminating. Following in their footprints, I shall distinguish between two fundamental approaches to valuing: descriptive and prescriptive. I have attempted to summarize their distinction in the following fashion. In *descriptive valuing,* the evaluator chooses the values of others as criteria and standards. The posture is not that these values are paramount, but that they are perceptions of intervention worth that are grist for the mill of decision–making. In *prescriptive valuing,* the evaluator herself "advocates the primacy of particular values", such as, for instance justice, equality and client needs, regardless of whether these values are adopted by any decision–making body or held by some stakeholding constituency. Prescriptive theories of valuing maintain that some values are superior to others whereas descriptive theories depict values held by others without contesting them or claiming that one value is best or better than some alternative ones.

Prescriptive theories give evaluators an external, critical perspective and intellectual authority that descriptive theories cannot match. They broaden evaluators' understanding of good government interventions by widening their understanding of what is good for the human condition generally.

Prescriptive valuing runs into problems because there is no correct prescriptive value theory around. It necessitates evaluators to take a stand on value issues. In accepting the goals of others as criteria of merit, on the other hand, the evaluator may maintain her scientific objectivity and stay out the thorny business of adopting a personal posture on valence issues.

Descriptive valuing is easier to handle than prescriptive values because all you have to do is to ask others. Prescriptive valuing is intellectually more demanding and requires training in ethics.

Descriptive theories are more consistent than prescriptive theories with the social and political organization of such Western democracies as Sweden, France, and the United States, which are based upon fostering a pluralism of values that compete against each other in political and administrative arenas. Using prescriptive valuing in these cases would impose one ethical view on a public intervention in political systems characterized by value pluralism.

When evaluators provide results that bear on the plurality of values in Western democracies or on specific values adopted by political interventions, they increase the chances that the information will be perceived as legitimate. Conversely, advocating a prescriptive ethic, and amassing data on that basis, will reflect neither the value pluralism nor the values adopted by interventions, and the likelihood that the information will be perceived as legitimate will be decreased, this making it less credible in policy. Descriptive theories are more legitimate and thus useful than prescriptive theories in this sense (Shadish, Cook, and Leviton 1991:47ff.).

Like Shadish, Cook, and Leviton, I believe that prescriptive values have a function to fulfill but that descriptive values ought to have priority most of the time in evaluation. Descriptive theories are more politically and socially practical in a system of pluralistic interests. My posture is rather conventional. Most evaluators embrace descriptive valuing. They portray values stated in program documents or held by stakeholders, apply these criteria to data about program performance, present the evaluation of different components separated from each other and leave the overall integration to the potential users of the information.

Aside from the general orientation to be taken (descriptive versus prescriptive valuing) the particular values preferred in each orientation must be justified. Descriptive value theories might be preordinate in the sense that the yardsticks are selected in advance. But the choice of yardsticks might also be made afterwards as in cases where evaluators just deliver information but leave the valuing to the information users.

In my brief exposition, I shall start with some suggested descriptive criteria of merit for effectiveness evaluation.

Effectiveness Criteria of Merit

The value component of public sector evaluation was long neglected because the answer appeared obvious: the evaluator should avoid setting up criteria of her own; the natural criteria of merit to apply are the initial, stated intervention goals.

Since programs are inaugurated to achieve some aims, it is natural to assess them in light of these aims. Even the standards issue can be resolved in a similar vein: if the aims are reached, the programs have been successful, if not they have failed. I shall not repeat in detail what I have already argued in chapter 4 on the pros and particularly cons of the goal–attainment approach. The strongest argument in favor of public intervention goals is that they have a special democratic status because they are institutionalized in a government decision, made by, for example, national diets or municipal assemblies under responsibility and according to the rules and procedures guiding public policy decision making in representative democracies.

With time, goal–attainment evaluators discovered practical difficulties. Some government services have very lofty goals that make them worthless as value criteria. Take national defence, for instance. The business of defence is to avoid war. The Swedes have avoided wars since 1813 but is war avoidance really a reasonable benchmark to use in judging defense efforts? It seems far too general to be applied as a criterion to evaluate the effectiveness and efficiency of military defense. Other programs have more specific goals but even these goals are plagued by haziness; particularly difficult to use are goal catalogues with no stated priorities among the goals. The crucial objection, however, is that goal–attainment evaluators tend to overlook unforeseen side effects. Since these spillovers are unanticipated, the evaluator will not be able to trace them, if she is guided by stated goals. And if she discovers them, the stated goals will not provide any value criteria for judging them either. The stated goal approach is obviously deficient on this account.

To resolve the issue, evaluation methodologists started to suggest alternative descriptive criteria of value. Figure 14.1 is a summary of some commonly suggested descriptive criteria for judging program effectiveness.

Responsiveness to client concerns has been suggested as an alternative to public policy and program goals. Is the program or the service acceptable to or highly appreciated by the recipients? This is the decisive issue in *client–oriented evaluation*.

The use of client criteria is grounded in political ideologies of the superiority of the market as compared to government provision of services. Since the public sector produces goods or services for consumers in the market place, responsiveness to client tastes is the major value criterion to be met. The client–orientation is also justified by democratic, participatory arguments.

FIGURE 14.1
Criteria of Merit for Effectiveness Evaluation

Descriptive criteria of merit:

1. Goal–attainment
   a. Goals of global conventions
   b. National policy goals
   c. National agency goals
   d. Regional agency goals
   e. Municipal policy goals or goals of municipal commissions
2. Client concerns, expectations, and conceptions of quality
3. Professional conceptions of merit
4. Citizens' expectations and values
5. Merit criteria of diverse stakeholding audiences
6. Goal–free evaluation (no value standard at all)

Prescriptive criteria of merit:

1. Contribution to problem–solving
2. Client needs
3. Equal distribution
4. Public interest

The client model is used particularly in local service provision such as medical service, crime prevention, child care, services to seniors, handicapped, and youth. It is also applied to cultural programs like libraries, museums, zoos, and theaters, recreation programs like national parks, swimming pools, number and quality of parks, soccer fields, tennis halls, and other services like trash hauling, street cleaning, snow removal, traffic noise, traffic congestion, and urban transit. Client criteria are reasonable to use, but within limits; they must be balanced against other criteria like goal attainment.

Another set of descriptive criteria are *professional* demands and goals. The pertinent profession is asked to provide yardsticks and judge the quality of the evaluand in peer reviews. Professionals include doctors in medical care, professors in basic research, nurses in services to seniors, and nuclear engineers in public nuclear power programs. The rationale for this approach is that the value structure in some fields is so complicated that only the expert practitioners themselves can perform the proper evaluations. For instance, only colleagues can judge the quality of basic science performed by their peers at physics departments in universities.

Occasionally, *citizens'* goals are also used as criteria, as when evaluators elicit the opinions of local residents on municipal library services, art exhibitions, sports recreation facilities, or public utilities like gas, electricity, water quality, drainage, and street lighting or public safety, for example, fire fighting, police protection, traffic enforcement and police patrolling. This approach is grounded in theories of participatory democracy. All the *stakeholders' goals,* expectations and worries concerning a particular intervention could also be used as criteria. The stakeholder approach is driven by theories of legitimate interest group representation.

The descriptive value criteria for output and outcome appreciation presented here raise several questions. Is the overview exhaustive? Which criteria of merit ought to be applied in a specific evaluation? Are there some criteria that necessarily must be considered in each evaluation? Should public service production, for instance, always be evaluated against client goals and expectations? How should client goals be balanced against program goals and professional goals? And finally, within each criterion of merit, which standards of performance should be used to tell us how well something must do on the particular criterion to be deemed excellent, passable, or deficient?

Descriptive public sector criteria are mostly plagued by ambiguity. The evaluator will run into problems, because they are unclear and do not point unambiguously to a distinct outcome. If program goals and other naturally occurring yardsticks such as client concerns are hazy, how can they be the cornerstones in the appraisal? The ensuing result would be fuzzy and vague, to say the least.

A radical response to the goal muddiness issue is suggested by the *goal–free model of evaluation.* Goal–free evaluation, according to my own idiosyncratic interpretation in this book, entirely disregards not only preordained intervention goals but also other before–the–fact criteria; it favors the pure study of implementation, output, and outcomes. Evaluation is transformed into ordinary, normal social science. In spite of this, I have put goal–free evaluation under "descriptive criteria of merit" for the following reason. Goal–free evaluation appears to adopt a just–give–them–the–facts philosophy. The role of the appointed evaluator is to account for results in terms of actual performance and actual outcomes without paying any attention to initial goals or other criteria of merit. But the results must be reported to somebody. I take it that the selection, clarification, and application of value criteria and standards is left to the potential recipients, who may use whatever values they deem applicable. In this sense, the goal–free model embraces a descriptive theory of valuing.

Prescriptive strategies have been suggested to avoid the problems of using descriptive criteria. Figure 14.1 provided four examples.

One such prescriptive strategy is to judge an intervention with respect to its contribution to *problem solving*. In this case, the evaluation criteria are not achievement of somebody else's goals and expectations but the extent to which policies and programs solve problems as defined by the evaluator. How can evaluators perform this function? There is no such thing as an objective problem formulation. Problems are concerned with values as well as with facts. It is impossible to specify a problem or its solution without explicitly or implicitly referring to some social values. If these values are those of some stakeholding constituency such as a political party or a government, the evaluator is back to descriptive valuing. Should the values on the other hand be those of the analyst herself, then she must face the task of grounding them in some appropriate ethical, political or other theory. This can be done, of course, but in the social fields there is little hope that such problem formulations will be widely accepted in pluralist democratic systems. And there is scant agreement in the literature concerning which theories should be used. Actually, defining a social problem is fundamentally a political enterprise. In my opinion problem definition is best left to political bodies.

Maybe things are different in fields like energy and environment where problem definitions seem to be less disputable and carry more weight. The thinning of the stratospheric ozone layer was discovered by scientists who also defined it as a problem and got their problem definition accepted by the global political community. The 1985 Vienna Convention and the 1987 Montreal Protocol with revisions might be evaluated against a definition of the ozone problem, not adopted goals.

Client needs are another prescriptive criterion. Needs are very different from wants and demands. To argue that somebody needs something is identical to maintaining that the person will be harmed or detrimentally affected if the thing is not obtained. Many needs theories lean toward a specific theory of justice. But there are several theories of justice. Justice is a central moral concern in evaluation but so are human rights, equality, liberty and utility. Why limit the concern only to justice? Limiting evaluation to needs interpreted as justice is problematic because there are several other candidates.

I agree with those stakeholders in modern democratic polities who dispute the assumption that evaluation should be needs based. Defining needs is no objective enterprise but a political one. Selecting criteria of merit from needs–based theories of justice may result in evaluations that differ dramatically from the terms used in public policy debates, which will minimize the usefulness of such evaluations. Similar types of reasoning may be directed against other prescriptive criteria such as *equal distribution* and the *public interest*.

All the effectiveness criteria displayed here, be they descriptive or prescriptive, have one thing in common: they pay no heed to costs. To remedy this omission, economists have devised cost criteria. The most pertinent cost measurements are productivity and efficiency. I shall examine them briefly in the next sections.

I agree with Shadish, Cook, and Leviton (1991:97f.) that most evaluation theorists have adopted the descriptive approach to criteria selection for two reasons. "One is that the job of making value judgments belongs to citizens or their elected representatives, so that it is wrong to impose an ethical system by choice of criteria. The second is that couching value judgments in terms used by stakeholders facilitates use of evaluation in debates and decisions."

My position is in line with theirs: both descriptive and prescriptive approaches are required, but descriptive valuing should be given priority. It is perfectly acceptable to answer questions about goal achievement, taking the policy and program goals as criteria and standards of evaluation. But it is also helpful and responsible to point out that the program is not attacking the real problem it was supposed to ameliorate. Both things can be done at the same time.

Productivity

Private business is often held up as an ideal for the public sector to emulate. In private business, profit is the criterion of merit and maximizing profit is the standard of success. In analogy to this, productivity maximization ought to be the standard of success for public interventions. Productivity is the ratio of outputs to costs, that is, outputs:inputs.

In chapter 4, it was shown that productivity can be measured in various ways, for instance as cost productivity and work productivity. We may use physical terms or money value above as well as below the dash in the algorithm. For simplicity, I shall express monetary value in U.S. dollars.

Water Pollution Control	Dollar cost per million liters treated
Water Treatment	Dollar cost per million liters treated
Income Tax	Dollar cost per dollar of tax collected
Passport Processing	Number of applications processed per man–year
	Total processing time per application in minutes
	Unit cost in dollars per application
Parks	Dollar cost per hectare maintained
Public Swimming Areas	Dollar cost per visitor
Building Standards Inspection	Man–hour cost per inspection
	Dollar cost per inspection
Fire Fighting, Prevention	Man–hour cost per capita
	Dollar cost per capita
	Man–hour cost per response
	Dollar cost per response
Urban Transit	Dollar cost per passenger trip

All interventions, large or small, incur costs. The development of an intervention creates costs, because alternatives must be probed, technical investigations must be performed, and reports must be written. After adoption, the program must be administered that requires operators, managers, executives, office space, office supplies, and technical equipment. Agency executives, managers, and front–line workers must be informed about the content of the program, for instance, through information meetings. Addressees must be informed about the existence and substance of public programs. Information brochures and folders must be composed and distributed, information disseminators contracted and trained. Regulations such as enabling legislation require personnel with technical competence who can scrutinize the applications. After applications have been approved, staff are needed to oversee, evaluate, and receive feedback on information. The same is true for economic incentives, disincentives, and information. Loans and subsidies are distributed on application, which requires staff for the processing of applications and making of decisions. Loans and subsidies by themselves also involve the distribution of economic resources and therefore costs. They also presuppose after–the–fact surveillance, performance review, and information feedback. The addressees of the interventions will also incur costs when they fill out the forms, participate in negotiations, and the like.

Productivity as a measure of public sector activities carries some technical advantages. Occasionally, costs are not terribly difficult to calculate since they reach the agencies in terms of monetarized funds.

However, dividing funds into appropriate relevant costs for each particular project may become an arduous task, because they are often
granted as lump sums for the program as a whole.

Yet these obstacles seems small in comparison to difficulties with
measuring the outputs, even though productivity only presupposes that
they are indicated in physical, not monetary terms.

In chapter 4, I discussed the case of municipal libraries to illustrate
the difficulties of finding valid output indicators. Is the number of
borrowed books really an exhaustive output measure? Many patrons
visit the library to read newspapers, magazines, and journals but this
does not show in the borrowing statistics. They frequent the reference
library to consult dictionaries and encyclopedias or the music department to listen to records, tapes, and discs. Libraries also provide some
information services. The number of books borrowed is not a fully
exhaustive output indicator.

There is also another intricacy involved in productivity evaluation.
A library may be held in esteem by the public at large even though
they never patronize it. It may have an intrinsic, potential, or expectation value. A comparison with scenic values illuminates the idea. The
Sarek National Park in Swedish Lapland is worth something to me
even though I have never visited it and maybe never shall. The same
goes for Muddus, Padjelanta, and other Lappish national parks. Yet I
view these national parks as precious jewels and want them to be
conserved. The same might be true for libraries as well. A distinguished municipal library is a worthwhile asset by itself, aside from
the number of books borrowed. This expectation value does not sur-
face in the statistics on books borrowed or the number of visitors
registered.

Or let me briefly mention a service like public child care. Which
output criteria ought to be used to value child care? And what constitutes good child care? In the Swedish political debate, the monetary
cost per number of day care places or the man–hour cost per day care
place are used as criteria of merit. These yardsticks, however, are less
satisfactory, since day care places can differ dramatically by quality.
There are important differences between day care centers, even in
Sweden, concerning didactics, teacher quality, atmosphere, and equipment. How should these quality aspects be captured and measured?

By this I only want to ascertain the general limits of productivity
measurement, and even then from within its own acknowledged premises.

Another important objection against productivity suggests that it is an internal metric, which does not apprehend what we really want to disentangle: namely, the effects that the program, its implementation and outputs have produced on the end–receivers or in society at large, the value of these results, and if the benefits are worth the costs. In the library example, borrowed books are not arresting by themselves; people often charge out books and shelve them at home without reading them. More important is the reading of the borrowed books. But what really matters are the borrowers' gains from their reading, which may be recreational or educational. What the cost–conscious, education–oriented library evaluator really wants to grasp may be if the value of the insights gained through borrowed books are worth the costs involved. But then she has left productivity measurement and entered the field of efficiency evaluation.

Proponents of productivity as a standard against which to evaluate public policies, programs, and services cannot escape the fact that productivity as an output yardstick is not an ideal measurement rod for assessing the worth and merit of public sector activities. Productivity measures quantities, while qualities tend to be overlooked. And the public institution may do wrong things, that is, the outputs may not produce the desired outcome.

Efficiency Criteria

The third family of merit criteria to be used in modern political and administrative evaluation is efficiency. Efficiency is often held to be *the* value of public administration. In his classic work *Administrative Behavior* (1976:186), Herbert Simon argued this point: "The criterion which the administrator applies to the factual problems is one of efficiency. The resources, the input, at the disposal of the administrator are strictly limited....It is his function to maximize the attainment of governmental objectives (assuming they have been agreed upon) by the efficient employment of the limited resources that are available to him." Efficiency has been cherished also in other contexts. Said George Bernard Shaw (1907:act 4): "There are only two qualities in the world: efficiency and inefficiency, and only two sorts of people: the efficient and the inefficient."

To repeat what was said in chapter 4, efficiency can be measured in two ways, as cost benefit or cost effectiveness. If measured in a cost–

benefit analysis, efficiency can be expressed as the ratio of the monetarized value of the results produced by the program to the monetarized costs. If equalized to what is measured in cost–effectiveness analysis, efficiency pays heed to monetarized costs as in cost–efficiency analysis, but the value of the effects is indicated in physical terms only (see figure 4.10).

The impacts produced by the program are not identical with any occurrences in the target area after its instigation. These occurrences may have been caused by something else. What evaluators must look for are effects produced by the program, period. On this account, efficiency assessment uses the same measure as effectiveness analysis. The major difference is that efficiency takes costs into account which is not the case in effectiveness analysis.

My discourse on effectiveness, productivity, and efficiency as value criteria in public intervention evaluation can be condensed to the overview provided in figure 14.2.

Assuming that productivity and efficiency measures can be developed and adopted, the benefits to civil service and the general public would seem to be extensive. First of all, awareness of results in itself stimulates people toward improvement of performance. Individuals tend to raise their sight when they see the effects of their endeavors. If there is continuous feedback on the basis of some objective result criterion, people will be motivated to improve their scores. This in turn will boost employee satisfaction and employee morale.

Measuring productivity and efficiency may also provide a basis for deemphasizing directives, norms, regulations, and even supervision itself. Working with a good set of productivity and efficiency measures, the employee can often become her own master. Objective cri-

---

FIGURE 14.2
Four Important Criteria of Merit in Program Evaluation

(i) Effectiveness	= degree of outcome goal–achievement, costs disregarded
(ii) Productivity	= output through cost
(iii) Efficiency (cost–benefit)	= monetarized value of program effects through monetarized program costs
(iv) Efficiency (cost–effectiveness)	= program effects in physical terms through monetarized program costs

teria, rather than a supervisor, guide an employee's labors and determine her accomplishments.

All of these factors can promote innovation, for once specific objectives have been set they should tend to become more important than the procedures for attaining them.

Points of Reference

To say something wise about the actual productivity and efficiency of particular programs, points of reference are needed. The actual productivity of a library, for instance, must be compared to something to give you an impression of how good the indicated productivity really is. That is, evaluators need standards of performance on the productivity criterion to tell what high or low productivity means.

The Israeli political scientist Yehezkel Dror (1968:28) has presented an overview of the most common value standards used in public policy evaluation. I have supplemented Dror's inventory by adding some performance standards of my own. With these additions, Dror's list looks as follows. To simplify, I have used productivity as a metric.

1. *The past.* How does the achieved productivity compare with that in the past? How much did one book loan cost in 1993 in municipality A compared with 1992, 1991 or even the long–term period of, say, 1982–1992?
2. *Intranational comparison.* How does the achieved productivity compare with that of similar institutions in the same national or regional area? How much did one book loan cost in 1993 in municipality A compared with similar measures for municipalities B, C, or D in the same country? Or how much did one book loan cost in library L compared with library M, N, and O in municipality A?
3 *International comparison.* How does the achieved productivity compare with that of similar institutions in other countries? How much did one book loan cost in 1993 in Finnish municipalities A, B, C, and D compared with similar measures for Swedish municipalities A, B, C, and D?
4. *Benchmark.* How does the achieved productivity fare in comparison with best empirical practice?
5. *Goals.* Does the achieved productivity meet the goals of the political bodies? Is the result in accord with municipal government goals?
6. *Client expectations.* Does the achieved productivity meet the demands of library clients?
7. *Stakeholder demands.* Does the achieved productivity meet the de-

mands of other library stakeholders? Are the costs per book loan acceptable to the municipal citizens, the librarians' union, or the library staff?

8. *Professional standards.* Does the achieved productivity meet accepted professional standards? How are the costs per book borrowed rated by the association of Finnish municipal libraries or by the librarians' professional organization? Does national and international expertise on library management judge the productivity as acceptable?

9. *Minimum.* Is the achieved productivity high enough to meet minimum demands?

10. *Optimum.* Is the achieved productivity as good as it could be according to an optimal model?

Effectiveness, Economic Criteria, and Procedural Values

Like all criteria of public program evaluation, effectiveness, productivity, and efficiency provide partial perspectives. They overlook or treat as givens other requirements normally demanded from public sector activities in contemporary democracies. In his *Bureaucracy,* James Q. Wilson (1989:126ff.) named these other requirements contextual goals. According to Wilson, contextual goals are produced by a desire either to ensure procedural fairness or to favor certain interests over others.

A procedural standard deeply rooted in Western public administration is *legal equity.* "When I now take a grip on the 'equity' notion, it is with a certain tremor," Torstein Eckhoff confessed in his inaugural lecture as a professor of the University of Oslo in 1957 (1989:242). "'Equity' is an expression, associated with such strong positive emotions that you feel like you are committing a sacrilege in attempting to analyze it. It is similar to words like 'freedom' and 'democracy' in the respect that nobody decently can declare himself an adversary to what the word stands for. But *what* it stands for, is seldom made clear, and it also varies a great deal."

I agree with Eckhoff's analysis and there is little reason in this context to dissect the concept in great detail. Let me only maintain that from an equity point of view, public policy and program evaluation first and foremost is directed at case management. For each case, we may require that the concerned individual shall be treated fairly by the pertinent authorities. She must be able to obtain the documents and other preparatory materials that the agency intends to use, and be offered a chance to argue her case before the formal decision is taken.

Afterwards, the individual must be given a justification for the decision and be notified on how to appeal it to a higher authority. Furthermore, equal cases must be treated equally. For instance, the civil servant in charge must neither give favors to relatives, party comrades, family friends or people from the same university, nor disfavors to enemies, people born in some special province, and political adversaries.

In *Bureaucracy,* Wilson (1989:126ff.) used American defense procurement programs to illustrate the case of contextual goals. The Defense Department, through the Defense Logistics Agency, each year acquires food, fuel, clothing, and spare parts worth billions of dollars, and administers close to $ 200 billion in government contracts. Congress and the president have repeatedly made clear their desire that the system be run efficiently. There are, however, legal fairness constraints placed on this efficiency. These procedural constraints are placed on the procurement process to ensure that contracts are awarded fairly, that is, in ways that allow all interested businesses to compete on equal terms. "The essential rules are that all potential contractors must be offered an equal opportunity to bid on a contract; that the agency's procurement decision must be objectively justifiable on the basis of written specifications; that contracts awarded on the basis of sealed bids must go to the contractor offering the lowest price; and that unsuccessful bidders must be offered a chance to protest decisions with which they disagree."

Characteristically, equity requirements make case management more time consuming. Procedural equity is expensive. Results–oriented criteria like productivity, efficiency, effectiveness will therefore conflict with equity and other criteria for procedural correctness. Trade–offs between procedural equity on the one hand and effectiveness, productivity or efficiency on the other cannot be performed through a scientific, technical calculus.

Other procedural criteria are *democratic values*. These are in principle also overlooked by effectiveness models and economic models. It has been shown that larger Scandinavian municipalities boast higher productivity in the production of social services than smaller ones. Against this it is often argued that smaller communities offer more favorable opportunities for citizens to participate in civic life and greater opportunities to keep an eye on public officials. No productivity study or any other evaluation for that matter, however impressive from a scientific and scholarly point of view, can explain in an objective fashion how a balance should be struck between these democratic values and productivity. The trade–off can only be made through public debate, opinion formation, compromise, and majority decisions, that is, through politics.

Still another set of contextual goals, emphasized by Wilson, are constraints purporting to *favor certain interests* over others. Again he (1989:126ff.) uses American defense procurement programs as cases. In the procurement processes, the Defense Department, through the Defense Logistics Agency, is legally forced to pay special attention to suppliers that are small businesses (especially small disadvantaged businesses), female–owned small businesses, handicapped workers, or disabled and Vietnam–era veterans, or are located in areas with a labor surplus.

Wilson concludes: "The [procedural fairness] motive might be described as an effort to produce a level playing field, the [favor–certain–interest] motive as an effort to tilt the playing field."

Still another requirement that might be used as a standard is *representativeness*. In some countries, public agencies are legally required to achieve a work force reflective of the diversity of the national population as whole. Administration should be a microcosm of the larger society, for instance with respect to race, languages, gender, and region. Korean civil service, for instance, has been evaluated from the point of view of regional balance in recruitment patterns. Such studies have found that people from the Kyongsang provinces are overrepresented in comparison to people from the Cholla provinces. While enhancing the legitimacy, such a socially representative public service may not be the technically most competent and efficient one.

Ideally, the evaluator would like to allocate one single value to the overall performance or character of the evaluand. For instance, efficiency would be combined with procedural fairness, representativeness, democratic values, and favor–certain–interest values into one overall value. This ambition, however, can never be fulfilled by scientific means. In the final analysis, global scoring necessitates political judgment. A way out of this quandary is to present the evaluation of each of the mentioned phenomena separately and leave the global scoring to the decision–makers as a political issue.

In the beginning more than in the 1990s, there was an obvious technocratic tendency in evaluation research. Short–sighted and ill–

conceived political games ought to be supplanted by long–range, sci-entifically based, rational decision making. But in my opinion, evalua-tion can never fully substitute for political judgment and should never be allowed to. In all authoritative allocation of values, to use David Easton's famous definition of the subject of politics, there are difficult balancing problems, which can only be settled through politics, not through technical calculi however reliably and thoroughly performed.

Let me on this account quote Lennart Lundquist (1990:18):

> In conflicts within as well as between different types of criteria of merit, there is no yardstick at hand which in an objective fashion lays out what values ought to apply. Neither is there always a sanction system which guarantees that all actors comply with a possible given criterion. How are priorities set in these cases? As a general rule, the problem cannot be solved through the application of techniques, however technically sophisticated. The only remaining way out is to decide through power. This means that somebody or something (e.g., elected political officials, parties to a negotiation or the market) with power to push through its will in the final analysis decides which criteria and standards ought to apply. This shows the obvious political nature of evaluation.

I strongly agree with Lundquist in his defense of politics against the exaggerated claims of evaluation research. Evaluation, however scien-tific and systematic, cannot and should not be a substitute for the full range of political play—controversy, discussion, and decision making. Evaluation has a considerable role to play, but cannot replace politics.

On one account, however, I wish to modulate Lundquist's conclu-sion in the above quotation. Instead of directly resorting to power in cases of disunity, I would commend power wielders to stress the dis-cursive, deliberative, debate–oriented trait in a democratic form of government. Power is the last retreat should differences remain after extended deliberations and negotiations between the parties in discord.

There is another solution to the criterion problem that is rarely addressed in evaluation theory. It suggests that the interest must focus not on results, but on procedures for making decisions on results. This institutional solution to the criterion problem suggests that the main emphasis should be placed on the building of institutions, which should conduct evaluations. Issues concerning who should participate in an evaluation and other rules concerning the evaluation enterprise would be central. The stakeholder scheme that Sweden has institutionalized in the previously presented SOU model would be a case in point (see chapter 4).

The institutional solution implies that the interest is moved from careful assessment of outcomes and results to painstaking assessment of organizational arrangements and rule systems for decision making. This marks an ironic return to process–oriented management and institutional models of evaluation, which modern evaluation, with its emphasis on results–oriented management and the direct study of intervention output and outcome, was once a reaction against.

15

Uses and Utility of Evaluation

> *"Long live economics and may it never be of any use."*
> —Toast at the Christmas party of the Cambridge economists
>
> *"The road to inaction is paved with research reports."*
> —Edward A. Suchman, Evaluative Research (1967)

That evaluation results should come to use is a dogma in the evaluation community. Furnishing potential recipients with well–underpinned information, wise judgments for reasoned afterthought, and efficient options for action is the proper task of evaluation. If utilization falters, evaluation flounders as well. Not only usefulness and utilization, but also utility are the hallmarks of a successful evaluation.[1]

The Growing Discontent with Evaluation

Yet nonutilization or underutilization of evaluation is a constantly recurring lament, more so perhaps in American than in Canadian and West European academic literature on evaluation. Decision–makers commission and fund evaluations but care little, if at all, about the resulting reports. Now and then, the issues are resolved before the evaluations are finalized. Programs that evaluators have found effective are cut back, while programs that evaluators have deemed ineffective are continued and even expanded. Evaluations are blatantly neglected.

A more sophisticated criticism admits that evaluations are used only as ammunition in battles between political factions, where allegiances are already formed and front lines already drawn. Evaluations are seized upon but only to strengthen or undermine established postures and stances. Other circumstances than facts on program impacts govern public sector decision making.

There are some truths to these criticisms. Evaluations are ignored or summarily dismissed. They are also employed as weapons in ongoing fights. Partly, however, the disappointment with evaluation is also due to exaggerated expectations.

Few things live up to the expectations held of them. And evaluation is no exception. In the 1960s, in both Europe and the USA, hopes were high. The sun of evaluation research had risen. In those days, the utilization issue–the last problem in my Eight Problems Approach to Public Policy Evaluation—was very simplistically addressed. Evaluation research should guide policy making and program administration in a more scientific direction, if not convert it into a scientific or sciencelike activity. Rule by the people or at least rule by elected politicians should be fortified by a healthy dose of expert advice. Technocracy should sustain democracy (Fischer 1990).

The transformation of governance into a researchlike enterprise is based on several premises concerning evaluation and its interaction with public sector decision making. First, evaluation ought to be an objective, value–free social science. This is achieved by taking the goals of others—mostly prestated policy and program targets—as organizers and criteria of assessment, and by focusing on the most efficient means to reach the given goals. In addition, to solve the means problem evaluation research must apply best available social science causal analysis methodology, preferably two–group experimental designs. Often, this requirement contradicts the way in which real–life intervention decisions are actually made. The solution to this contradiction is a radical metamorphosis of public sector decision making. To meet the methodological requirements of scientific causal analysis, public decision making must be converted into a two–step procedure: first, provisional tryouts organized as two–group randomized experiments to allow for scrupulous evaluation; second, utilization of the evaluation results to inaugurate the best means to achieve the stated ends.

In the reformed world of the radical experimentalists, public sector decision–makers respond without delay to the findings of evaluation research, digest them and act accordingly. Evaluation is perceived as a science and utilization is viewed as a linear process through which corroborated scientific findings on the most appropriate means are transmitted into a well–oiled decision–making machinery, where they are received, adopted and acted upon by public officials partly turned into social engineers. Utilization is interpreted according to the instrumental planning model.[2]

The utopia of radical experimentation, where utilization occurs in a straightforward, linear and mechanical manner, contrasts starkly with the real world of government where evaluations "wind up as litter in the bureaucratic mill," to quote Carol Weiss' (1972:11) expressive formulation. Why is it that evaluation does not get a hearing? This question is closely related to a larger, increasingly important one: the use of science and social inquiry in government decision making. Actually, a new academic growth industry has emerged devoted to the study of the utilization of science, social research, and evaluation. There is a substantial, rapidly multiplying literature on the subject of linkages between science and politics, which can be easily seen from the bibliographies assembled (Dynes and Marvel 1987; Rich 1981:65ff., 137ff., 169ff., 207ff.). Several overviews of this thriving scholarship have been produced.[3] Journals like *Science Communication* (formerly *Knowledge: Creation, Diffusion, Utilization*), *Knowledge and Policy,* and *Public Understanding of Science* testify to the scope of the current research on knowledge utilization in public and corporate decision making.

To probe deeper into the utilization issue, we must clarify what is meant by utilization; otherwise, we can neither sequester use from nonuse nor discern various types of use. And if we do not know exactly what utilization is, how can we be so sure that there is too little of it? Therefore five types of utilization will be discerned: instrumental, conceptual, interactive, legitimizing, and tactical. We must also circumscribe who the recipients are. In addition, it seems meaningful to clarify in what sense the term evaluation can be employed. I shall start with the concept of utilization, and then say something about users and evaluation, and end with some recipes for improved utilization.

The Engineering Model of Evaluation Utilization

The engineering model for utilization of evaluation—conceived as an ideal to reach out for—has been a propelling force behind the notion of evaluation as a device for reining in the demons of politics and make Leviathan more domesticated and rational (Albœk 1988:23ff.; Fischer 1990). The constituent features of the engineering model are sketched in figure 15.1.

Although the engineering model is applicable to all levels of political life, I shall assume here—for pedagogical reasons—that the national politicians set the goals.

In the sequel, the engineering model will be interpreted as a theory of how the interplay between politics, administration, and evaluation

FIGURE 15.1
The Engineering Model for Utilization of Evaluation

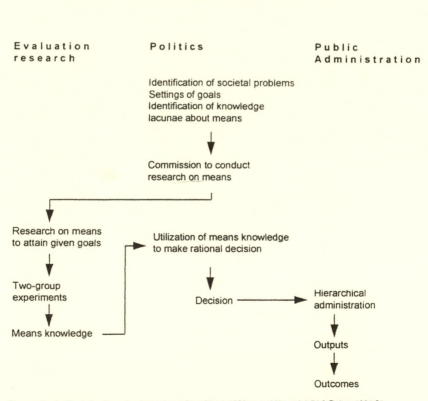

Source: Inspiration to the figure has been drawn from Albœk 1988:xx and Naustdalslid & Reitan 1994:51.

research actually unfolds. It will not be regarded as an ideal to be achieved.[4] As an empirical theory, the engineering model is based on the so–called rational organization model according to which organizations are instruments to attain ends. Being rational means selecting the most efficient means to reach a given end. The essential features of the rational organization model can be understood as a series of steps in a problem solving process joined to an assumption about perfect implementation of the decision to solve the problem: problem identification, goal determination, outlining of alternative means to reach the goals, valuation of the alternatives, selection of the most efficient alternative to reach the goal, and implementation of the decision so that intended outcomes will be achieved.

According to the engineering model, intervention decisions are taken in two stages. The first, preliminary stage suggests that conceivable measures are rigorously tested in carefully designed, small–scale pilot trials. The findings from the pilot trials are fed back into the political system which in a second stage on basis of the findings will arrive at a decision about the full–scale introduction or discarding of the program.

The engineering model asserts that problems are identified in the political system, that politicians set goals to remedy the problem and point to areas where their knowledge of appropriate means is too scant. Then researchers are commissioned to ascertain the most efficient means to reach the contemplated goals. The researchers work with best available research designs and methodologies, preferably two–group randomized experimentation to ensure that the most efficient means to achieve the given purposes are discovered. In other words, the researchers conduct one or several experiments on a minor scale. When this is finished they deliver objective and secure knowledge about means back to the political system. The politicians will use this safe instrumental knowledge to make a rational decision, binding for all citizens in the nation. The decision is then transmitted to the public administration, which faithfully and expeditiously will implement it so that the coveted outcome will be produced.

In the engineering model evaluation is used in an *instrumental* fashion. By instrumental is meant that the evaluation findings are utilized as means in goal–directed problem solving processes. Evaluation research sets no goals, neither does it discover or clarify problems. The proper role of evaluation is, given politically decided goals and before the reform is inaugurated across the board, to elicit, through the use of experimentation, the most efficient means to reach the indicated goals. Since the goals have been determined by the politicians, the evaluators can pursue factfinding about means in a purely value neutral and objective fashion (Fischer 1990). Popper's words comes to mind: "Piecemeal social engineering resembles physical engineering in regarding the *ends* as beyond the province of technology" (1957:3).

At this point, I shall attempt to deepen the discussion by joining instrumental evaluation use to theories of mass media influence on society. To illustrate how mass mediated persuasive appeals actually work on the audience according to two significant theories of this field, I shall use a three–step staircase scheme. Mass media effects are usually studied in three domains: the knowledge domain, the attitude domain, and the action domain. While the knowledge domain concerns perceptions of reality and the attitude domain pertains to values and valuations, the action domain involves practical action. The order in which the domains occur in the real world is subject to dispute. Some scholars maintain that the cognitive component (knowledge domain) precedes the affective (attitude domain), which in turn antedates the conative one (action domain). Others argue that action comes first, while attitudes and knowledge change later to legitimize the actions (Devine and Hart 1989). The two theories are represented in figure 15.2.

Learning theory, the dominant doctrine in the field, invokes a staircase hierarchy in which the stages come in the cognitive—affective—conative order. Knowledge comes first and results in attitude change, which conditions action.

FIGURE 15.2
Learning Theory and Dissonance–Attribution Theory

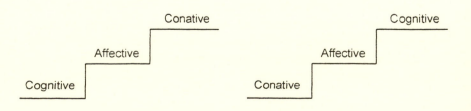

Learning according to learning theory typically seems to occur when the audience is involved in the topic of the information effort and when there are clear differences between the alternatives. The diffusion of new products and other tangible innovations provides the best illustration of such conditions. New commodities offer clear alternatives and the audiences most interested in them are involved. In these circumstances, audience members first become aware of the product, then develop an interest in it and assess its worth, and finally adopt or discard it. The notion that knowledge comes first, then attitudes, and then action implies a kind of rationality that, by and large, seems pretty close to the philosophy underlying evaluation use in the engineering model.

According to the competing *dissonance–attribution theory,* the steps are taken in exactly the reverse order: first comes behavior, then attitude modification, and finally learning. This sequence has typically occurred in situations in which the audience has been involved but the alternatives have been almost indistinguishable. The consumer is forced to behave—make a choice—on the basis of some nonmedia or nonmarketing communication source. Then she changes her attitude in order to bolster that choice—often on the basis of experience with the chosen alternative. Finally, learning itself occurs on a selective basis, in order to support the original choice by response to the messages that are supportive of it.

While admitting that information activities can have a cognitive effect in promoting the original choice behavior and attitude change, dissonance theorists contend that the main information effect is in terms of reducing dissonance or providing information for attribution or self–perception *after* action and attitude transformation have occurred. The dissonance theory seems far away from instrumental use in the engineering model. On the other hand, it appears to represent fairly well what we know about political information processes. It resembles legitimizing use of research and evaluation, a topic to which I shall return further ahead.

How realistic is the engineering model, construed as an empirical theory? There are probably circumstances in which reality does not differ much from the engineering model. There seems to be cases where the political system has set exceptionally clearcut targets and by means of evaluation succeeded in achieving these in ways that resemble instrumental use.

In most situations, however, real life deviates markedly from the engineering model. Evaluations may have significant consequences but not in the linear sequence asserted by the instrumental view. The roles of evaluation in political and administrative contexts are more many–sided, subtle and complex (Wittrock 1991; Weiss 1979).

Most of all, the deviations pertain to the actions of the commissioners and the users–the politicians, the parties, the agencies. They also revolves around what evaluation transmits and the communication between evaluation and politics.

Four Other Types of Utilization of Evaluation

If applied according to the *enlightenment model,* evaluation results are incorporated gradually into the user's overall frame of reference; evaluation is used in thinking (Weiss 1979:209) but not in action. Enlightenment is also referred to as *conceptual use.*

In the enlightenment model, politicians and other stakeholders have received cognitive and normative insights through the evaluation, but these insights have not been directly instrumental and transformed into action. After due consideration of the findings, program officials conclude that the proposals for action should be brushed aside. Although the recommendations are not observed, the whole procedure contributed to a thorough scrutiny of the premises of the program, the illumination of problems, and a deeper understanding of program merits and limitations. This is the meaning of enlightenment use (Weiss 1981:20f.).

To enhance our understanding, I shall join the enlightenment model to a more elaborated impacts hierarchy than the one pictured in figure 15.2 above. William McGuire's (1989:44ff.) so–called Communication/Persuasion Model is probably one of the most detailed hierarchies of communication consequences so far invented. I have arranged the twelve response stages of the model into a staircase, shown in figure 15.3.

McGuire (1989:48) contends that the twelve steps constitute the output side of the persuasion process. The list "shows the successive response substeps required if the communication is to be effective; for example the public must be exposed to the message and, having been exposed to it, must attend to it, like it, learn what and how, agree, store and retrieve, and decide on the basis of it, down to behaving on the basis of that decision (step ten), getting reinforced for so behaving,

FIGURE 15.3
Response Steps in Communication Processes

Step 12. Post–behavioral consolidating
Step 11. Reinforcement of desired acts

Step 10. Behaving in accord with decision
Step 9. Deciding on basis of retrieval
Step 8. Information search and retrieval
Step 7. Memory storage of content and/or agreement
Step 6. Yielding to it (attitude change)

Step 5. Skill acquisition (learning how)
Step 4. Comprehending it (learning what)
Step 3. Liking, becoming interested in it
Step 2. Attending to it
Step 1. Exposure to the communication

Source: W. J. McGuire, *Theoretical Foundations of Campaigns,* 1989:44ff.

and engaging in postcompliance activity (such as proselytizing others or reorganizing one's related beliefs) that consolidates the new position induced by the communication."

A user who has advanced from step one through ten has applied the evaluation instrumentally. Yet if the evaluation only passed step one through five, that is, if the recipient has been exposed to the evaluation, attended to it, become interested in it, comprehended it and acquired some skills through it that he did not have before, but neither yielded to nor acted as a consequence of it, the user has applied the evaluation in an enlightening manner.

Evaluation findings, then, may have been consulted by the user, even painstakingly studied by him, and made him much more informed than before but neither triggered any action, nor swayed any attitudes. This is enlightenment use.

Concepts used in evaluations can and do aid and structure policy discussions. At a general level many of the concepts of evaluation research are part of the *lingua franca* of policy makers. Within specific problem contexts particular constructs are drawn on to provide a vocabulary to help organize and clarify discussion and debate. Think of the policy effects of such category labels as "policy instruments," "side effects," "determinants of policy outcomes,""management by objectives," and "counterfactual cases." The process by which evaluation percolates through legislative assemblies, agencies, and commissions and influences policy makers' ways of thinking is subtle, but nevertheless not to be disregarded. This structuring ability is also enlightenment use.

Carol Weiss, whose works are constantly cited in papers and books on research utilization and evaluation use, also discerns a third category, *interactive utilization* of evaluation. Public policy designers are engaged in hobnob search processes with a number of different actors, where evaluators constitute one group only and their knowledge just one set among many. Participants may include administrators, interest group representatives, planners, journalists, clients, political appointees, friends, party members, and exercised citizens. The dialogue may serve the purpose of intellectual penetration of a societal problem. However, since disagreements are a commonplace in such "policy primeval soups," to borrow a phrase divulged by John W. Kingdon, the exploration procedure will also contain conflict building and conflict resolution. The process from evaluation to future decision in the political system is not linear and unidirectional but unorganized, messy and interactive in a fashion that escapes diagrammatic representation.

Interactive use involves the application of evaluation–informed knowledge in conjunction with further research–based data and other forms of background like common sense, conventional wisdom, intuition, and recipients' own first–hand experiences (Weiss 1979:206f.).

In interactive use, public officials endorse "the Open Mouth Principle." They taste, swallow, and digest various kinds of information of which data on program results, program costs, and program structure form only a minor part. Decision–makers cannot consider outcomes and cost efficiency only but have to be mindful of legality issues, ethical appropriateness, congruence with due process and democratic values. They must ponder the costs of transforming the program, the type of staff needed to implement the change, the stances of client groups and intermediators, and what their fellow party associates believe. They must always calculate the political consequences of their actions, including their chances of reelection.

In my view, instrumental as well as enlightening and interactive application are reasonable utilizations of evaluation. The utilization concept should therefore be clarified in these three directions. But there are two additional, seemingly destructive uses, which are crucial for understanding the political system's way of handling evaluation.

The engineering model posits that government comes up with an unequivocal problem definition and sets lucid, well–ordered goals. Then it gives a clear assignment to researchers to uncover efficient means to reach the goals. But politics is not an academic seminar passionately devoted to solving problems by reasoned argument. Politics is a system of power struggle and resolution of disagreements. Political parties fight each other but so do government agencies, bureaus, municipal commissions, and interest organizations. Not even the state proper is a unitary actor with one, clearly expressed will. Rather it consists of a conglomerate of ministries, agencies, commissions, companies and other actors with different desires and knowledge needs. Knowledge needs are often power conflicts barely masked as demands for more information. Research is asked for not to meet a genuine interest to know more about the world but to use as ex post rationalization, to legitimize decisions and resolutions based on other considerations. This is the power approach, the *legitimizing* approach, to evaluation.

In legitimizing use, evaluation is seized upon to justify established positions grounded in other considerations, such as for instance political ideology, electoral hopes, coalition expediency or personal idiosyncracies. Evaluation is used to strengthen one's positive or negative stances on either issues or political adversaries and allies. Some evaluation results, deemed suitable to serve political purposes, are appropriated as additional evidence in conflict situations and in political struggles to bolster the case at stake. Other results, believed to be damaging, are either ignored or summarily dismissed. The *de facto* task of evaluation is to deliver ammunition for political battles, where alliances are already formed and frontlines already exist.

Legitimizing use of evaluation bears some striking resemblance to the Dissonance–Attribution Theory presented in figure 15.2. The Dissonance Theory embraces the view that knowledge enters the stage *after* the action has been taken to dissolve *ex post facto* the tensions created by it. Also in the twelve–steps staircase in figure 15.3 there are stages where knowledge comes in after–the–fact to fortify actions already performed. Steps eleven and twelve are the cases in point.

Let us reflect for a moment on the following scenario. For overall ideological and expedient electoral reasons, the parties in office have unanimously decided to drastically cut the program. But they need well–underpinned evidence to bolster the pending formal decision. An evaluation is appointed for the express purpose of scrutinizing those parts of the program already known to be less than satisfactory. The portions that seem to work well and are strongly supported by the clients are not subjected to investigation. In spite of the bias built into the terms of the evaluation, the results turn out not to be unequivocally negative. But the politicians in power seize upon the negative results only and use them as an official pretense to push through the reduction. The evaluation is used to provide legitimacy for a position already adopted. It is employed as an external cover to reinforce, alternatively hide, the real motivations for the cuts in the program.

Legitimizing use is a broad category, which also covers the following case. An agent with no influence over the appointment of an evaluation is using some of its findings as support for his old stance on the program. The evaluation in this case provides him with new arguments—new ammunition—for a position already taken.

The fifth form of evaluation utilization to be expounded here, *tactical utilization,* asserts that evaluation is requested to gain time or avoid responsibility. The important fact is not the eventual findings, but that an evaluation is appointed and under way. The process of doing evaluation, not the findings of this process, is used.

Let us consider a situation where decision–makers want to cover up faulty results, whitewash failures, avoid public debate and deflect criticism. An evaluation is appointed to render the activity an appearance of rationality and placate angry critics. The rationale is that an evaluation is appointed and under way, not that it eventually will produce substantive results. The evaluation process is aimed at fulfilling a tactical function. (As an aside I might add that tactical use was referred to in chapter 6 as Potemkin villages.)

In sum, evaluation can be used in at least five ways: instrumentally, conceptually, interactively, as legitimization, and tactically.

Individuals and Collectivities as Users, Direct and Indirect Use

In discussing use, it is also important to distinguish between *individual use* and collective use. Evaluation can be used among individuals in an organization without producing any action at the collective level (Wittrock 1991; Nydén 1992). In the political and administrative context, utilization is mostly supposed to occur among *collective* actors. Governments, opposition parties, ministries, agencies, agency sections, or bureaus are the potential recipients. This raises the issue of the role of knowledge in collective decision making, an issue that cannot be dealt with here.

Another equally apparent yet momentous distinction is the one between direct and indirect use. In *direct use* the recipient is personally exposed to the evaluation, either by taking part in investigative work or by being exposed to the findings through evaluator briefings or via published literature. *Indirect use* occurs when the transmission is mediated through some third link in the communication process between evaluators and users.

Use transpires although decision–makers neither join the evaluation team, nor are briefed about results or exposed to written reports. Often, decision–makers can afford little time to take part in fact–finding investigations or peruse the written documents emerging from them. Yet, under happy circumstances their advisors and staff may probe the material to produce easy–to–digest oral briefings. Consequently, evaluation findings may reach decision–makers and be used by them through indirect channels. The mass media are probably prominent transmitters through their recycling of pertinent literature. Consultants constitute another important intermediating group.

Evaluations Might Have Numerous Users

The instrumental theory of utilization—but to some extent also the enlightenment theory—assumes that the politicians who commission the evaluation also are the plausible users. The engineering model, for instance, presupposes a uniform political sphere and unequivocal assignments to conduct evaluations. I have already discussed the rather self–evident assertion that politicians are no homogeneous batch. Politics means conflict resolution rather than rational problem solving. On occasion, an evaluation may be neglected by the governing parties but attended to and used by the parliamentary opposition. In his inquiry into the Swedish Secretariat for Futures Studies, Björn Wittrock (1980) has shown that the so–called Energy and Society Study conducted in the middle of the 1970s was basically ignored by those who commissioned it—the framers of the major energy policy decisions—but assiduously employed by opponents of the official policy.

The theory of interactive, legitimizing and tactical use all make the highly probable assertion that evaluations may have several users and that the state is not a unitary actor. Aside from program framers, top–level management, senior administrators, middle–level managers and program staff, conceivable recipients of evaluation include political opponents of the program, third party implementers, addressees and their organizations, informal implementers like associations, the evaluation community, and pertinent researchers. In addition, the mass media always take an interest in evaluations, particularly if they smell the scent of potentially criticisms of political incumbents.

There is also a time complication in utilization. Adopting a short–term time perspective, protagonists of instrumental use suppose use to occur in some immediate pending decision. Yet, results may be used in the long-range perspective as well. Nothing impedes evaluators from providing more general knowledge of policy control mechanisms, chains of implementation, institutional arrangements, side–effects, and audience behavior, which in the long run alone—that is, through the education of students—may become consequential in decision making.

Users Learn from Process as well as Findings

The instrumental critique basically assumes that reporting alone will do the job. It happens that utilization researchers show a written report to probable users and ask if they have seen or read it. Often, the respondents allege that they have heard about the report but not read it. The conclusion follows that the evaluation has not been used.

The reporting perspective on utilization is evidently too narrow, particularly when confined to written final reports. Not only should evaluation refer to findings—expressed orally, in writing or in graphics—but to preceding investigatory processes as well. Evaluation is a process-product concept in the sense that it may refer both to the product—the oral briefing or the written report—and to the working process antedating the reporting. Many studies indicate that evaluations actually are used, provided the concept is stretched to cover also the investigatory operations leading to the oral or written reports. The mere decision to undertake an evaluation can serve as an implicit threat that stricter control is impending and make the evaluatees change their behavior. Disseminations of the questions to be posed in an impending evaluation may provide important signals to subordinates about what their superiors expect from them. Questions usually reveal what standards and criteria will be employed in the review. Users acquire crucial insights into the program by participating in the conduct of the evaluation and without even consulting the final results. In evaluation processes, evaluators often act as educators of the users.

In tactical use, as previously discussed, evaluation processes are used, not the results.

Strategies for Enhancing Utilization of Evaluation

How does evaluation get a hearing in governmental decision making? The literature is replete with admonitions. The basic–science road would be to publish the best approximation to truth, attend to the resulting scholarly debate, and let the political process handle the rest. However, I shall discuss situations in which evaluators adopt a consciously active role to use. In this active mode, the broad approaches with subapproaches in figure 15.4 will be covered.

The diffusion–centered strategy considers faulty utilization a question of improved transmission of evaluation results. Production–focused strategies attempts to transform the evaluators and their evaluation procedures to increase evaluation use. In user–oriented strategies, finally, the main preoccupation is to render the recipients more evaluation–friendly and susceptible to evaluations.

The point of departure for the construction of the three first parts of the strategy scheme has been a brief article in which Andrew D. Seidel (1983:52ff.) differentiated between the communication, the linkage, and the collaboration strategies for promoting the use of knowledge in decision making. However, I have changed both the terminology and the content of Seidel's original contribution and added a few points of

---

FIGURE 15.4
Strategies to Enhance Utilization of Evaluation

1. Diffusion–centered Strategy
   a. Reporting Method
   b. Linkage Method
2. Production–focused Strategy
3. User–oriented Strategy
4. Metaevaluation (Synthesis Analysis)
   a. Evaluation of another evaluation (also as self–evaluation)
   b. Summarizing and synthesizing of several Evaluations
   c. Evaluation of the general evaluation function

my own. In addition, I shall also treat metaevaluation as an approach to improved evaluation use.

The *diffusion–centered strategy* is concerned with making dissemination of evaluation findings as effectual as possible. There is nothing wrong with evaluation as long as it is carried out with best available methodologies. The bottleneck is that the recipients must know about the results before they can use it.

Within the diffusion–centered strategy, I have discerned two subapproaches: the reporting method and the linkage method. Concentrating on evaluation papers, tracts, and oral briefings, the reporting method attempts to broadcast evaluation output as widely as feasible and make it as recipient–friendly as possible, without compromising on either methodology or facts. The point of the linkage method is the same but here the efforts are institutionalized into formal groups, appointed commissions or some permanent documentation system.

Starting with the *reporting method,* I have collected and organized some possibilities of streamlining and broadcasting evaluation outputs, suggested by Seidel (1983:52ff.) and other communication experts. The results are shown in figure 15.5.

It is adamant for the success of the reporting method that the evaluator is resolutely committed to utilization, locates the potential users, attempts to avoid unintelligible writing, shuns no effort to fashion her papers and briefings in a user–friendly manner, and assumes the role of an ardent advocate of her results.

The purpose of the second diffusion–centered subapproach, *the linkage method,* is to promote dissemination by opening up channels into the recipient organization in a sustainable, organized, and systematic fashion. The linkage method involves permanent use of some intermediary agent between evaluators and practitioners.

Advisory commissions are one possible link. Besides the evaluators, such bodies are usually composed of the potential primary recipients of the evaluation, the evaluation sponsors, and producers of other evaluations. The commission members may offer valuable advice concerning how the findings should be diffused within their respective organizations. In addition, they might also function as disseminators themselves.

Another option is to involve opinion leaders. Defined as credible and influential members of their respective communities, opinion leaders operate as gate keepers in particular communication networks, who

FIGURE 15.5
The Diffusion–Centered Strategy: The Reporting Method

- Reports should display some startling fact that makes people sit up and think;
- Reports ought to be pointed and brief;
- Each written report should be confined to one trenchant issue; if complex, the results should be presented in several brief reports instead of one comprehensive treatise;
- Reports should contain a short and sharp executive summary;
- Potential evaluation clients should be located, preferably in advance;
- Written reports should be fashioned in user language rather than in jargon designed to make simple ideas difficult to grasp;
- Accounts of results should be accompanied by graphics;
- Crucial results should be highlighted stylistically, through the use of clear headings, subheadings, and an appropriate overall organization of the analysis; substantive findings ought to be presented first, methods afterwards; the major substantive results should be stated in unequivocal terminology prior to reservations, not the other way around; it is important that the executive summary starts with the major substantive findings;
- Reasoning on methods should be reduced to an absolute minimum in the bulk of the report; instead methodological considerations ought to be appended as attachments;
- Findings, insights and recommendations ought to be disseminated continually and to many audiences before the final essay is completed;
- Reports should include recommendations for action;
- Reports should be prompt and timely;
- Appropriate managers and other stakeholders should receive copies of written preliminary papers and the final essay;
- Results should be communicated in person;
- Evaluators should become involved in the selling of their findings;
- Evaluators should be around in case managers may want to talk;
- Evaluators should talk briefly and often;
- Evaluators should tell stories, performance anecdotes, to illustrate the points;
- Evaluators should engage in public debate.

can obstruct, filter, delay or precipitate flows of information. Dissemination will increase if such gate keepers are appointed members of advisory commissions.

Still another possibility would be to engage an information transfer specialist. Appointed a member of the advisory commission, her task would be to suggest mechanisms for the fostering of communication between evaluators and users.

Also computerized routines and systems designed to make evaluation results better known to conceivable recipients are included in the linkage substrategy. Efforts to incorporate evaluations into new documentation systems and data bases are cases in point.

In sum, the diffusion strategy starts from the assumption that faulty utilization is due to noise and other communication barriers between producers and consumers of evaluation. There might be something to this assumption. It is obvious that before recipients can use any information, they must know about it. It helps, too, if they understand it. Occasionally, evaluation reports are both incomprehensible and little disseminated. Therefore, amelioration of the dissemination function and the prerequisites for communication is important. The diffusion–centered strategy does not necessitate any changes either in evaluation methodology or in the facts to be reported. Neither does it demand any changes on the recipient side. This seems to explain the popularity of the diffusion strategy. Yet it should be emphasized that utilization of evaluation is not a question of user–friendly reporting and intensified dissemination efforts only. The broadcasting of evaluation results cannot guarantee utilization. There are much more difficult obstacles to utilization than information barriers.

The *production–focused strategy,* the second major approach to utilization improvement, suggests that evaluation outputs should be made more user–friendly through efforts directed at the evaluation process. The assumption is that evaluations are dismissed or shelved because they are irrelevant, if not faulty. Production strategists do not primarily worry about how to improve communication of substantiated findings or dissemination of oral or written information. The adjustments must probe deeper. The evaluation process as such must be adapted to meet the demands and desires of the conceivable recipients.

One possibility is to adapt evaluation to the stages of program development. To illustrate this important idea, I shall use a four–stage scheme developed by Lee J. Cronbach, as it is summarized in the Shadish, Cook, and Leviton volume (1991:336):

> The *breadboard* stage comes first. The ideas for a program have been provisionally incorporated into field activities on a small scale and are being routinely tinkered with to improve design. The *superrealization* stage is when a suitable design has been constructed and a demonstration study is initiated under conditions that maximize the likelihood of success—designers of the model deliver services with no slippage from the plan, expenditures per recipient are high, service recipients are carefully chosen for cooperativeness, and the catchment area is partly cut off from outside perturbations. In the *prototype* stage a program is

implemented under conditions that mimic those under which the program would be introduced as policy. Finally, the *operating program* stage is when the program is permanently up and running.

The assumption appears to be that the evaluation must be accommodated to the various stages of program maturity. The four different stages require four different evaluations.

Another feature of the production strategy is responsiveness to user worries. The responsive evaluator should care for the user's questions, not the questions of academic interest only. Various plausible users have diverse information wants in the different stages of intervention maturity. Preferably, the likely recipients—for example, responsible officials at the policy level, program level and local delivery level, program clients, scholars and journalists—should frame the questions and then leave them to the evaluator for investigation.

The use of manipulable variables as contingent factors is also recommended. Users are only attentive to contingencies that can be influenced through human action, or more specifically, the user himself. This usually means that suggestions aiming at a complete restructuring of society should be avoided. The underlying notion is that evaluations must be theoretical in order to become practically applicable. Theory in this context stands for explanatory theory. Only when we know what factors condition a beneficial or detrimental outcome, the appropriate conclusions for the future can be drawn. To this end, the responsive evaluator should concentrate on contingencies that humans may change, that is, manipulable variables.

Some people go even further and maintain that evaluators should focus on not only manipulable but feasible variables. It is patently insufficient to come up with manipulable variables, which no politically responsible person would like to change. Suggested modifications must be politically acceptable.

Still another ingredient in the production–oriented strategy is to adapt evaluation methodology to user needs. On this account, evaluation theorists disagree. Some theorists argue that case studies which attempt to picture the program as a comprehensive whole are best adapted to utilization whereas others maintain that sample surveys and questionnaires are more prone to produce use. Michael Patton asserts that evaluation methods and designs are more conducive to utilization than the scientific quality of the findings. It is particularly adamant that the utilization–focused evaluator choose softer, process–oriented anthropological methods which ensure close evaluator–user interaction. She ought to apply open–ended interviews and frame the major issues to be investigated in an interactive dialogue with commissioners and users. Then the odds are increased that utilization will happen.

A more far–reaching specimen of the production–focused approach claims that the recipients, or some sample of them or their trusted representatives, should be consulted by the evaluators throughout all stages of evaluation and utilization. In addition to problem identification, planning for data collection, actual data collection, data processing, and report writing, cooperation should spill over into dissemination and utilization as well. This enhances the probability that the users become committed to the findings, which increase the possibility that they will use the findings or recommend others to do so. It also enables the evaluators to implement their findings. This comes rather close to so–called action research.

The stakeholder–consultation substrategy is strongly endorsed by evaluation theorists, who are frantically preoccupied with utilization. Michael Q. Patton, who has composed treatises on "utilization-focused evaluation," effectively commends this strategy as a vehicle of ensuring that the evaluation will pose questions relevant to potential primary users.

The stakeholder–consultation approach displays several advantages. The crucial rationale is that the chances of providing the right kind of information to recipients will increase. Through active participation, conceivable recipients may ensure that the evaluation will be responsive to issues that real users want to have illuminated.

Another merit is that learning may occur in the evaluation process, that is, long before the publication of the final tract. By participating in all stages of the evaluation, users will become committed to the results, which will enhance the likelihood that they will use them or recommend others to use them. Often the users will take the results as their own, and claim that they have been thinking along these lines all the time.

Yet there are drawbacks with the stakeholder–consultation substrategy. Researchers risk becoming involved in political processes. The problems that will be addressed may be of minor interest from a research perspective. In choosing between objectivity and usefulness, the second may be preferred. From the point of view of academic

research, it is important to separate objectivity and truth from usefulness and use. Invalid knowledge may be used, and valid knowledge
may remain unused. Evaluation should not be transformed into something entirely politicized.

An even more radical approach claims that the evaluation should be
performed by the recipients themselves, or their trusted representives.
This is typical of the Swedish policy commission model, presented in
chapter four.

The third and final approach to improvement of utilization, the
user–oriented strategy, engenders making potential evaluation clients
more susceptible to utilization.

Richard Stankiewicz has expounded some thoughts on research utilization, which can be applied to evaluation utilization as well.
Stankiewicz discerns five factors that may influence the user's capacity of receiving and applying information:

- the recipient's general stance toward change;
- the emphasis afforded by the organisation to analytical functions and
  activities;
- the evaluation capacity of the recipient organization;
- the emphasis afforded by the recipient organization on the development
  of staff professionalism; and
- the existence of an active strategy to develop and sustain contacts with
  external evaluation communities.

The interpretation of this is that utilization of evaluation concerns
both individual users and structural features of the utilizing organization.

There are studies that show that to become utilized evaluations need
some champion in the recipient organization. Users might also be
educated in evaluation. The major approach in this area would be to
incorporate evaluation into the management system of the organization. Evaluation should be institutionalized as an ongoing internal affair, like in management by results or management by objectives.

A different possibility is to adjust the policy formation process to
the demands of evaluation research for two–group experimentation.
As we have seen, this presupposes the implementation of a two–stage
approach to public policymaking: first a provisional small–scale tryout
accompanied by stringent evaluation, then inauguration across the country of the best alternative elicited through the tryout.

In addition to the three approaches to enhanced utilization hitherto discussed, I shall add a fourth, *metaevaluation*. Metaevaluation might refer to three different operations:

1. evaluation of another evaluation, either ongoing or completed;
2. a procedure for summarizing and synthesizing the findings of several evaluations of the same program or of an array of similar programs;
3. evaluation of the general evaluation function of an organization or a unit.

Heeding the advice of Scriven, I suggest that the evaluator conducts self–evaluation of her own evaluation, preferably the final report, before it is left to the commissioner. Self– evaluation amounts to quality control, for instance, by applying Scriven's Key Evaluation Checklist (Shadish, Cook, and Leviton 1991:81ff.). By removing remaining weaknesses, this self–evaluation may contribute to improved use of the final report. Another strategy is to encourage critical commentaries from enlightened and passionate scholars.

I also recommend metaevaluation in the sense that the findings of several evaluations should be summarized and synthesized. Often one is struck by the number and diversity of evaluation studies that have been produced in a single public policy sector or on an individual program. Evaluation research is usually designed to solicit practical answers to particular questions. The many evaluation studies have embraced a variety of methodological approaches and data gathering techniques. As a result, when previous studies are viewed in isolation from each other, the lessons learned often appear insignificant, inconclusive, and even contradictory. However, if the findings of past efforts are meticulously synthesized, they may cumulate to a surprising extent. Accordingly, they can be used to build more general explanations of what works and what does not. This could also be done at a cross–national level. A synthesis of results seems to be more useful to decision–makers than a single evaluation effort. In this fashion, metaevaluation—or synthesis analysis—is an approach to improved utilization of evaluation.

Also metaevaluation in the third sense of auditing of the evaluation function as suggested by Hudson, Mayne, and Thomlison (1992:195ff.) might improve future utilization. Metaevaluation in this sense is often included in a larger evaluation management philosophy suggesting the following. Instead of actually carrying out substantive evaluations,

senior management should concentrate on auditing the evaluation function in subordinate bureaus. While lower–level branches are instructed
to do self–evaluation of their own performance, higher authorities assumes the task of conducting evaluations of their subordinates' evaluation work. Senior management, for instance, may decide that lower
levels ought to perform self–evaluation and summarize the findings in
an evaluation essay. The task of senior management would then be to
evaluate the evaluation report.

Summing Up

Utilization is central to evaluation. The point of departure for my
discussion of utilization has been the engineering model according to
which evaluation is used instrumentally. Yet instrumental use seems
to be a rare species in public life. Besides instrumental use, I have
therefore discerned not only enlightening and interactive use but also
legitimizing and tactical use. Those who inquiry into utilization of
evaluation must evidently search for all five types of utilization.

But are all the five uses something that utilization–sensitive evaluators always should attempt to promote or at least abide by?

That instrumental and interactive use is something to be coveted by
scrupulous evaluators is obvious. In addition, enlightenment use also
belongs to the category of attractive utilization. But what about legitimizing use? Is that something that the utilization–conscious evaluator
ought to applause or tolerate? As for university–based evaluators, for
instance, can they tolerate that their efforts are used as ammunition in
political battles to bolster postures already adopted? Most academic
researchers would probably argue that legitimizing use is less desirable than, for instance, instrumental and interactive use. I do not entirely concur with this conclusion. I cannot fault political parties employing well–founded evaluation results to bolster their own case or
undermine those of their adversaries. After all, evaluation should count
but politics ought to decide. Legitimizing use must be placed within
the range of uses that even academic evaluators should endure.

Remains tactical utilization. Is tactical use something that university–based evaluators should covet? Should the purpose of evaluation
activities, albeit a minor one, be that evaluation activities are designed
to allow politicians to gain time or give the outside world the impression that they are committed to a worthy cause, although in fact they

do not perceive the matter in this perspective at all? I cannot see that tactical use is something that researchers should nurture, or even tolerate, as researchers. If they do, they act as political animals, not as scientists defiantly searching for truth. Contrariwise, it is an important task for academic evaluators to unveil eventual tactical purposes underlying an evaluation.

Final Word

"Evaluation is the liveliest frontier in American social science," Lee Cronbach wrote more than a decade ago. While this fascination with evaluation has subsided in the United States since Cronbach made his statement, it is probably still on the rise on the European continent. The methodological debate is comprehensive and probing. The production of new books and articles on evaluation is considerable. New journals appear, and professional organizations are created in several countries. The demand for education in evaluation is growing as is the clamor for people with evaluation expertise. Throughout the 1990s, a knowledge of evaluation will be an obvious asset for young people, who seek their future in government and public administration.

However, evaluation has its limits and problems. One such problem is to find out where results–oriented management is appropriate and justifiable and in which areas we should stick to the more traditional process–oriented management. A related problem is where to let the professions or the clients do the evaluations and what influence on up–coming decisions these professional and client–oriented evaluations should have. A third problem is under what circumstances evaluations should be performed; obviously they should not be undertaken regardless of costs. Evaluation may also be outright damaging as when an front–end operators strives to apply quantitative performance measures, which do not faithfully represent the general mission of their organization.

In the present work, the limits to evaluation set by a democratic constitution and a democratic public life has been particularly emphasized. For specific reasons, the demand for rational, social sciencelike evaluation must be subordinated to the requirements of a democratic body politic. Standard scientific methodology claims that innovative programs and policy instruments must be tried out through two–group experiments before they can be enacted across the board, but democratic politics may demand that reforms are inaugurated across the board without delay. Instrumental use of evaluation may demand immediate remedial action on programs, but the representatives of the people may believe differently and have a democratic mandate to do so. Higher value should be assigned to democratic control, widespread participation, and accommodation among various legitimate interests than to removing public sector decision making from the public clash of conflicting stakeholders to promote efficiency and rationality.

Democracy and sciencelike evaluation is a thorny topic, vastly underplayed in evaluation literature. Many books do not even mention it. This significant problem apparently needs further clarification.

Notes

1. "'Utilization' contains eight more letters and four more syllables than 'use,' and means almost the same thing. Its extra bulk may lend 'utilization' a kind of scientistic authority. At any rate, most of the writers reviewed here use the longer word, particularly those trying to develop a more precise, technical definition" (Karapin 1986:261).
2. An incisive criticism of instrumental evaluation and other technocratic thought is provided in Fischer 1990.
3. See, for instance, Weiss 1977; Alkin et al. 1979; Lindblom and Cohen 1979; Premfors 1979; Cronbach et al. 1980; Weiss and Bucuvalas 1980; Larsen 1980; Braskamp and Brown 1980; Leviton and Hughes 1981; Glaser et al. 1983; Dunn et al. 1984; and Heller 1986.
4. The engineering model is not conceived of as a heuristic tool, either. It is not interpreted as an instrument to facilitate empirical investigations, that is, it is not regarded as an ideal type like the perfect market in economic theory or the hierarchical model in administrative theory. While this interpretation would be perfectly reasonable, I shall brush it aside for the time being and depart from the notion that the engineering model purports to depict reality.

Glossary of Key Concepts in Evaluation[1]

Accountability: The aim of doing evaluation in order to provide information pertaining to the issue of whether stewards have exercised their delegated powers and discharged their duties properly. Accountability evaluation enables the delegating body to hold the persons to whom powers and responsibilities are delegated responsible for what they have achieved, particularly the worth of an intervention. Also to challenge the strategic direction of the intervention. Besides → improvement, accountability is the basic purpose for which evaluation should be performed.

Action Research: Investigation where the aim is not only to collect information and arrive at a better understanding, but to do something practical as well. Usually, action research is concerned with social change or has as its object to improve the efficiency of an organization such as the state.

Ad Hoc Policy Commission: A nonpermanent body in the Swedish system of government, appointed by the cabinet to evaluate past programs and propose new solutions to problems; the participants include representatives of numerous → stakeholding audiences, who are expected to work within the terms specified by the government.

Addressees: The targets of public interventions. Also clients, recipients, participants, audiences, beneficiaries.

---

[1] Each word following an arrow also appears as an entry in this Glossary.

After–the–Fact Evaluation: Assessment undertaken once the intervention is adopted, albeit provisionally. → Evaluation Ex Post.

Ambiguity: A technical term signifying the property of a word or some other linguistic expression to carry two or more different meanings. The word evaluation is ambiguous because it can mean both the process of evaluating and the product of that process in the form of an oral or written report. → Vagueness.

Analytical Scoring: The allocation of grades to diverse components of an ‹ evaluand, without any effort to provide a single overall score.

Arranger: Actor who decides to undertake and fund some activity, for example, an evaluation. Arrangers can contract out to or direct other bodies to actually carry out the activities.

Baseline Data: Information on target variables and other relevant parameters pertaining to the period before the intervention was adopted.

Basic Knowledge: The aim of undertaking evaluation for generating a body of fundamental research findings. Basic knowledge is best understood as a side purpose of doing evaluation, the major aims being → accountability and → improvement.

Before–the–Fact Evaluation: Assessment of considered but not yet adopted interventions. → Evaluation Ex Ante.

Beneficial Side Effect: A consequence of a public intervention occurring outside the targeted area and deemed favorable by some stakeholder.

Black–Box Evaluation: A term, usually employed pejoratively, that refers to global summative evaluation, in which an overall and frequently brief evaluation is provided, without any data on implementation processes between external inputs into the organization and results (implementation is treated as a black box) or any suggestions for improvements, causes of troubles, and so on (Scriven 1991:74).

Capture Theory: A theory of public administration according to which whole agencies or individual officers are seduced to act in manners favorable to the regulatees (addressees) instead of pursuing the public interest. Also regulatory capture theory.

Ceteris Paribus: Literally "all other things equal"; the problem of holding constant all other factors but the one(s) the impact of which on some dependent variable will be investigated.

Chain of Implementation: Graphic representation of the theory or theories undergirding the intervention. See → Intervention Theory, → Theory of the Intervention Field.

Client–Oriented Evaluation: Assessment proceeding from the goals, expectations, concerns, objectives, or even needs of program participants.

Clients' Judgments: A→ shadow controls design for → impact assessment in which program clients are asked to determine the effects of the program.

Cognitive Map: A specific way of representing a person's (causal) assertions about some limited domain, such as a policy problem.

Communication–Oriented Explanation of Utilization: A theory suggesting that deficiencies in the utilization of evaluations are due to faulty communication between evaluator and evaluation recipients.

Comprehensive Evaluation: An effectiveness model of evaluation in which assessments are directed at results as well as inputs and implementation. The Countenance Model is a typical comprehensive evaluation. → Effectiveness Assessment.

Conceptual Use: The activity of employing information (science, evaluation) to enhance understanding of some issue but not for instrumental action. Synonym: → Enlightening Use, enlightenment. → Instrumental Use, → Legitimizing Use, → Tactical Use.

Concern: In → stakeholder evaluation "any matter of interest or importance to one or more parties about which they feel threatened, that they think will lead to an undesirable consequence, or that they want to substantiate in a positive sense" (Guba and Lincoln 1981:92). Also → Issue.

Control Group: A group of units of analysis with characteristics → equivalent (similar) to another, experimental group to whom the intervention is given, while it is withheld from the control group.

Control-Series Design: A → quasi–experimental approach to the → impact issue.

Coping Strategies: Actions taken by street–level bureaucrats to survive the simultaneous pressure from above and below (M. Lipsky). One such strategy is "creaming," that is, treating the most promising cases in order to get a good performance record.

Cost–Benefit Evaluation: An economic evaluation model using the ratio of outcomes produced by the intervention to costs incurred to produce the outcomes, where both outcomes and costs are expressed in terms of money.

Cost–Effectiveness Evaluation: An economic evaluation model using the ratio of outcomes produced by the intervention to costs incurred to produce the outcomes, in which outcomes are expressed in physical terms and costs in terms of money.

Counterfactual: A conditional statement the first clause of which expresses something contrary to fact, as "If the program had not been there, the outcome would not have happened."

Counterfinality: The property of producing effects that run counter to the original intentions such as spawning reverse impacts in the targeted area; occasionally also generating unintended side effects outside the targeted area.

Criteria [of Merit]: The evaluative yardsticks against which the value, worth, or merit of the government intervention is assessed. → Standards.

Decision-Centered Evaluation: Assessment using a pending decision or decision situation as organizer.

Demonstration Program: Intervention specifically designed to implement a new program on trial.

Descriptive Theory of Valuing: An approach to valuing in which evaluators use as evaluative yardsticks the merit criteria of others, such as for instance premeditated intervention goals. Alternative: → Prescriptive Theory of Valuing.

Design: A logical model of proof that allows the making of valid, causal inferences (Nachmias 1979:21). Research designs purport to address the causal issue in evaluation research. → Randomized, → matched, → generic, → reflexive, → statistical and → shadow controls are the major designs.

Desk-Drawer Syndrome: The phenomenon that potential users put evaluations aside without consulting them.

Detrimental Side Effect: Anticipated or unanticipated consequence of a public intervention deemed unfavorable by some stakeholder or observer.

Diffusion–Centered Strategy: An approach to enhancing the utilization that includes user–friendly presentation of evaluation findings, widespread broadcasting of results, and evaluator commitment to dissemination.

Direct Use: Utilization linked to the recipients' personal exposure to the evaluation, either by participating in the investigatory team, or by being informed through oral or written reporting.

Documentary Methods: A data collection device involving the use of information amassed for other purposes such as statistics, or data produced by the process itself like client records and other written documents, accessible through textual analysis. Alternatives: → Observation Methods,→ Interrogatory Methods.

Economic Policy Instruments: A major type of government tools involving either the handing out or the taking away of material resources; taxes, fees, subsidies, and grants are cases in point. Alternatives: → Regulation, → Information.

Eight Problems Approach to Evaluation: A list included in the present book enumerating the primary problems to be addressed in evaluation; the first two issues concern the evaluation as such, the following five the intervention, whereas the last problem concerns the feedback from the evaluation.

Effectiveness Assessment (Evaluation): The activity of finding out and appraising actual program impacts without taking costs into account. Also efficacy evaluation and → impact assessment. Effectiveness assessment also covers evaluation of outputs. If costs are brought in, we are dealing with efficiency assessment.

Efficiency: An economic model of evaluation using the ratio of the value of the outcome produced by the intervention to the costs incurred. Cost–Benefit and Cost–Effectiveness are cases in point.

Emergent Design: Sampling technique suggesting time sequencing of selection of units of analysis. Also cascading or rolling design. Opposite: preselected sample.

Enabling Legislation: Governmental regulatory technique in which permits are granted in certain specified cases provided the applicant can show that his planned activity will satisfy certain criteria; also a technique of conferring new legal powers or capacities.

Engineering Model: A theory of the interplay between politics, evaluation research, and public administration in which political officials discover problems, set goals, and commission researchers to find the most efficient means to reach the given goals; the researchers apply best available research designs and methodologies—preferably two–group randomized experimentation—to ensure that the most efficient means to achieve the given goals are discovered; the politicians use the knowledge elicited by the researchers to make rational decisions, which in turn are faithfully and expeditiously implemented by the public administration so that the coveted outcome will be produced.

Enlightening Use: See → Conceptual Use.

Equivalence: The extent to which preprogram (baseline, benchmark) equation has been achieved between two groups, usually called experimentals and controls.

Evaluability Assessment: A technical expression, denoting a preevaluation procedure designed to determine whether ongoing interventions are in shape for a full–blown impact assessment carried out under experimental conditions. Also exploratory evaluation.

Evaluability, Concern for: In the natural sense, the process of determining whether interventions are susceptible to assessment.

Evaluand: A neologism in the English language, evaluand is a technical term for whatever is being evaluated, by analogy with "multiplicand," "analysand," and so on (Scriven 1991:139). In the present book, I have used "evaluand" sparsely because particularly "government intervention" still seems to be more commonly understood.

Evaluation: In the present tract, a shorthand for careful retrospective assessment of the administration, → output and → outcome of public interventions—public policies, programs, program ingredients, projects, reforms, activities—which is intended to play a role in future practical action situations.

Evaluation Consumer (Client): The person, group, or agency who either commissions or uses the evaluation.

Evaluation Ex Ante: Assessment of considered but not yet adopted public interventions; ex ante evaluation is not included in the present book. → Before–the–fact Evaluation.

Evaluation Ex Post: Assessment of ongoing and terminated public interventions; also *post hoc* or after–the–fact evaluation.

Evaluation, General Meaning: The process of determining the merit, worth, or value of things, and the result of that process.

Evaluation Research: Retrospective assessments of social interventions using social science methodology for the purpose of contributing to future public policy debate and decision making.

Exemption Method: A regulatory technique to free an individual or a group from an obligation or liability to which others are subject.

Expert Assessment: A → shadow controls design to → impact assessment in which expertise is used to produce information on intervention effects.

Explanandum: In philosophy–of–science language, the phenomenon to be explained; the same as dependent variable(s) in variable language.

Explanans: In philosophy of science, that which is explaining; explanatory factors; the same as independent variable(s) in variable language. Also determinants, contingencies.

Explanatory Evaluation: Appraisal containing explanations.

Ex Post [Facto]: (literally "from the thing done afterward"): done, made, formulated after the fact and on the basis of current premises, conditions, or knowledge: retrospective, retroactive.

Ex Post Facto Design: A matched controls approach to impact assessment, where the control group is identified after–the–fact, that is, only after the program has been introduced. In general, research that collects data pertaining to a period after an intervention has started.

External Evaluation: Evaluation produced by some body outside the agency in charge of the program to be evaluated. When external evaluations are also arranged by and reported to an outside body, they are external in a very strong sense of the term.

External Validity: The extent to which research findings can be generalized to larger populations, like other interventions, and applied to different settings, for example, if results from experiments carried out in highly artificial environments can be transferred to real–life settings (Campbell and Stanley 1966:5ff.). → Internal Validity, → Validity.

Extraneous Confounding Factors: Nonintervention variables resulting in effects that obscure or exaggerate the true effects of an intervention; also called external conditions.

Eye–Wash: Attempt to justify a weak program by deliberately selecting for evaluation only those aspects of it that appear successful and avoiding aspects that look bad (Suchman 1967).

Feasibility Analysis: A technical term in → evaluability assessment signifying the last two steps, concerned with identifying users of a prospective full evaluation and achieving agreement to proceed with such an evaluation.

Formative Evaluation: Evaluation undertaken for the purpose of improving ongoing program activities in contrast with → summative evaluation.

Front–End Evaluation: Evaluation of or in the first stages in the basic intervention process, that is, initiation through decision (see figure 2.2). Front–end evaluation can be carried out either *ex ante* or *ex post.*

Functional Scope: the width of the → evaluand.

Generic Controls: A → design for → impact assessment according to which the effects of the permanent intervention among targets are compared with established norms about typical changes occurring in the larger population.

Goal–Achievement Measurement: Simple evaluation focusing on the whether government intervention aims actually are fulfilled (but ignoring whether the intervention has contributed to the fulfillment).

Goal-Attainment Evaluation: An effectiveness evaluation model focusing on whether the intervention goals have been achieved and to what extent the intervention has contributed to actual goal achievement.

Goal–Based Models: A common name for evaluation designs based on preordained intervention goals; → goal–attainment evaluation and → side–effects evaluation belong to this category.

Goal-Free Evaluation: According to Scriven, who coined the term, an evaluation focusing on global results of the program, assessing them against the needs of program clients while carefully avoiding all attention to premeditated program goals. In this book, goal–free evaluation has been consciously reinterpreted to signify any investigation focusing on global intervention results without considering intervention goals, stakeholder concerns, or client needs. Evaluation using clients' goals and expectations is called → client–oriented evaluation.

Global Scoring: The allocation of a single grade to the character or performance of an → evaluand (Scriven 1991:177).

Hawthorne Effect: The tendency of people being investigated to react positively or negatively to the fact that they are investigated, thereby making it difficult to identify the effects of the program itself; impact generated by measurement instruments. Also guinea pig effect, reactive measurement effect.

Hidden Agenda: Goals and objectives behind a government intervention not disclosed to the general public. In politics, hidden agendas are often concerned with strategic goals, that is, winning the next election, keeping the political party together, and strengthening the ties between the parties of a governing coalition.

Hierarchy Theory of Bureaucracy: A classic picture of public administration showing that policy and program decisions are always perfectly executed; it could also be interpreted normatively to mean that policy and program decisions should always be faithfully implemented or heuristically as an ideal type. Also conventional theory of bureaucracy.

Impact Assessment: The activity of estimating the effects of an intervention; also the result of such an activity. Theoretically, intervention effects can be traced anywhere in general governance processes. In public sector evaluation, however, effects are measured either at the addressee level or at the level of the surrounding society. Also → effectiveness assessment, efficacy assessment.

Impact Theory: All empirical and normative presuppositions undergirding a public intervention according to the initial framers and other stakeholders. Also → Intervention Theory.

Implementation: The act of carrying out or accomplishing something; also the state of been carried out (accomplished) or the state of being executed.

Improvement: The aim of undertaking evaluation to improve program operations and service delivery. Besides → accountability, the basic rationale of evaluation.

Inadvertent Confounding: Illustrative cases are the → Hawthorne effect, guinea pig effects, interviewer effects.

Indirect Use: Utilization that occurs when the transmission from evaluation to recipient is mediated by some third link between the two.

Information: A fundamental policy instrument involving measures undertaken to influence addressees through the transfer of knowledge, communication of reasoned argument, persuasion, advice.

Information as (Policy Instrument): Information as a policy instrument in its own right as opposed to information as a meta–policy instrument.

Information on (Policy Instruments): Information on the existence, meaning, and so forth, of other policy instruments; also called information as a meta–policy instrument.

Input–Oriented Management: Management technique according to which the principals' goals are targeted at the input side of subordinate agencies, that is, the allocation of funds, or the hiring of people.

Instrumental Use: Utilization occurring when recipients adopt the evaluation's recommendations for action—in the form of commended means to reach given ends—and act accordingly.

Interactive Use: Utilization involving the application of evaluation–based intelligence in conjunction with research–informed knowledge on alternative prospective lines of action and other forms of experience like common sense, conventional wisdom, and intuition (Weiss 1979:206f.).

Internal Evaluation: Evaluation produced within the institution in executive charge of the→ evaluand; self–evaluation. Internal evaluations can be externally arranged and used.

Internal Validity: The extent to which the program explanation is safe, that is, not jeopardized by competing influences and circumstances. Underlying internal validity is the question: Does the evaluation design prove that the program and only the program actually has produced the measured change in the target variable(s)? → External Validity, → Validity.

Interrogatory Methods: Strategy of amassing data through questioning the appropriate people by conducting interviews, disseminating questionnaires and the like. Alternatives: → Documentary and → Observation Methods.

Interrupted Time–Series Design: A case of the → reflexive controls approach to impact appraisal, embodying repeated periodic measurements on one and the same group before and after the intervention. If the time series shows a type of "interruption" somewhere after the intervention was launched, this might be attributed to the intervention.

Intervention (Public Intervention): A generic term for government action or government measure. Other terms include program, policy, reform, project, activity, and service.

Intervention Field: See → Theory of the Intervention Field, → Intervention Theory.

Intervention Theory: All empirical and normative suppositions that public interventions rest upon; also referred to as program theory, the program's theory of action, the impact model, the policy theory, or the reasoning undergirding the program (activity). One intervention may be based upon several intervention theories; actually, this is often the case in public policy, since, for instance, every party to the intervention coalition may have supported the intervention for different reasons. → Theory of the Intervention Field.

Interviewer Effect: The tendency for answers provided by the respondent and recorded in a questionnaire to vary depending on which interviewer is assigned to the respondent; synonymous to interviewer variance.

Issue: In stakeholder evaluation "any statement, proposition, or focus that allows for the presentation of different points of view; any proposition about which reasonable persons may disagree; or any point of contention" (Guba and Lincoln 1981:92). See also Concern.

Labeling: A type of informative policy instrument engendering the technique of attaching a slip of paper, cloth, or other material to product to indicate its manufacturer, content, or other appropriate information. See Mandatory disclosure.

Legitimizing Use: When evaluation results are seized upon by recipients to bolster and rationalize positions already taken. → Enlightening, → Instrumental, → Interactive and → Tactical Use.

Linkage Method: A strategy of improving the utilization of evaluation by introducing some intermediary agent between the evaluators and the potential recipients of the evaluation. The linkage strategy includes appointment of advisory committees, transmission through opinion leaders, and the hiring of information transfer specialists.

Main Effect: The major subject–matter impact that some stakeholder, usually decision–makers or program managers, deliberately wants to achieve through the intervention.

Management by Objectives (MBO): A managerial doctrine according to which top–management ought to set clear outcome or maybe output goals, involve the subordinates at all levels in the breaking down of these goals into measurable objectives, give subordinates leeway to choose among appropriate means to reach these objectives, take pains to monitor the progress toward the goals, evaluate the results in terms of effectiveness and efficiency, and disseminate the evaluation results to all people involved (and maybe also award successful and punish unsuccessful subordinates).

Mandatory Disclosure: Governance technique requiring private citizens or organizations to furnish information to one another or to the general public. → Labeling. Also mandatory labeling.

Matched Controls: Experimental two–group design in which equation between the groups is achieved through matching, that is, selection according to premeditated criteria.

Matching: The technique of creating equalization between two groups through selection according to premeditated criteria.

Matchmaking: A custom, particularly widespread in India and Korea, where parents try to find suitable marriage partners for their sons and daughters.

Metaevaluation: The word embodies three meanings: (i) evaluation of another evaluation; (ii) evaluation of the evaluation function in organizations; and (iii) summary of findings from several evaluations.

Meta–Process: Process directed at other processes. In relation to the public intervention process, evaluation can be seen as a meta–process. Also Secondary Process. In evaluation of evaluation, evaluation is oriented toward evaluation processes which in turn are directed at intervention processes; consequently, evaluation of evaluation is a metameta–process. Also Meta-evaluation.

Mismatch Theory: A theory according to which implementation is hampered due to attitudinal or belief mismatch between implementors and addressees on the one hand and intervention intentions on the other concerning ends and means.

Missing Link of Policy Analysis: An expression used by Erwin Hargrove about implementation analysis, meaning that before–the–fact analyses of implementability of a reform ought to be carried out in addition to conventional before–the–fact, black–box, cost–benefit analysis.

Monitoring: The process of checking what is happening in the implementation and results stages of the → evaluand without raising questions about intervention impact on outcomes. The five steps of monitoring are: 1. reconstruct → intervention theory; 2. select where empirical checks should be set in; 3. collect and analyze data; 4. apply merit criteria and performance standards to the findings, and 5. analyze → evaluand and its intended implementation from a general governance perspective.

Naturalistic Evaluation: Assessment procedure with no ambition to adapt the government intervention to methodological evaluation requirements. In the opposite, nonnaturalistic case, the intervention is modified to suit demands of evaluation research. The classic experiment with two randomized groups is a paradigm case of a nonnaturalistic, "artificial" evaluation strategy.

Nonexplanatory Evaluation: Evaluation containing assessments but no explanations.

Null Effects: No discernable impacts within the target area.

Obligation to Notify: Regulatory technique in which an activity is forbidden until a government authority is notified about it.

Observation Methods: Data collection strategy in which the investigator through site visits makes observations with his own eyes. In direct observation, the evaluator openly admits she is an evaluator, in participant observation, the participation in the process to be judged is a pretense to enable the collection of unbiased data. → Interrogatory, → Documentary Methods.

One-Group, Before-and-After Design: A case of → reflexive controls in which one preprogram and one postprogram measurement are compared to each other to find any traces of program effects.

Optional Policy Instruments: Governance tools enabling subordinate bodies to take some measure, should they deem it practical or purposeful to do so. In Swedish governance, for instance, the national parliament enacts optional policy instruments (*fakultativa styrmedel*), which municipalities may or may not use. The opposite would be obligatory or mandatory policy instruments.

Organizer of an Evaluation: The basic question to be posed in an evaluation.

Outcome: Intervention effects on participants and on the surrounding social and natural world. Immediate, intermediate, and ultimate outcomes are often discerned. The custom that outcome stands for effects on participants whereas effects on society are called impacts is not adopted in the present work.

Output: Things coming out of organizations, usually from their administration systems. In the public sector, outputs may be services delivered, goods distributed, permissions and licenses granted, grants and loans disbursed, campaign messages divulged.

Peer Review: Evaluation carried out by equals, usually prominent colleagues of the same profession.

Perverse Effect: A consequence in the target area contrary to the one intended and coveted. Also reverse or regressive effect.

Placebo: A dummy treatment introduced to the control group in some experimental situations to avoid the → Hawthorne effect.

Policy Analysis: The study of the nature, causes, and effects of alternative public policies and programs that address specific societal problems. While including policy and program *ex post* evaluation, policy analysis is mainly focused on *ex ante* evaluation and the study of policy causes.

Policy Theory: → Intervention Theory.

Portrayal: An information–rich account of a government intervention using pictures, thick descriptions, quotations, and funny anecdotes.

Post Hoc Ergo Propter Hoc: Literally "After this, therefore because of this"; the fallacy of imputing all outcomes to a particular, preceding factor.

Postdata Designs: Strategies for → impact assessment in which scores on the result variable are available only from the time subsequent to the introduction of the program.

Postponement: Attempt to delay action by pretending to seek facts through evaluation (Suchman 1967).

Postprogram–Only Control Group Design: A → randomized or → matched controls design in which postmeasurements but no premeasurements are available.

Posture: Attempt to use evaluation as a "gesture" of objectivity and to assume the pose of scientific research (Suchman 1967).

Potemkin Village: Sham villages reputed to have been erected on the order of Prince Potemkin, a favorite of Empress Catherine II of Russia, for Catherine's tour of the Crimea in 1797; a facade, a front. Evaluation might be rigged as a Potemkin Village.

Pseudo–Evaluation: Evaluation guided by (hidden) strategic motives such as eye–wash and postponement.

Predata Designs: Strategies for impact assessment in which scores on the result variable are only available from the time period prior to the installment of the program.

Preordinate Evaluation: Appraisal with a predetermined, not emergent, design.

Preprogram Evaluation, Preformative Evaluation: Evaluation applied in the planning stage of an intervention, which typically includes program evaluability improvement in the sense of → baseline data collection, and fashioning a program design that facilitates later postprogram evaluation. Contrary to → evaluability assessment, preprogram evaluation is not concerned with ongoing but with not–yet–adopted interventions.

Prescriptions: → Regulations phrased in the affirmative, laying down a course of action to be followed; synonyms: directions, dictates, decrees.

Prescriptive Theory of Valuing: Approach to the valuing component of evaluation advocating the primacy of particular values, as opposed to → descriptive theories which use the values of others as yardsticks.

Pretest-Posttest Comparison Group Design: A → matched controls approach to impact assessment.

Primary User: Agent to whom the evaluation is first reported and who is supposed to act on the information contained in the evaluation.

Process Evaluation: Assessment trying to explain intervention outcomes through the use of a broad, configurative conception of → impact assessment, including analyses of processes between intervention instigation and intervention outcomes, situational surroundings, and factors effective in the intervention formation phase.

Process–Oriented Management: An administrative doctrine according to which principals issue rules and regulations directed at decision–making processes in their executives in the hope of thereby influencing outputs and outcomes. Objectives are targeted at internal administrative procedures, not results.

Process–Product Concept: A concept referring to the process as well as the product of the process. Words ending with "–tion" are usually process–product concepts, like, for instance, "evaluation" which refers to the process of determining the merit, worth, and value of things as well as the results of that process in the form of, for example, written reports or oral briefings. Evaluation produces evaluations.

Producer: Agent who carries out some activity, for example, an evaluation, in the sense of being responsible for data gathering, data analysis, and reporting, maybe also the design of the evaluation.

Production–Focused Strategy: A strategy to enhance the utilization of evaluation suggesting that evaluations should be made more recipient–friendly through efforts directed at adapting the evaluation process to the demands and desires of the conceivable users. The key buzzwords of this strategy include: responsiveness to user preoccupations, manipulable or even feasible variables, interactive methodology, and user inclusion in the evaluation team.

Production–Oriented Explanation of Utilization: In production–oriented explanation, properties of the knowledge producers, and their products are the major clues to weak and strong utilization.

Productivity: The ratio of output per unit of input.

Program Analysis: A technical term in → evaluability assessment, signifying the first four steps in which the nature of the current program is determined.

Program–Administrator Judgments: → Shadow controls design in which program administrators such as street–level bureaucrats and program managers are used to pass judgments on the impacts of the program.

Program Field Theory: → Theory of the Intervention Field.

Program–Oriented Evaluation: According to the Swedish National Audit Bureau, a specific assessment strategy through which *one* particular program was assessed from its instigation via the chain of implementation through the final outcomes. Also → System–Oriented Evaluation.

Program Theory: → Intervention Theory.

Prohibitions: → Regulations phrased in the negative, forbidding an action, activity, and the like; synonyms: proscriptions, bans, interdictions.

Prospective Evaluation: The same as Evaluation *Ex Ante.*

Quasi-Experiment: Literally "resembling experiment"; two-group design for data collection with → matched groups.

Radical Rationalism: A managerial doctrine according to which public policies ought to be based on thorough planning, careful prognoses, meticulous before–the–fact impact statements and the like and enacted as large, comprehensive programs.

Random Sampling: A process of sample selection in which each individual or element in the population is assured an equal and independent chance of being included. Also called random selection, selection at random, or selection by chance.

Randomization: The allocation of a set of units to two groups according to some method that safeguards that each unit has an equal probability of being chosen. Randomization ensures that initial differences, that is, prior to any intervention, between experiment group and control group is attributable to chance variations and not to systematic bias or differences between the groups. Also random assignment.

Randomized Experiment: Data collection design involving two randomly selected groups where the treatment is administered to one but not the other.

Reflexive Controls: A one–group data–gathering design for → impact assessment in which targets who have received the intervention are compared to themselves, as measured before the intervention; the investigation group is used as its own control group because preprogram scores serve as controls in relation to postprogram scores. Something is reflexive if it has a relation to itself.

Regulation: Besides economic policy instruments and information, a fundamental type of policy instrument involving measures taken to influence people by means of verbally formulated rules, mandating targets to act in accordance with what is ordered in these rules.

Reporting Method: A strategy of improving utilization by turning interim or final evaluation reporting more user–friendly and by actively involving the evaluator as an advocate and promotor of the findings.

Responsive Evaluation: Evaluation with an → emergent design, in contrast with → preordinate evaluation the design of which is predetermined (Scriven 1991:315). The idea is that evaluators must be responsive to the concerns and issues of some stakeholding constituency and through interactive communication let these affect the final design of the study.

Results: In public policy, a technical term covering either outputs, or outcomes, or both.

Results–Oriented Management (Management by Results): A managerial doctrine according to which management should be based on the continuous and systematic feedback to principals and subordinates of reliable information on results, primarily defined as outcomes, secondarily as outputs. → Management by Objectives

Secondary Effects: Second-level or intermediary consequences.

Serendipity Problem: The possibility that an unexpected side effect of a measure taken to solve a problem can turn out to be the major gain or loss or concern.

Serendipitous Results: Unexpected consequences of intentional actions.

Shadow Controls: A design for → impact assessment in which the evaluator asks others to estimate the net impact of the public intervention or at least what would have happened should the intervention not have been instituted (the → counterfactual case).

Side Effects: All consequences, intended or unintended, anticipated or unanticipated, not included among the main effects; in public intervention evaluation, impacts occurring outside the target area of the intervention; also called spillovers, spin-off effects, by–effects.

Side–Effects Evaluation: Assessment considering actual attainment of prespecified goals as well as intended and unintended side effects.

Sine Ira et Studio: "With neither anger nor partiality," motto for the neutral, technical bureaucracy, first formulated by Tacitus.

Snowball Rolling: A qualitative, inductive data collection technique in which the findings in one stage of the investigation will determine what to search for in the next. Each new discovery is allowed to lead to the next in order to maximize the possibility of understanding how the program functions *in situ*. Evaluator responsiveness to stakeholders' concerns, issues, worries, questions, and perceptions are essential traits in this data gathering methodology. Responsiveness is usually achieved through eye–ball to eye–ball interaction between evaluator and evaluatees.

Solomon Four-Group Design: Experimental → design purportedly enabling experimenters to control for extraneous confounding factors as well as → Hawthorne effects.

Stakeholder: A person or group that has an investment, share, or interest in something, as in a business or industry. In evaluation, an actor with a particular interest in a policy, or program and its evaluation. Program stakeholders have interests in the program as such, whereas evaluation stakeholders have an interest in its evaluation only.

Stakeholder Evaluation: Assessment where the concerns and interests of parties involved and interested in the program and its evaluation are used as points of departure and organizers.

Standards [of Performance]: A set of marks on a criterion of merit that tells what is unacceptable, barely acceptable, promising, and excellent program performance on the criterion.

Statistical Controls: A design for impact assessment in which participant and nonparticipant targets of the permanent intervention are compared, statistically holding constant differences between participants and nonparticipants.

Straw Man Fallacy: The error of describing the position taken in a debate in such extremist way that it is difficult to conceive of anybody ever having held it in order to make her own position appear more moderate.

Substantive Goals: Goals pertaining to the subject matter of the program in contrast with strategic and procedural goals.

Summative Evaluation: Retrospective evaluation, conducted for the benefit of some external audience or decision–maker. The term notwithstanding, summative evaluations can be done on programs that are still running (Scriven 1991:340). "The distinction between formative and summative evaluation has been well summed up by Bob Stake:'When the cook tastes the soup, that's formative; when the guests taste the soup, that's summative'" (169).

Synthesis Analysis: The activity of summarizing the findings of several evaluations of one or more programs. Also the result of this effort. Synthesis analysis is one type of → metaevaluation.

System–Oriented Evaluation: In the language of the Swedish National Audit Bureau, an assessment concerned with the interplay of several individual programs directed at the same social activity. An example would be an assessment of agricultural policy, which certainly comprises numerous programs.

Tactical Use: Utilization ensuing when evaluation is requested to gain time or avoid responsibility, the important fact being that an evaluation is commissioned and underway, not that its findings shall be applied.

Target Variable: The action(s) or condition(s) that a public intervention wants to affect.

Targets: The intended addressees of an intervention. Also participants, clients, recipients, beneficiaries, maleficiaries, or regulatees.

Tertiary Effects: Third-level consequences; consequences of second–order or intermediate consequences.

Theory of the Intervention Field: All factors except the public intervention that exert causal impact upon the behavior or conditions that the public intervention seeks to modify. → Intervention Theory.

Threats to Validity: Problems that occur in conducting research (evaluation) that can interfere with determining whether the results are valid. → Validity.

Triangulation: The use of several different measures or measurement instruments to obtain information about the same action, condition, thing.

Unanticipated Effects: Results found to have occurred as consequences of an intervention but were not foreseen and expected when the intervention was designed and adopted. Social facts that are results of human action but not of human design, to slightly paraphrase Adam Ferguson.

Unintended Consequence: An effect of a human action—such as a government intervention—that was not pursued.

Unobtrusive Measures: Measurements taken or data collected for other purposes than for the current study. Unobtrusive measures minimize the possible reactions of people who know they are under scrutiny (→ Hawthorne Effect).

User–Oriented Explanation of Utilization: A theory claiming that recipient properties have impacts on evaluation use.

User–Oriented Strategy: An approach to improved utilization recommending attempts to make potential evaluation clients more susceptible to utilization.

Vagueness: The property of a word or a linguistic expression of having a fuzzy borderline. → Ambiguity.

Validity: The extent to which a finding is well–grounded, justified, well–underpinned. → External Validity, → Internal Validity, → Threats to Validity.

References

Monographs and Articles from Journals

Albæk, Erik, 1988, *Fra sandhed til information: Evalueringsforskning i USA—før og nu*. Copenhagen: Akademisk Forlag.

Alkin, Marvin C., Richard Daillak, and Peter White, 1979, *Using Evaluations: Does Evaluation Make a Difference?* Newbury Park, Calif.: Sage.

Allison, Graham T., 1980, "Implementation Analysis: The 'Missing Chapter' in Conventional Analysis Illustrated by a Teaching Exercise," in Leif Lewin, and Evert Vedung, eds., *Politics as Rational Action: Essays in Public Choice and Policy Analysis,* 237–60. Dordrecht, Holland: D. Reidel.

Anderson, Scarvia B., and Stanley Ball, 1978, *The Profession and Practice of Program Evaluation*. San Francisco: Jossey-Bass.

Anderson, Scarvia B., Samuel Ball, and Richard T. Murphy, 1974, eds., *Encyclopedia of Educational Evaluation*. San Francisco: Jossey–Bass.

Arvidsson, Göran, 1986, "Performance Evaluation," in Franz–Xaver Kaufmann, Giandomenico Majone, and Vincent Ostrom, eds., 625–43.

Baldwin, David A., 1985, *Economic Statecraft*. Princeton, N.J.: Princeton University Press.

Bardach, Eugene, and Robert A. Kagan, 1982, *Going by the Book: The Problem of Regulatory Unreasonableness*. Philadelphia: Temple University Press.

Barrett, Susan, and Colin Fudge, eds., 1981, *Policy and Action: Essays on the Implementation of Public Policy*. London: Methuen.

Berger, Peter L., and Richard John Neuhaus, 1977, *To Empower People: The Role of Mediating Structures in Public Policy*. Washington, D.C.: American Enterprise Institute.

Berk, Richard A., Robert F. Boruch, David L. Chambers, Peter H. Rossi, and Ann D. Witte, 1985, "Social Policy Experimentation: A Position Paper," *Evaluation Review* 9: 387–440.

Berman, Paul, 1978, "The Study of Macro- and Micro-Implementation," *Public Policy* 26: 157–84.

———, 1980, "Thinking about Programmed and Adaptive Implementation: Matching Strategies to Situations," in Helen M. Ingram, and D. Mann, eds., *Why Policies Succeed or Fail,* 205–27. Newbury Park, Calif.: Sage.

313

Bernstein, Ilene N., and Howard Freeman, 1975, *Academic and Entrepreneurial Research: The Consequences of Diversity in Federal Evaluation Studies.* New York: Russell Sage Foundation.

Bernstein, Marver, 1955, *Regulating Business by Independent Commission.* Princeton, NJ.: Princeton University Press.

Bickman, Leonard, ed., 1990, *Advances in Program Theory.* San Francisco: Jossey–Bass.

Björkman, Johan, 1971, *Kortsiktiga effekter av trafikinformation.* Stockholm: Stockholm School of Economics.

Boudon, Raymond, 1982, *The Unintended Consequences of Social Action.* London: Macmillan.

Braskamp, L. A., and A. D. Brown, eds., 1980, *Utilization of Evaluative Information.* New Directions for Program Evaluation No. 5. San Francisco: Jossey-Bass.

Brewer, John, and Albert Hunter, 1989, *Multimethod Research: A Synthesis of Styles.* Newbury Park, Calif.: Sage.

Campbell, Donald T., 1969, "Reforms as Experiments," *American Psychologist* 24: 409–29. Reprinted with minor revisions in James A. Caporaso, and Leslie L. Roos, eds., 1973, 167–225.

———, 1970, "Considering the Case against Experimental Evaluations of Social Innovations," *Administrative Science Quarterly* 15: 110–13.

———, 1982, "Experiments as Arguments," *Knowledge: Creation, Diffusion, Utilization* 3: 327–37.

Campbell, Donald T., and Julian C. Stanley, 1966, *Experimental and Quasiexperimental Designs for Research.* Chicago: Rand McNally.

Caporaso, James A., and Leslie L. Roos, eds., 1973, *Quasiexperimental Approaches: Testing Theory and Evaluating Policy.* Evanston, Ill..: Northwestern University Press.

Chelimsky, Eleanor, 1978, "Differing Perspectives of Evaluation", *New Directions for Program Evaluation,* 2–18.

———, 1985, ed., *Program Evaluation: Patterns and Directions.* Washington, D.C.: American Society for Public Administration.

Chen, Huey–Tsyh, 1990, *Theory–Driven Evaluations.* Newbury Park, Calif.: Sage.

Ciarlo, James A., ed., 1981, *Utilizing Evaluation: Concepts and Measurement Techniques.* Newbury Park, Calif.: Sage.

Collier, John Jr. and Malcolm Collier, 1986, *Visual Anthropology: Photography as a Research Method.* Albuquerque: University of New Mexico Press.

Cook, Thomas D., and Donald T. Campbell, 1979, *Quasi-Experimentation: Design and Analysis for Field Setting.* Boston: Houghton Mifflin.

Cronbach, Lee, 1982, *Designing Evaluations of Educational and Social Programs.* San Francisco: Jossey-Bass.

Cronbach, Lee J., and Associates, 1980, *Toward Reform of Program Evaluation: Aims, Methods, and Institutional Arrangements.* San Francisco: Jossey–Bass.

Davis, Howard R., and Susan E. Salasin, 1975, "The Utilization of Evaluation," in Elmer L. Struening, and Marcia Guttentag, eds., *Handbook of Evaluation Research* 1: 621–66.

Derlien, Hans–Ulrich, 1990a, "Genesis and Structure of Evaluation Efforts in Comparative Perspective," in Ray C. Rist, ed., 1990, 147–75.

———, 1990b, "Program Evaluation in the Federal Republic of Germany," in Ray C. Rist, ed., 1990, 37–51.

Deutscher, Iring, 1976, "Toward Avoiding the Goal-Trap in Evaluation Research," in Clark C. Abt, ed., *The Evaluation of Social Programs,* 249–68. Newbury Park, Calif.: Sage.

Devine, Patricia, and Edward R. Hart, 1989, "Message Strategies for Information Campaigns: A Social– Psychological Analysis," in Charles T. Salmon, ed., *Information Campaigns: Balancing Social Values and Social Change*, 229–58. Newbury Park, Calif.: Sage.

Doern, G. Bruce, and Richard W. Phidd, 1983, *Canadian Public Policy: Ideas, Structure, Process.* Toronto: Methuen.

Downs, Anthony, 1967, *Inside Bureaucracy.* Boston: Little, Brown.

Dror, Yehezkel, 1968, *Public Policymaking Reexamined.* Scranton, Pa.: Chandler.

Dunn, William N. et al., 1984, "Designing Utilization Research," *Knowledge: Creation, Diffusion, Utilization,* 387–404.

Dunsire, Andrew, 1978, *Implementation in a Bureaucracy: The Execution Process* and *Control in a Bureaucracy: The Execution Process,* I–II. Oxford: Martin Robertson.

Dynes, Patrick S., and Mary K. Marvel, 1987, *Program Evaluation: An Annotated Bibliography.* London: Garland Publishing.

Eckerberg, Katarina, 1987, *Environmental Protection in Swedish Forestry: A Study of the Implementation Process.* Umeå: Department of Political Science, Research Report 1987:12.

Eckhoff, Torstein, 1983, *Statens styringsmuligheter, særlig i ressurs-og miljøspørsmål,* Oslo: Tanum-Norli.

Eckhoff, Torstein, 1989, *Juss, moral og politikk.* Oslo: Universitetsforlaget.

Eckhoff, Torstein, and Knut Dahl Jacobsen, 1960, *Rationality and Responsibility in Administrative and Judicial Decision–making.* Copenhagen: Munksgaard.

Edwards III, George C., and Ira Sharkansky, 1978, *The Policy Predicament.* San Francisco: W. H. Freeman.

EFN–rapport 1985:13, *Solvärme och värmepumpar: en utvärdering av det statliga energiforskningsstödets effektivitet.* Stockholm: Liber.

Elmore, Richard, 1978, "Organizational Models of Social Program Implementation," *Public Policy* 26: 2, 185–228.

———, 1980, "Backward Mapping: Implementation Research and Policy Decisions," *Political Science Quarterly* 94: 601–16.

Elmore, Richard, Gunnel Gustafsson, and Erwin Hargrove, 1986, "Comparing Implementation Processes in Sweden and the United States," *Scandinavian Political Studies* 21: 209–33.

Elster, Jon, 1978, *Logic and Society: Contradictions and Possible Worlds.* Chichester: Wiley.

Engwall, Lars, ed., 1992, *Economics in Sweden: An Evaluation of Swedish Research in Economics.* London: Routledge.

Etzioni, Amitai, 1975, *A Comparative Analysis of Complex Organizations: On Power, Involvement, and Their Correlates.* New York: Free Press, rev. ed.

Fairweather, George W., and Louis G. Tornatzky, 1977, *Experimental Methods for Social Policy Research.* Oxford: Pergamon Press.

Fernández–Ballesteros, Rocío, 1992a, "A Model for Planning Evaluation Research," in John Mayne, Marie–Louise Bemelmans–Videc, Joe Hudson, and Ross Conner, eds., 205–13.

———, 1992b, *Introducción a la Evaluación psicológia I–II.* Madrid: Ediciones Pyrámide, S.A.

Fischer, David Hackett, 1970, *Historians' Fallacies: Toward a Logic of Historical Thought.* New York: Harper and Row.

Fischer, Frank, 1990, *Technology and the Politics of Expertise.* Newbury Park, Calif.: Sage.

Fitz-Gibbon, Carol Taylor, and Lynn Lyons Morris, 1975, "Theory–Based Evaluation," *Evaluation Comment,* 1–14.

Foss Hansen, Hanne, 1989, "Moderniseringens effektivitet," *Nordisk Administrativt Tidsskrift* 70: 189–212.

Franke–Wikberg, Sigbrit, and Ulf P. Lundgren, 1980, *Att värdera utbildning: Del 1: En introduktion till pedagogisk utvärdering.* Stockholm: Wahlström and Widstrand.

Friberg, Lennart, 1973, *Styre i kristid: Studier i krisförvaltningens organisation och struktur 1939–1945.* Stockholm: Allmänna Förlaget.

Gaskell, George, and Bernward Joerges, 1987, *Public Policies and Private Actions: A Multinational Study of Local Energy Conservation Schemes.* Aldershot, England: Gower.

Gerlich, Peter, 1983, *Hochschule und Effizienz: Anstösse zur universitären Selbstreflexion.* Wien: Passagen Verlag.

Glaser, Edward M., Harold H. Abelson, and Kathalee N. Garrison, 1983, *Putting Knowledge to Use: Facilitating the Diffusion of Knowledge and the Implementation of Planned Change.* San Francisco: Jossey-Bass.

Goodsell, Charles, 1981, *The Public Encounter: Where State and Citizen Meet.* Bloomington: Indiana University Press.

Gray, Andrew, and Bill Jenkins, 1990, "Policy Evaluation in a Time of Fiscal Stress: Some Reflections from the British Experience," in Ray C. Rist 1990, 73–87.

Gray, Andrew, Bill Jenkins, and Bob Segsworth, 1992, *Budgeting, Auditing, Evaluating: Functions and Integration in Seven Governments.* New Brunswick, N.J.: Transaction Publishers.

Grip, Gunvall, 1987, *Vill du frihet eller tvång? Svensk försäkringspolitik 1935–1945.* Stockholm: Almqvist and Wiksell International.

Guba, Egon G., and Yvonna S. Lincoln, 1981, *Effective Evaluation: Improving the Usefulness of Evaluation Results Through Responsive and Naturalistic Approaches.* San Francisco: Jossey-Bass.

———, 1989, *Fourth Generation Evaluation.* Newbury Park, Calif.: Sage.

Hadden, Susan, 1986, *Read the Label: Reducing Risk by Providing Information.* Boulder, Colo.: Westview Press.

Hadenius, Axel, 1986, *A Crisis of the Welfare State?* Stockholm: Almqvist and Wiksell International.

Hadenius, Karin, 1990, *Jämlikhet och frihet: Politiska mål för den svenska skolan.* Stockholm: Almqvist and Wiksell International.

Ham, Christopher, and Michael Hill, 1984, *The Policy Process in the Modern Capitalist State.* Brighton: Wheatsheaf.

Hanf, Kenneth, and Theo A. J. Toonen, eds., 1985, *Policy Implementation in Federal and Unitary Systems.* Dordrecht: Martinus Nijhoff.

Hargrove, Erwin C., 1975, *The Missing Link: The Study of Implementation of Social Policy.* Washington, D.C.: Urban Institute.

———, 1983, "The Search for Implementation Theory," in Richard Zeckhauser, and D. Leebaert, eds., *The Role of Government in the 1980's.* Durham, N.C.: Duke University Press.

Hayek, Friedrich A., 1978, *New Studies in Philosophy, Politics, Economics, and the History of Ideas.* Chicago: University of Chicago Press.

———, 1979, *The Counter Revolution of Science.* Indianapolis, Ind.: Liberty Press, 2nd ed.

Heller, Frank, ed., 1986, *The Use and Abuse of Social Science.* Newbury Park, Calif.: Sage.

Hellstern, Michael, and Hellmut Wollmann, eds., 1983, *Experimentelle Politik—*

Reformstrohfeuer oder Lernstrategie, Bestandsaufnahme und Evaluierung. Opladen: Westdeutscher Verlag.

Hemenway, David, 1985, *Monitoring and Compliance: the Political Economy of Inspection*, Greenwich, Conn.: JAI Press.

Herman, Joan L., ed., 1987, *Program Evaluation Kit*. Newbury Park, Calif.: Sage, 2nd ed. [Consists of the following volumes: 1. *Evaluator's Handbook*, 2. *How to Focus Evaluation*, 3. *How to Design Program Evaluation*, 4. *How to Use Qualitative Methods in Evaluation*, 5. *How to Assess Program Implementation*, 6. *How to Measure Attitudes*, 7. *How to Measure Performance and Use Tests*, 8. *How to Analyze Data*, 9. *How to Communicate Evaluation Findings*.]

Hirschman, Albert, 1991, *The Rhetoric of Reaction: Perversity, Futility, Jeopardy*. Cambridge, Mass.: Harvard University Press.

Hjern, Benny, and David O. Porter, 1981, "Implementation Structures: A New Unit of Administrative Analysis," *Organization Studies* 2: 211–27.

Hjern, Benny, and Chris Hull, 1982, "Implementation Research as Empirical Constitutionalism," *European Journal of Political Research* 9: 105–15.

Hofstee, Willem K. B., 1992, "From the Citizen's Point of View: the Positioning of Program Evaluation," in John Mayne, Marie-Louise Bemelmans–Videc, Joe Hudson, and Ross Conner, eds., 277–83.

Hood, Christopher C., 1976, *The Limits of Administration*. London: Wiley.

––––––, 1983, *The Tools of Government*. London: Macmillan.

––––––, 1986, "The Hidden Public Sector: The'Quangocratization of the World?", in Kaufmann, Franz–Xaver, Giandomenico Majone, and Vincent Ostrom, eds., 185–207.

Hoogerwerf, Andries, 1990, "Reconstructing Policy Theory," *Evaluation and Program Planning* 13: 285–91.

––––––, 1992, "Policy Evaluation and Government in the Netherlands: Meta Evaluation Research as One of the Solutions," in John Mayne, Marie-Louise Bemelmans–Videc, Joe Hudson, and Ross Conner, eds., 215–27.

House, Ernest R., 1980, *Evaluating with Validity*. Newbury Park, Calif.: Sage.

Houston, Tom R., 1972, "The Behavioral Sciences Impact-Effectiveness Model," in Peter H. Rossi, and Walter Williams, eds., 51–71.

Howlett, Michael, 1991, "Policy Instruments: Policy Styles, and Policy Implementation: National Approaches to Theories of Instrument Choice," *Policy Studies Journal* 19: 1–21.

Hudson, Joe, John Mayne, and Ray Thomlison, eds., 1992, *Action–oriented Evaluation in Organizations: Canadian Practices*. Toronto, Ontario: Wall and Emerson.

Jenkins, Bill, and Andrew Gray, 1992, "Evaluation and the Consumer: the UK Experience," in John Mayne, Marie–Louise Bemelmans–Videc, Joe Hudson, and Ross Conner, eds., 285–99.

Johansson, Jan, 1992, *Det statliga kommittéväsendet: Kunskap, kontroll, konsensus*. Stockholm: Acad. diss., Dept of Political Science.

Jonung, Lars (with Jan Rydenfelt), 1984, *Prisregleringen, företagen och förhandlingsekonomin*. Stockholm: SNS Förlag.

Jørgensen, Torben Beck, 1981, *Når staten skal spare*. Copenhagen: Nyt fra Samfundsvidenskaberne.

Judd, Charles M., and David A. Kenny, 1981, *Estimating the Effects of Social Interventions*. Cambridge: Cambridge University Press.

Karapin, Roger S., 1986, "What's the Use of Social Science? A Review of the Literature," in Frank Heller, ed., *The Use and Abuse of Social Science*. Newbury Park, Calif.: Sage, 236–65.

Katz, Elihu, and Brenda Danet, 1973, *Bureaucracy and the Public: A Reader in Official–Client Relations.* New York: Basic Books.

Kaufman, Herbert, 1967, *The Forest Ranger: A Study in Administrative Behavior.* Baltimore: Johns Hopkins Press.

Kaufman, Roger, and Susan Thomas, 1980, *Evaluation without Fear.* New York: New Viewpoints.

Kaufmann, Franz–Xaver, Giandomenico Majone, and Vincent Ostrom, eds., 1986, *Guidance, Control, and Evaluation in the Public Sector.* Berlin: Walter de Gruyter.

Kelman, Steven, 1981, *Regulating America, Regulating Sweden: A Comparative Study of Occupational Safety and Health Policy.* Cambridge, Mass.: MIT Press.

Kosecoff, Jacqueline, and Arlene Fink, 1982, *Evaluation Basics: A Practitioner's Manual.* Newbury Park, Calif.: Sage.

Lamoreaux, Naomi R., 1984, "Regulatory Agencies," in Jack P. Greene, ed., *Encyclopedia of American Political History.* New York: Scribner.

Lane, Jan-Erik, 1983, "The Concept of Implementation," *Statsvetenskaplig Tidskrift* 86: 17–40.

———, 1987, "Implementation, Accountability, and Trust," *European Journal of Political Research* 15: 527–46.

Larsen, Judith K., 1980, "Knowledge Utilization: What Is It?" *Knowledge: Creation, Diffusion, Utilization* 1: 421–42.

Launsø, Laila, and Olaf Rieper, 1993, *Forskning om og med mennesker: Forskningstyper og forskningsmetoder i samfundsforskningen.* Copenhagen: Nyt Nordisk Forlag Arnold Busck, 2nd ed.

Leviton, Laura C., and Edward F. X. Hughes, 1981, "Research on the Utilization of Evaluations: A Review and Synthesis," *Evaluation Review: A Journal of Applied Social Research* 5: 525–48.

Lewin, Leif, 1988, *Det gemensamma bästa: Om egenintresset och allmänintresset i västerländsk politik.* Stockholm: Carlssons.

Light, Richard J., and David B. Pillemer, 1984, *Summing Up: The Science of Reviewing Research.* Cambridge, Mass.: Harvard University Press.

Lindblom, Charles E., and David K. Cohen, 1979, *Usable Knowledge: Social Science and Social Problem Solving.* New Haven, Conn.: Yale University Press.

Linder, Stephen, and B. Guy Peters, 1989, "Instruments of Government: Perceptions and Contexts," *Journal of Public Policy* 9: 35–38.

Lipsky, Michael, 1980, *Street-level Bureaucracy.* New York: Russel Sage.

Love, Arnold, 1991, *Internal Evaluation: Building Organizations from Within.* Newbury Park, Calif.: Sage.

Lundquist, Lennart, 1976, "Några synpunkter på begreppet politisk planering," *Statsvetenskaplig Tidskrift*: 121–39.

———, 1985, "From Order to Chaos: Recent Trends in the Study of Public Administration," in Jan-Erik Lane, ed., *State and Market: The Politics of the Public and the Private.* Newbury Park, Calif.: Sage.

———, 1987, *Implementation Steering: An Actor-Structure Approach.* Lund: Studentlitteratur.

———, 1990, *Kriterier för utvärdering av offentlig verksamhet.* Turku: Meddelanden från Ekon.–Statsvet. fakulteten vid Åbo Akademi, ser. A:305.

Lundqvist, Lennart J., 1980, *The Hare and the Tortoise: Clean Air Policies in the US and Sweden.* Ann Arbor, Mich.: University of Michigan Press.

Madaus, George F., Michael Scriven, and Daniel L. Stufflebeam, eds., 1983, *Evaluation Models: Viewpoints on Educational and Human Services Evaluation.* The Hague: Kluwer–Nijhoff.

March, James G., and Johan P. Olsen, eds., 1976, *Ambiguity and Choice in Organizations*. Bergen: Universitetsforlaget.

Mayne, John, Marie–Louise Bemelmans–Videc, Joe Hudson, and Ross Conner, eds., 1992, *Advancing Public Policy Evaluation: Learning from International Experiences*. Amsterdam: Elsevier.

Mayntz, Renate, ed., 1980, *Implementation Politischer Programme: Empirische Forschungsbereichte*. Königstein: Athenäum.

———, ed., 1982, *Implementation Politischer Programme: Ansätze zur Theoriebildung*. Opladen: Westdeutscher Verlag.

Mazmanian, Daniel A., and Paul A. Sabatier, 1981, *Effective Policy Implementation*. Lexington, Mass.: Lexington Books.

Mazmanian D. A., and P. A. Sabatier, 1983, *Implementation and Public Policy*. Glenview, Ill.: Scott, Foresman, and Co.

McGuire, William J., 1989, "Theoretical Foundations of Campaigns," in Ronald E. Rice, and C.K. Atkin, eds., *Public Communication Campaigns*, 45–65. Newbury Park, Calif.: Sage.

Meijer, Hans, 1956, *Från uppslag till betänkande: studie i kommittépolitik och kommittéarbete*. Lund: Gleerup.

Merton, Robert K., 1957, 1968, *Social Theory and Social Structure*. London: Collier–Macmillan (1968 enl. ed).

Meyers, William R., 1981, *The Evaluation Enterprise: A Realistic Appraisal of Evaluation Careers, Methods, and Applications*. San Francisco: Jossey-Bass.

Mitnick, Barry M., 1980, *The Political Economy of Regulation: Creating, Designing, and Removing Regulatory Forms*. New York: Columbia University Press.

Modeen, Tore, and Allan Rosas, eds., 1988, *Indirect Public Administration in Fourteen Countries*. Åbo: Åbo Academy Press.

———, eds., 1990, *Indirect Public Administration in the Fields of Education Pensions*. Åbo: Åbo Academy Press.

Montjoy, Robert S., and Laurence J. O'Toole, 1979, "Towards a Theory of Policy Implementation: An Organizational Perspective," *Public Administration Review* 39: 465–76.

Municio, Ingegerd, 1982, "Implementationsforskning: En litteraturöversikt," *Statsvetenskaplig Tidskrift* 85: 183–90.

Murray, Charles, 1984, *Losing Ground: American Social Policy, 1950–1980*. New York: Basic Books.

Nachmias, David, 1979, *Public Policy Evaluation: Approaches and Methods*. New York: St. Martin's.

Nakamura, Robert T., and Frank Smallwood, 1980, *The Politics of Policy Implementation*. New York: St. Martin's Press. Textbook.

Nilstun, Tore, 1988, *Expertbedömningar: Om teori, ideal och verklighet vid utvärdering av sektors FoU*. Stockholm: Byggforskningsrådet, BVN skritserie 1988:1.

Nilstun, Tore, and Göran Hermerén, 1984, *Utvärderingsforskning och rättsliga reformer: En analys av orsaker och effekter*. Lund: Studentlitteratur.

Nioche, Jean–Pierre, 1982, "De l'évaluation à l'analyse des politiques publiques," *Revue Française de Science Politiques* 32: 32–61.

———, 1992, "Institutionalizing Evaluations in France: Skating on Thin Ice?," in John Mayne, Marie-Louise Bemelmans-Videc, Joe Hudson, and Ross Conner, eds., 1992, 23–36.

Nioche, Jean–Pierre, and R. Poinsard, eds., 1984, *L'évaluation des politiques publiques*. Paris: Economica.

Niskanen, William A., 1971, *Bureaucracy and Representative Government*. Chicago: Aldine–Atherton.

Nydén, Michael, 1992, *FoU, utvärdering och användning: En studie av utvärdering av forskning och utvecklingsarbete, dess organisation och användning.* BVN Skriftserie 1992:1. Stockholm: Svensk Byggtjänst.

Öhman, Arne, and Bo Öhngren, eds., 1991, *Two Faces of Swedish Psychology: 1. Frontiers in Perception and Cognition: An Evaluation of Swedish Research in Cognitive Psychology.* Uppsala: Swedish Science Press.

Ormala, Erkki, ed., 1987, *Evaluation of Technical Research and Development: Experience of Practices and Methods in the Nordic Countries.* Helsinki: Nordic Cooperative Organization for Applied Research.

Orwell, George, 1970, "Politics and the English Language," *The Collected Essays, Journalism, and Letters of George Orwell. Volume IV. In Front of Your Nose, 1945–1950*, 156–170. Harmonds-Worth, Middlesex: Penguin Books.

Palmlund, Ingar, ed., 1986, *Utvärdering av offentlig verksamhet: den offentliga förvaltningens roll i samhället.* Stockholm: Liber.

Patton, Michael Quinn, 1986, *Utilization-Focused Evaluation.* Newbury Park, Calif.: Sage, 2nd ed.

———, 1987, *How to Use Qualitative Methods in Evaluation.* Newbury Park, Calif.: Sage.

———, 1990, *Qualitative Evaluation and Research Methods.* Newbury Park, Calif.: Sage, 2nd ed.

Peters, Guy, 1982, *American Public Policy: Process and Performance.* New York: Franklin Watts.

Petersson, Olof, and Donald Söderlind, 1992, *Förvaltningspolitik.* Stockholm: Publica.

Popper, Karl R., 1957, *The Poverty of Historicism.* London: Routledge and Kegan Paul.

———, 1974, *Conjectures and Refutations: The Growth of Scientific Knowledge*, 5th ed. London: Routledge and Kegan Paul.

Premfors, Rune, 1979, "Social Research and Public Policy Making: An Overview," *Statsvetenskaplig Tidskrift* 82: 281—90.

———, 1983, "Social Research and Governmental Commissions in Sweden," *American Behavioral Scientist* 27: 623—42.

———, 1986, "Utvärderingar i offentliga beslutsprocesser," in Ingar Palmlund, ed., 1986, 81–94.

———, 1989, *Policyanalys: Kunskap, praktik och etik i offentlig verksamhet.* Lund: Studentlitteratur.

Pressman, Jeffrey, and Aaron B. Wildavsky, 1984, *Implementation: How Great Expectations in Washington are Dashed in Oakland; etc.* Berkeley, Calif.: University of California Press, 3rd ed. 1st ed. 1973.

Program Evaluation Kit, see Herman.

Rasmussen, Erik, 1987, *Complementarity and Political Science: An Essay on Fundamentals of Political Science Theory and Research Strategy.* Odense: Odense University Press.

Redford, Emmette S., 1952, *Administration of National Economic Control* New York: Macmillan.

Rich, Robert, ed., 1981, *The Knowledge Cycle.* Newbury Park, Calif.: Sage.

Riecken, Henry W., and Robert F. Boruch, eds., 1974, *Social Experimentation: A Method for Planning and Evaluating Social Intervention.* New York: Academic Press.

Ripley Randall B., and Grace A. Franklin, 1986, *Policy Implementation and Bureaucracy.* Chicago, Ill.: Dorsey, 2nd ed.

Rist, Ray C., ed., 1990, *Program Evaluation and the Management of Government: Patterns and Prospects across Eight Nations.* London: Transaction Publishers.

Rivlin, Alice, 1971, *Systematic Thinking for Social Action*. Washington D.C.: Brookings.

Rosenbloom, David H., 1989, *Public Administration: Understanding Management, Politics, and Law in the Public Sector*. New York: Random House, 2nd ed.

Rosenthal, Robert, 1984, *Meta-Analytical Procedures for Social Research*. Newbury Park, Calif.: Sage.

Rossi, Peter H., and Howard E. Freeman, 1985, 1989, *Evaluation: A Systematic Approach*. Newbury Park, Calif.: Sage, 3rd ed., 4th ed.

Rossi, Peter H., and Walter Williams, eds., 1972, *Evaluating Social Programs: Theory, Practice, and Politics*. New York: Seminar Press.

Rothstein, Bo, 1986, *Den socialdemokratiska staten: Reformer och förvaltning inom svensk arbetsmarknads- och skolpolitik*. Lund: Arkiv.

———, 1991, "Demokrati, förvaltning och legitimitet," in B. Rothstein, ed., *Politik som organisation*, 42–84. Stockholm: SNS Förlag.

Rutman, Leonard, 1977, ed., *Evaluation Research Methods: A Basic Guide*. Berverly Hills, Calif.: Sage.

———, 1980, *Planning Useful Evaluations: Evaluability Assessment*. Newbury Park, Calif.: Sage.

Rutman, Leonard, and George Mowbray, 1983, *Understanding Program Evaluation*. Newbury Park, Calif.: Sage.

Rydén, Bengt, ed., 1983, *Makt och vanmakt: Lärdomar av sex borgerliga regeringsår*. Stockholm: SNS Förlag.

Sabatier, Paul, and Daniel Mazmanian, 1980, "The Conditions of Effective Implementation: A Guide to Accomplishing Policy Objectives," *Policy Analysis* 5: 481–504.

———, 1981, "The Implementation of Public Policy: A Framework for Analysis," in D. Mazmanian, and P. Sabatier, eds., *Effective Policy Implementation*. Lexington, Mass.: D.C. Heath.

Sætren, Harald, 1983, *Iverksetting av offentlig politik: En studie av utflytting av statsinstitusjoner fra Oslo 1960–1981*. Oslo: Universitetsforlaget.

Sahr, Robert C., 1985, *The Politics of Energy Policy Change in Sweden*. Ann Arbor: University of Michigan Press.

Salamon, Lester M., 1981, "Rethinking Public Policy: Third Party Government and the Changing Forms of Government Action," *Public Policy* 29: 255–75.

———, 1989, *Beyond Privatization: The Tools of Government Action*. Washington, D.C.: Urban Institute Press.

Sandahl, Rolf, 1992, "Evaluation at the Swedish National Audit Bureau," in John Mayne, Marie-Louise Bemelmans-Videc, Joe Hudson, and Ross Conner, eds., *Advancing Public Policy Evaluation: Learning from International Experiences*, 115–21. Amsterdam: Elsevier.

Scheirer, Mary Ann, 1981, *Program Implementation: The Organizational Context*. Newbury Park, Calif.: Sage.

Scriven, Michael, 1973, "Goal-Free Evaluation," in Ernest R. House ed., *School Evaluation: The Politics and Process*. Berkeley, Calif.: McCutchan.

———, 1974, "Pros and Cons About Goal-Free Evaluation," *Evaluation Comment* 3: 1–4.

———, 1980, *The Logic of Evaluation*. Inverness, Calif.: Edgepress.

———, 1991, *Evaluation Thesaurus*. Newbury Park, Calif.: Sage, 4th ed.

Seidel, Andrew D., 1983, "Producing Usable Research: A Selected Review," *Policy Studies Review* 3: 52–56.

Seidman, Harold, and Robert Gilmour, 1986, *Politics, Position, and Power: From the Positive to the Regulatory State*. New York: Oxford University Press, 4th ed.

Selznick, Philip, 1980, *TVA and the Grass Roots: A Study of Politics and Organization*. Berkeley: University of California Press.

Shadish Jr., William R., Thomas D. Cook, and Laura C. Leviton, 1991, *Foundations of Program Evaluation: Theory and Practice*. London: Sage.

Shaw, George Bernard, 1992, in *Oxford Dictionary of Quotations*, Fourth Edition, 636:26, Angela Partington, ed. Oxford: Oxford University Press.

Sieber, Sam D., 1981, *Fatal Remedies: The Ironies of Social Intervention*. New York: Plenum Press.

Simon, Herbert A., 1976, *Administrative Behavior: A Study of Decision–Making Processes in Administrative Organizations*. London: Collier–Macmillan, 3rd ed.

Sjöblom, Stefan, 1991, *Kostnadsvariationer i kommunal serviceproduktion–det allmänna biblioteksväsendet*. Åbo Akademi: Meddelanden från Ekon.–statsvet. fakulteten Ser. A:355.

Skinner, Burrhus Frederick, 1969, *Contingencies of Reinforcement: A Theoretical Analysis*. Englewood Cliffs, N.J.: Prentice Hall.

Skocpol, Theda, 1985, *Bringing the State Back In*. Cambridge: Cambridge University Press.

Smith, Adam (1937, 1776), *Wealth of Nations*. New York: Random House.

Smith, M. F. "Midge," 1989, *Evaluability Assessment: A Practical Approach*. Dordrecht: Kluwer.

Söderlind, Donald, and Olof Petersson, 1988, *Svensk Förvaltningspolitik*. Uppsala: Diskurs, 2nd ed.

SOU 1967:11–13, *Programbudgetering*. Stockholm: Liber.

————1976:49, *Offentligt utredningsväsende*. Stockholm: Liber.

Stake, Robert E., 1975, *Evaluating the Arts in Education: A Responsive Approach*. Columbus, Ohio: Merrill.

Statskontoret, ed., 1977, *Om Planering vid Statliga Myndigheter: Metoder, Organisation, Erfarenheter, Synpunkter*. Stockholm: Statskontoret.

Stigler, George J., 1971, "The Theory of Economic Regulation," *Bell Journal of Economics and Management Science* 2: 3–21.

Stjernquist, Per, 1973, *Laws in the Forest: A Study of Public Direction of Swedish Private Forestry*. Lund: CWK Gleerup.

Stone, Clarence N., 1980, "The Implementation of Social Programs," *Journal of Social Issues* 36:4, 13–34.

————, 1985, "Efficiency versus Social Learning: A Reconsideration of the Implementation Process," *Policy Studies Review* 4:3, 484–96.

Struening, Elmer L., and Marcia Guttentag, eds., 1975, *Handbook of Evaluation Research* 1–2. Newbury Park, Calif.: Sage.

Stufflebeam, Daniel L., 1983, "The CIPP–Model for Program Evaluation," in George F. Madaus, Michael Scriven, and Daniel L. Stufflebeam, eds., 117–41.

Suchman, Edward A., 1967, *Evaluative Research: Principles and Practice in Public Service and Social Action Programs*. New York: Russell Sage.

————, 1972, "Action for What? A Critique of Evaluative Research," in Carol H. Weiss, ed., *Evaluating Action Programs*. Boston: Allyn and Bacon.

Svensk Författningssamling. Stockholm: Liber.

Tarschys, Daniel, 1986, "För döva öron? Politikern och utvärderaren", in Ingar Palmlund, ed., 20–26. Stockholm: Liber.

Thorslund, Sverker, 1974, *Erfarenheter av trafikinformation via massmedia: Trafikanternas problem före, under och efter högertrafikomläggningen som objekt för informationsarbete*. Stockholm: Stockholm School of Economics.

Van Horn, Carl E., 1979, *Policy Implementation in the Federal System*. Lexington, Mass.: D.C. Heath.

Van Horn, Carl E., and Donald S. Van Meter, 1977, "The Implementation of Inter-governmental Policy," in Stuart S. Nagel, ed., *Policy Studies Review Annual* 1: 97–120, Newbury Park, Calif.: Sage.

Van Meter, Donald S., and Carl E. Van Horn, 1975, "The Policy Implementation Process: A Conceptual Framework," *Administration and Society* 6: 445–88.

Vasquez, John A., ed., 1986, *Evaluating U.S. Foreign Policy*. New York: Praeger.

Vedung, Evert, 1979, *Kärnkraften och regeringen Fälldins fall (Nuclear Power and the Downfall of the Fälldin Government)*. Stockholm: Rabén, and Sjögren.

———, 1982a, *Energipolitiska utvärderingar 1973–1981* (Energy Policy Evaluations 1973–1981). Stockholm: Liber, Delegationen för energiforskning, rapport nr 52.

———, 1982b, *Political Reasoning*. Newbury Park: Sage.

———, 1988, Review of Rasmussen 1987 "Complementarity and Political Science", *Politica* 20: 360–63.

———, 1991, *Utvärdering i politik och förvaltning* (Evaluation in Politics and Public Administration). Lund: Studentlitteratur.

———, 1992, "Five Observations on Evaluation in Sweden," in John Mayne *et al.*, *Advancing Public Policy Evaluation: Learning from International Experiences*, 71–84. Amsterdam: Elsevier.

———, 1993, *Statens markpolitik, kommunerna och historiens ironi (Governmental Land Use Policies, the Municipalities, and the Irony of History)*. Stockholm: SNS Förlag.

———, 1996, *Statliga informationskampanjer: Svenska energisparprogram* (Public Sector Information Campaigns: Swedish Energy Conservation Programs). Uppsala University: Department of Government. Unpublished manuscript.

Vernon, Richard, 1979, "Unintended Consequences," *Political Theory* 7: 73.

Wagner, Jon, ed., 1979, *Images of Information*. Newbury Park, Calif.: Sage.

Webb, Eugene J., 1966, *Unobtrusive Measures: Nonreactive Research in the Social Sciences*. Chicago: Rand McNally.

Weber, Max, 1974, *From Max Weber: Essays in Sociology*. Edited with an Introduction by Hans H. Gerth, and C. Wright Mills. London: Routledge and Kegan Paul. First published in 1948. Reprinted in 1952, 1957, 1961, 1964, 1967, 1970, and 1974.

Weiss, Carol H., 1972a, *Evaluation Research: Methods of Assessing Program Effectiveness*. Englewood Cliffs, N.J.: Prentice-Hall. Often used text. Directed to programs.

———, 1972b, *Evaluating Action Programs: Readings in Social Action and Education*. Boston, Mass.: D.C. Heath.

———, 1977, *Using Social Research in Public Policy Making*. Lexington, Mass.: D.C. Heath.

———, 1979, "The Many Meanings of Research Utilization," *Public Administration Review* 39: 426–31.

———, 1981, "Measuring the Use of Evaluation," in James A. Ciarlo, ed., 17–33.

Weiss, Carol H., and Michael J. Bucuvalas, 1980, *Social Science Research and Decision-Making*. New York: Columbia University Press.

West, William F., 1985, *Administrative Rulemaking: Politics and Processes*. Westport, Conn.: Greenwood Press.

Wholey, Joseph S., 1977, "Evaluability Assessment," in Leonard Rutman, ed., 41–56.

———, 1983, *Evaluation and Effective Public Management*. Boston, Mass.: Little, Brown and Co.

Wholey, Joseph S., John W. Scanlon, Hugh G. Duffy, James S. Fukumoto, and Leona M. Vogt, 1970, *Federal Evaluation Policy: Analyzing the Effects of Public Programs*. Washington D.C.: The Urban Institute.

Wholey, Joseph S., and Kathryn E. Newcomer, and Associates, 1989, *Improving Government Performance: Evaluation Strategies for Strengthening Public Agencies and Programs*. San Francisco: Jossey–Bass.

Wildavsky, Aaron, 1973, "If Planning Is Everything, Maybe It's Nothing," *Policy Sciences* 4: 127–53.

————, 1979, *Speaking Truth to Power: The Art and Craft of Policy Analysis*. Boston: Little, Brown, and Co.

————, 1985, "The Self–Evaluating Organization," in Eleanor Chelimsky, ed., *Program Evaluation: Patterns and Directions*, 246–65. Washington, D.C.: American Society for Public Administration. [Reprint of article in PAR 1972, 509–520.]

Williams, Walter, 1976, "Implementation Analysis and Assessment," in Walter Williams and Richard F. Elmore, eds., *Social Program Implementation*, 267–292, New York: Academic Press.

————, ed., 1982, *Studying Implementation: Methodological and Administrative Issues*. Chatham, N.J.: Chatham House.

Wilson, James Q., 1978, *The Investigators: Managing FBI and Narcotics Agents*. New York: Basic Books.

————, 1989, *Bureaucracy: What Government Agencies Do and Why They Do It*. New York: Basic Books.

Winter, Søren, 1990, "Integrating Implementation Research," in Dennis J. Palumbo, and Donald J. Calista, eds., *Implementation and the Policy Process: Opening Up the Black Box*, 19–38. London: Greenwood Press.

Wittrock, Björn, 1980, *Möjligheter och gränser: Framtidsstudier i politik och förvaltning*. Stockholm: Liber.

————, 1991, "Social Knowledge and Public Policy: Eight Models of Interaction," in Peter Wagner, ed., *Social Sciences and Modern States: National Experiences and Theoretical Crossroads*. Cambridge: Cambridge University Press.

Wittrock, Björn, and Stefan Lindström, 1984, *De stora programmens tid: Forskning och energi i svensk politik*. Stockholm: Akademilitteratur.

Wittrock, Björn, Peter deLeon, and Helga Nowotny, 1985, *Choosing Futures: Evaluating the Secretariat for Futures Studies*. Stockholm: Forskningsrådsnämnden.

Woodside, Kenneth, 1986, "Policy Instruments and the Study of Public Policy," *Canadian Journal of Political Science* 19: 775–94.

Yin, Robert K., 1982, "Studying the Implementation of Public Programs," in W. Williams, ed., 36–72.

Periodicals

Administrative Science Quarterly.

Educational Evaluation and Policy Analysis. Sponsored by the American Educational Research Association.

European Journal of Psychological Assessment.

Evaluation: The International Journal of Theory, Research, and Practice. New journal that will accept theoretical and practical contributions. Published by Sage Publications.

Evaluation and Program Planning. Issued quarterly by the Eastern Evaluation Research Society, which is affiliated with the American Evaluation Association (AEA).

Evaluation Practice, sponsored by the American Evaluation Association. Apart from articles, this journal contains a debate department and a section on full bibliographical references to current articles and evaluation reports and a presentation of each on one line each. Always followed by a separate newsletter called "Evaluation Practice News" with professional openings and personal notices.

Evaluation Review: A Journal of Applied Social Research. Formerly *Evaluation Quarterly.* Probably the main journal in the field.

Evaluation Studies Review Annual. Yearbook on 500–800 pp, starting in 1976. Published by Sage, Newbury Park, California.

International Review of Administrative Sciences. Belgium. One of the most quoted journals in the field of public administration.

Journal of Law and Society. Crossdisciplinary journal for debate on law and regulations.

Journal of Policy Analysis and Management. Official voice of the Association for Public Policy Analysis and Management (APPAM). The association was founded in 1979.

Journal of Public Policy. Published quarterly by Cambridge University Press.

Knowledge and Policy (formerly *Knowledge in Society*). Besides *Science Communication* probably the foremost journal devoted to knowledge diffusion and knowledge utilization. Associated with the European Evaluation Society (EES).

New Directions for Program Evaluation (NDE). An official publication of the American Evaluation Association and probably one of the best in the field. NDE publishes empirical, methodological, and theoretical works on all aspects of evaluation and related fields. Substantive areas include any field, such as tax policy, energy, environment, education, job training, public health. Also included are such topics as product evaluation, personnel evaluation, policy analysis, and technology assessment. Each issue of NDE is devoted to a single topic, with contributions solicited, organized, reviewed, and edited by a guest editor.

Policy and Politics. A leading British journal in the field of public policy studies. Published by the School for Advanced Urban Studies, Bristol.

Policy Sciences: An International Journal Devoted to the Improvement of Policy Making. Started in 1970. An important international journal on planning, policy analysis and evaluation.

Policy Studies. Published by the Policy Study Institute, London, "the leading independent research organization in the United Kingdom undertaking studies of economic, industrial and social policy and the workings of political institutions. The Institute's aim is to inform public policy by establishing the facts."

Policy Studies Journal. Very valuable. Published by the Policy Studies Organization. See also Policy Studies Review.

Public Administration. Published by the Royal Institute of Public Administration. Issued four times a year. Articles on public administration and political and administrative decision–making processes.

Public Administration Review. Published bimonthly by the American Society for Public Administration.

Public Interest. Journal on public policy in neoconservative spirit. Quarterly.

Public Policy. Issued between 1940 and 1981. Later, the journal came to be associated with the J. F. Kennedy School of Government, Harvard.

Public Productivity and Management Review. Formerly *Public Productivity Review.* Jointly sponsored by the Section on Management Science and Policy Analysis of the American Society for Public Administration and The National Center for Public Productivity at Rutgers University.

Public Understanding of Science. Published quarterly.

Science Communication (formerly *Knowledge: Creation, Diffusion, Utilization*). Published four times annually, this international and interdisciplinary journal examines the nature of expertise and the translation of knowledge into practice and policy. The journal welcomes submissions from authors from the social sciences, policy sciences, economics, and history, and organizations such as universities, government, and the private sector. Preference is given to articles that bridge the gap between theory and practice.

Professional Associations

American Evaluation Association (AEA). An international association of practical and theoretical evaluators. Members are working at universities, research institutes, government agencies, and consulting firms. *Evaluation Practice* and *New Directions for Program Evaluation* are published quarterly. Sponsors an annual conference with numerous parallel sessions and distribution of prizes and awards.

American Society for Public Administration (ASPA) has a section called "Management Science and Policy Analysis". Supports the publication *Management Science and Public Policy Analysis*.

Association for Public Policy Analysis and Management (APPAM) is an organization for US schools of public policy. Annual conference. *Journal of Policy Analysis and Management* is published four times a year.

Canadian Evaluation Association. Similar to its US counterpart. Annual conference. Sponsors the *Canadian Journal of Evaluation*.

European Consortium for Political Research (ECPR). Association of European political science departments. Work is done in permanent workshops. Once a year all workshops meet in an arrangement called "Joint Sessions of Workshops". The ECPR supports the *European Journal of Political Research,* operates a summer school in social science data analysis at the University of Essex, and publishes the quarterly newsletter "ECPR News."

European Evaluation Society. Formed in 1994. Newsletter. Annual conference. Members have access to *Knowledge and Policy*.

International Association for Impact Assessment. A nonprofit organization designed to bring together those concerned with environmental impact assessment (EIA), risk assessment, social impact assessment (SIA), technology assessment (TA), and other forms of impact assessment. IAIA, through it members, works to integrate contributions from from practitioners and researchers from diverse disciplines, improve analytical techniques, promote high quality performance in the field, advance the training of impact assessors, provide peer review on request, and share information through professional meetings and timely publications. Membership is open to all. *Impact Assessment Bulletin*, appearing under the auspices of the IAIA, is published quarterly.

Policy Studies Organization. Major U.S. professional association, which sponsors the two leading periodicals *Policy Studies Journal* and *Policy Studies Review*.

The Network the Evaluators (Nätverket Utvärderarna), Swedish association based at the National Bureau of Statistics (SCB), Stockholm.

Index